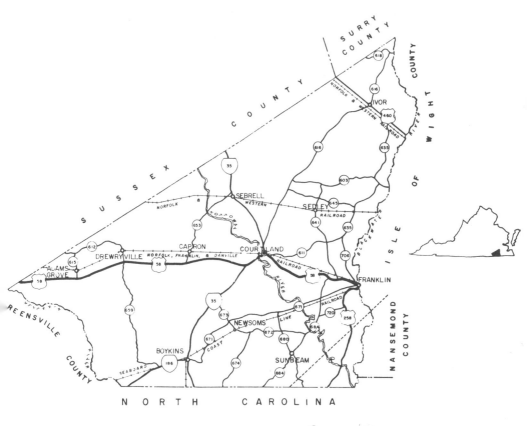

Southampton County
Virginia

Southampton County
Virginia

Thomas C. Parramore

Published for the
Southampton County Historical Society
by the
University Press of Virginia
Charlottesville

THE UNIVERSITY PRESS OF VIRGINIA
Copyright © 1978 by the Rector and Visitors
of the University of Virginia

First published 1978

Endpapers: Adapted from a map drawn by Mrs. J. R. W. Street,
Franklin, Va., and printed in *Bicentennial Calendar,* 1975.

Library of Congress Cataloging in Publication Data

Parramore, Thomas C.
   Southampton County, Virginia.

   Includes bibliographical references and index.
   1. Southampton Co., Va.—History. I. Southampton
County Historical Society. I. Title.
F232.S7P37   975.5′552   77-28828
ISBN 0-8139-0754-3

Printed in the United States of America

To

John Crump Parker
In grateful appreciation
of his untiring efforts and
fervent interest in behalf of
the Southampton County Historical Society

Contents

Illustrations

Preface

A glance at a map of the counties of Southside Virginia is enough to indicate that Southampton was created out of the general southwesterly migration that proceeded from the James River settlements in the seventeenth and eighteenth centuries. Genealogists are well acquainted with the gradual movement of successive generations across Isle of Wight and Norfolk counties, through Nansemond, Southampton, Greensville, Surry, Mecklenburg, and other Virginia counties into North Carolina, Tennessee, and the states beyond. Tracks of the ancestors of thousands of American families black and white can still be traced back across this great avenue of expansion to sources that antedate the arrival of the *Mayflower*.

Unsuited by historical and environmental circumstances to developing the system of large plantations and the important tobacco and cotton economy which is usually associated with the Old South, Southampton remained rural and provincial until well after the Civil War, when the peanut and timber industries propelled it into the mainstream of Virginia and southern commercial growth. A network of rail links with the outside world finally accomplished in the late nineteenth century what the steamboat and sailing vessel had failed to achieve.

The history of Southampton is strewn with fascinating dualities: two natives of the antebellum county who became governors—within a decade of one another—of North Carolina; two natives who became celebrated generals in the Civil War—on opposite sides; two black men who became—one by intention, the other by happenstance—perhaps the most celebrated symbols of the antislavery movement; two wars in which a narrow and sluggish stream would become a critical lifeline in the struggle of opposing armies.

The history of Southampton County reflects vividly the overriding significance in American life of the continuing drama of race relations. No other part of the United States has experienced with such devastating finality the ultimate consequences of slavery's evil. Probably no other Americans have been forced to live with so terrible a specter of racial antipathy as haunts the daily existence of the Southamptonian and permeates his relationships with other human beings.

In the preparation of this volume, I have had the benefit of the industry and zeal of Edgar B. Jackson, a Southamptonian who spent years in accumulating data toward a history of the county. All of Mr. Jackson's voluminous files were made available to me, along with his further generous assistance and advice. No doubt a history of the county would have been delayed many years but for the devoted effort given by Edgar Jackson to its realization.

I also owe a debt of thanks to others who provided me with aid and counsel in my own research and writing. John C. Parker has extended the benefit of his considerable knowledge together with friendly support and encouragement. Gilbert W. Francis and Frank Story Cutchin have smoothed my way through scores of difficulties. Edward Trice and Daniel Balfour are among those who have provided useful data on various historical topics. The members of the Southampton County Historical Society's Book Committee, along with their special advisory members, have been helpful with suggestions throughout the term of the project. Finally, I am grateful for the support of my wife, Barbara, and daughters Lisa and Lynn, who made it possible for me to pursue my interest and fulfill my commitments.

Southampton County
Virginia

1

The Passing of the Nottoways

Trader Man

It must have been toward ten o'clock on that August evening in 1650 when the Nottoways were startled by the dreadful noise in the woods north of the village. The familiar harmony of night sounds had been abruptly broken by the bellowing of some alien creature and a shudder of warning rippled through the cabins of Chounerounte's town. Within moments after the first chilling shout the Indians had abandoned their homes and fled into the adjacent swamp: no such sound had ever come from those woods before, and surely no friendly visitor would shatter the peace of the forest in this way.

Edward Bland and his expedition, hallooing lustily through the Virginia forest on that summer night, were bound from Fort Henry on no warlike mission. They wanted from the Nottoways only a night's lodging before continuing their journey toward the Tuscarora country farther south. But the instincts of the Indians measured well the threat posed by the sound of the approaching white men, for it was the first knell of doom for the Nottoway tribe. Snatched unwillingly out of their womb of isolation from the English, the Nottoways, four hundred strong in 1650, were to be reduced by half within another eighty years. By the close of the eighteenth century they would amount to a wretched remnant, their blood diluted by foreign taint and their culture eroded beyond recognition. But it was neither an ignoble surrender nor a fumbling collapse. Defying the will of an impatient Destiny, the Nottoways dared to make him wait.

The brief recorded history of the Nottoways begins with their first appearance in Edward Bland's journal on August 27, 1650. Commissioned by Virginia authorities to open a trade with the Tuscaroras on Roanoke River, Bland set out from Fort Henry (now Petersburg) on a route leading almost due south through the Nottoway and Meherrin nations. For more than forty years these small tribes, backwater communities of perhaps five hundred Iroquois, had been all but unknown to the English settlers.[1]

From sketchy accounts left by Bland and a few others, the seventeenth-century Nottoways are believed to have occupied three villages in what is today Sussex County. The two visited by Bland, on Stoney Creek and Rowantee Branch of Nottoway River, were under the authority of two brothers named Oyeocker and Chounerounte. A day's journey to the south, on the Meherrin River, was a town of Meherrin Indians, also visited by Bland. It was a region of extensive pine barrens, but Bland found cornfields on both sides of the Nottoway River producing two crops a year. Few fish came so far upstream, but the Indians lived well enough on deer and other game animals besides a wide variety of edible plants.[2]

Bland's account leaves the clear impression of a people not yet touched by the ways and technology of the whites. Aside perhaps from Captain Floods,[3] official interpreter for the southern Indians, the Meherrins and Nottoways had probably never seen a white man before the arrival of Bland's expedition. Situated along a main trad-

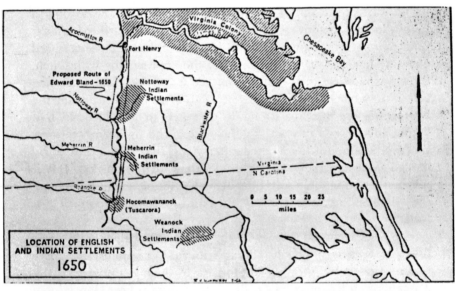

English and Indian settlements. Archaeologist's map indicates where major tribes of early historical period resided. Note also route of Bland's expedition. (Reprinted, by permission, from Lewis R. Binford, "An Ethnohistory of the Nottoway, Meherrin, and Weanock Indians of Southeastern Virginia," *Ethnohistory* 14 [Summer-Fall, 1967])

ing path between the Powhatans and Tuscaroras, the Nottoways and Meherrins were well acquainted with colonial policy but little if at all affected by it.[4] They had taken no part in the Indian uprisings of earlier years and were so little accustomed to fighting that they neglected to fortify their villages. Their oval bark huts were suitable for hospitality but useless for defense.

A striking illustration of their lack of acquaintance with English goods was the request made to Bland by a group of Meherrins on August 29 to "heare some . . . guns go off."[5] The English obliged, but other Indians at a distance, unaware of the demonstration, were frightened into the woods by the musket blasts. The time was soon at hand, however, when the harsh report of the musket would replace the silent flight of the arrow for the Nottaways and Meherrins. With the passing of the traditional weapons, the inevitable decline of Indian culture would begin.

The later history of the Nottoways and Meherrins, however, is not one of spineless retreat and rapid decay. The last half of the seventeenth century would see both tribes drawn into close association with the whites and increasingly under the influence of European culture. Forced to cooperate with Virginia authorities to the point of making war on other tribes, they adopted only such European ways as could not be resisted. For more than a hundred years after the first wave of English migration had swept over and past them, the Nottoways and Meherrins could still claim a recognizable identity with their ancient heritage.

The Blackwater Line

In 1634 Virginia's western boundary, the limit of English colonization, was set at a line running southeast from Fort Henry through the Blackwater Swamp. This meant that colonists were forbidden to settle on the west or south side of the Blackwater River. For the time being the fields and hunting grounds of the Nottoways and Meherrins were safe from interference and there was no real threat from the English against their tribal integrity.

The greater immediate danger to the small frontier tribes now became those stronger Indian groups farther west who had not

come to terms with the European presence. Neither the Nottoways, with their ninety warriors, nor the Meherrins, with barely
fifty men who could be sent into battle,[6] were in a position to resist
a stout attack. Their only chance for survival was to take sides with
the stronger force, and this, as the uprisings of 1622 and 1644 had
clearly shown, was with the English.

The decision to cast their lot with the English may have been
unavoidable for the Meherrins and Nottoways, but it led to demands that tore savagely at the fabric of their society. When Virginia authorities asked friendly tribes for aid against the Susque-
hannas on the northeast border in 1675, the twenty men sent by the
Nottoways and Meherrins were the only help they received.[7] Two
years later, when the Virginia government proposed a general
treaty between itself and various frontier groups, the Meherrins
and Nottoways were obliged to consent though it placed them in a
difficult and dangerous position. The treaty of 1677 left them tributaries to a government that placed no great value on their existence.

By the terms of this treaty the border tribes friendly to the English
were molded into a buffer zone between the white colony and the
hostile tribes of the upcountry. The Nottoways, Meherrins, and
other Indians of this frontier zone were expected to give warning to
the English of approaching danger and assist them in defending
against it. In return the Indians signing the treaty were confirmed in
the possession of land which had always been theirs and promised
protection from injury by whites. They were also authorized to bring
intertribal disputes to Williamsburg, the colonial capital, for settlement.[8] But the buffer tribes must also bear the first shock of attack
in time of war and the greatest injury from it.

The unhappy one-sidedness of the treaty was soon apparent. In
1681, harassed by attacks from hostile tribes, the Nottoways were
forced to give up their lands and move southward away from danger. But their new location on Assamoosick Swamp in modern Surry
County proved equally dangerous, and they appealed to the Virginia authorities for the aid to which they were entitled. Colonial
officials provided little but sympathy, and in 1694 the Nottoways
were compelled to move again, this time to the mouth of Assamoosick Swamp in what was to become Southampton County.[9]

In the meantime another small tribe had briefly occupied lands near the site of the present Courtland. About the year 1653 the Weanocks, formerly settled at the headwaters of Wiccacon Creek in North Carolina, came north to a place they called Warekeck on the south bank of the Nottoway River. Some families of Weanocks also settled at Three Forks and on the north side of the river near Assamoosick Swamp, all of them paying annual rent to the Nottoways for the use of the land. But the Weanocks, almost continually at war with one tribe or another, were fated never to remain long at any place. Attacked by the Nansemonds in 1662, with the loss of their chief and six other men, they petitioned Virginia authorities for permission to come within English lines. It is from the report of the militia force sent to escort them to the east of Blackwater that we have our scanty knowledge of the Weanock tribe.

Far more than the Nottoways or Meherrins, the Weanocks had already come under the influence of the white colonists. The Weanock chief had occupied "an English built house" (probably a frame structure), and there was an English-type apple orchard in the village. The Weanocks had not surrendered fully to colonial ways, for the militia reported accompanying them to their burial ground three or four miles west of the village where they placed the body of the chief "on a scaffold . . . covered with skins and matts." But they could no longer defend themselves, and a pathetic group of stragglers had to be rescued some days later from "a piece of a puncheon fort" five or six miles from Warekeck.[10]

Two years spent inside English lines did nothing to promote self-sufficiency among the Weanocks. Returning to Warekeck in 1664, they abandoned it soon afterward following a battle with the Potchiaks. They moved from the Nottoway River back to their old homes near the head of Wiccacon Creek only to be driven away by the Tuscaroras. In the next few years they were driven from the Meherrin River by another Tuscarora attack before throwing up a village on the Blackwater in modern Surry County—as close to the English as they could get. Assaulted even there by the Tuscaroras and Nottoways, the fugitive Weanocks soon ceased to function as a tribe. Their remaining families went to live in the 1690s with the Nottoways and Nansemonds.[11]

The Meherrins managed to outlast the Weanocks by about half a century. After residing during the 1680s on Tararra Creek near the present Boykins, they moved in 1691 to the mouth of the Meherrin River in North Carolina. William Byrd, leading his dividing-line expedition westward past the Meherrin town in 1728, found only a handful of them still living. Within another three decades even this small band had vanished, probably by intermarriage with the whites and blacks and by merging with other tribes.[12] Among the early tribes of the Blackwater frontier, only the Nottoways were able to construct a pattern for long-term survival.

The Buffer Zone

The lifting of the Blackwater barrier in 1705 by the Virginia House of Burgesses only legalized the invasion of Indian territory that had probably started several years earlier. Bursting through Virginia's statutory confines, white settlers pushed quickly onto the Indian hunting grounds and laid claim to lands even before the colonial government could recognize their titles. The Nottoways found themselves restricted by the act of 1705 to two tracts of land within the area they had occupied since 1694. The first of these was a circle six miles in diameter with the Nottoway "great town" at its center, on the east side of Assamoosick Swamp. The second was a six-mile square on the north side of the Nottoway River near Buckhorn Swamp. The latter tract included an island at the mouth of Raccoon Swamp on which stood the "Quiokoson house" where the Nottoway placed the bodies of their notable dead.[13] Within these two reservations the Nottoways were soon surrounded by the farms of the hundreds of settlers pouring across the Blackwater.

The policy of settlement had not gone so far by 1711 as to cut the Nottoways off from possible combinations with more warlike tribes. At the outbreak of the Tuscarora War in the autumn of 1711 Governor Alexander Spotswood became alarmed that the Indians of the buffer zone might join forces with the Tuscaroras. In order to discourage such a possibility, the governor in early October ordered a muster of the militia of three counties at the main Nottoway town. One of these units was that of Isle of Wight County, within which were the lands of the Nottoways.

The governor arrived at the Nottoway town and on October 20, with some 1,600 troops assembled, held a meeting with representatives of the tribes of the buffer zone. As a guarantee of the support of the Indians, he demanded that two sons of chief men of each tribe be sent to Williamsburg. By this means, the boys could be kept as hostages until the fighting ended and they could also be educated at the Indian School at the College of William and Mary as a step toward Christianizing both them and their tribes. Probably with little choice in the matter, the Nottoways agreed to send two boys, as did the Nansemonds and Meherrins. Though the Nottoways seem to have done no fighting in the four years of the war, they served the colony by seizing Tuscaroras who sought refuge within the Nottoway reservation.[14] The crushing defeat of the Tuscaroras doubtless confirmed the Nottoways in the wisdom of their own policy.

By the time the war ended in 1715 the Nottoways were growing hogs for themselves and for market and finding employment with the whites as guides, hunters, and so on. A peace treaty of 1713 formalized the good will that had existed between the Nottoways and the colonists for many years.[15] But despite these concessions to European influence, the Nottoways were far from yielding to the foreign culture, as Spotswood himself would soon discover.

In the hope of using them as a defensive force on Virginia's frontier, Spotswood in 1714 sought to bring the small tribes of friendly Indians together in a fortified town. The fort he erected near the present Lawrenceville, called Fort Christanna, was to be garrisoned by twelve white soldiers who would lead the Indians into battle whenever an attack was threatened. A school was established there under Rev. Charles Griffin, who would help to Christianize the Indian children and supervise their adaptation to "civilized" society.

Although the remains of several tribes were assembled at Fort Christanna, the Nottoways declined the invitation. Spotswood, in an effort to force them to come in, decreed that all trade with the Indian country must be carried on through the fort. But the Nottoways, unwilling to forfeit their reservation lands, defied the pressure, offering as a reason that they did not choose to associate with the Siouan tribes who made up the community. The Nottoways appear to have sent a few children for schooling under Griffin, but the gov-

ernor's plan no longer seemed necessary after peace was signed with
the hostile tribes in 1718. The House of Burgesses refused to support
the project further and the Christanna site was abandoned, though
other groups of Indians lived there from time to time until about
1750. [16]

Some idea of the character of Nottoway life during the first third
of the eighteenth century can be gathered from the journals of Virginia's lively diarist, William Byrd. During visits to the Nottoway
town in 1711 and 1728 Byrd made observations that indicate something of the extent to which the Indians had been able to retain
their traditional values and ways even as they slowly adopted English practices. Byrd's was neither an admiring nor a sympathetic
view, but his comments remain useful and important in understand-
ing what were already "the only Indians of any consequence," as
Byrd termed them, "now remaining within the limits of Virginia." [17]

In contrast to the Weanocks, who had at least one "English built
house" as far back as the early 1660s, the Nottoways of 1728 still
lived in bark cabins. In company with Governor Spotswood, Byrd
had lodged in such a cabin during his visit of 1711 and had found
it an uncomfortable experience. His view was confirmed in 1728
when he and his dividing-line surveyors were entertained in quarters
which were "no other than close arbours made of Saplings, arched
at the top, and cover'd so well with Bark as to be proof against all
Weather." Though such a structure held back the rain and wind,
the want of a hole in the roof left only the door as an outlet for smoke.
This deficiency, Byrd claimed, kept "the whole family Warm, at the
Expense of both their Eyes and Complexion." The only furniture
in these cabins were the hurdles or frames covered with deerskin
mats which served as beds.

Although the last recorded attack on them had been by some
Senecas in 1705, the Nottoways now had a stout fort, near the walls
of which stood their dwellings. Even as Byrd's party approached the
town they were surprised by female scouts who were "station'd on
an Eminence" to give warning. This they did by "continu'd Whoops
and Cries, which cou'd not possibly have been more dismal at the
Sight of their most Implacable Enemies." Escorted into the Nottoway fort, Byrd found it to be in the shape of a square about a hundred yards on each side. A wall or palisade of logs some ten feet high

formed the outer defense, the barrier "leaning a little outwards, to make a Scalade more difficult." At intervals along the wall were loopholes for firing upon the enemy. Within were emergency cabins with sufficient room for the two hundred people of the tribe.

The emphasis on scouts and fortifications showed that the Nottoways had altered their pattern of life considerably since they had been visited by Edward Bland eighty years earlier. But the changes were toward another mode of Indian life rather than toward white patterns. The likelihood of further war was small, but there were still occasional incidents of bloodletting among the Nottoways, Toteros, and Saponi, and the residents of the town could not afford to let down their guard. A further evidence of this defensive posture was the dance to which Byrd was treated during his evening at the village. When the spectators assembled, the young men appeared wearing what seemed to Byrd "Hideous" paints and markings. To the rhythm of a gourd war drum with a skin stretched tautly across it, the men sang and kept "exact time with their feet, while their Hands and Arms were screw'd into a thousand Menacing Postures."

The dress of the Nottoways was still thoroughly traditional. The women, who dressed in their finest apparel for the war dance, came in loosely worn red and blue "Match-Coats." Their hair was braided with small blue and white cylinders of conch shells "drilled through and Strung like Beads" and hanging gracefully in large rolls on their shoulders. They kept their skin soft with bear's oil, which also served as a protection against insects, and wore many necklaces and bracelets. Byrd thought the Indian women "Straight and well-proportioned" and having "an air of Innocence and Bashfulness." Although the Virginian thought them neither pretty enough of face nor clean enough of person for his taste, his fellow surveyors spent the night in warm pursuit of the women.

Nottoway women, including the old Weanock queen, did all of the domestic and field work of the tribe while the men occupied their time mostly in hunting and fishing. Before marriage a girl might enjoy a long series of flirtations and affairs, but once married, she not only remained faithful to her vows but could not be "provokt by a Brutish or even a fumbling Husband to go astray."

Byrd had little appreciation of Nottoway culture and labeled the community lazy and undisciplined. Although his prejudice in the matter was obvious, the restricted living space and condition of dependence which now marked their existence may have been taking its toll on the Nottoways. There were few animals left for hunting or trapping and the commerce in furs had moved away to the west. If the Nottoways were to survive for long on a reservation they would have to give up the old methods of food gathering and learn to farm.

Simmons Town

The show put on by the Nottoways for their visitors in 1728 was almost the "last hurrah" of a doomed people. Their Quiokoson House was already in disuse and the island on which it stood was deserted.[18] There was enough of the English language spoken among them that the colonial interpreter could be discharged in 1734[19] and no others reappointed. But more disheartening was the growing burden of debt that afflicted members of the tribe and their difficulty in procuring needed supplies. Producing very little of value for commerce, besides a few handicrafts, furs, hogs, and so on, they could not readily obtain articles of English trade.

By 1734 the problem was acute enough to cause the Nottoways to petition the legislature for the right to sell land in the neighborhood of their Assamoosick "great town," which had been abandoned. The act granting their request appointed a commission of trustees to supervise the sales, and such a board was to participate in all future land transactions of the Nottoways. The act noted that the Nottoways had been "reduced by warrs sickness and other casualties to a small number and among those that remain many are old and unable to labour or hunt, so that one of the said tracts will be sufficient for them and more than they are able . . . to cultivate, or make use of."[20]

Probably the words of the legislators gave a color to the situation that was not altogether accurate. To the extent that the Nottoways still depended upon hunting and the gathering of wild foods, the reservation lands were less than ample. They were beginning to learn farming, but the decision to sell land was no doubt based on something other than the lack of need or use for it. They required seeds, tools, draft animals, even food itself. Every acre of hunting land sold was another spur to agriculture, but the new methods would be learned only with difficulty and after much disappointment.

During the middle and latter part of the eighteenth century the Nottoways sent one appeal after another to the legislature for the right to lease or sell other lands, and all seem to have been granted. One deed of sale followed another as the reservation fell to a mere fragment of what it had once been. In 1744 the last Nansemond Indians, following in the wake of the Weanocks and Meherrins, concluded their tribal history by coming to live with the Nottoways. [21]

Even as late as 1751 the Nottoways were able to fashion a display of tribal dignity and purpose that was sufficient to attract the attention of the urbane residents of colonial Williamsburg. The occasion was the arrival at Williamsburg on August 12, 1751, of a Cherokee chief and thirty attendants to negotiate with the government about trade relations. The Cherokees had been in town only a day or two when a report was circulated that a band of Nottoways, considered mortal enemies of the Cherokees, was approaching Williamsburg. As the Cherokees armed themselves for battle, alarmed whites contemplated the spectacle of a war in their streets. But the Nottoways, arriving on August 15 under a white flag of truce, made known their peaceful intentions. To the music of ceremonial drums, representatives of both tribes exchanged greetings in the marketplace, marched to the courthouse, and joined in speeches and smoking the peace pipe. [22] Their differences adjusted, they held a dance in the evening and next day left town well satisfied with the results of their conference.

Soon after the outbreak of the French and Indian War in 1756 Governor Dinwiddie issued a call for three hundred Virginia Indians to serve with the English forces. A force of Nottoway and Tuscarora men, led by Lt. James Baker of Nansemond County, was recruited and marched to Fort Duquesne in Pennsylvania. [23] Two years later the Virginia House of Burgesses took note of the bravery of several of the Nottoways in "the action before Fort Duquesne" (in which Baker was killed) and the destitute condition

of their families. The Burgesses voted awards of £10 sterling to Tom
Step and £5 each to Billy John, School Robin, and Aleck Scholar.
It was also ordered that the treasurer "purchase a silver gorget [a
neck ornament] and suit of clothes to be presented to Captain
Thomas Step . . . as a mark of distinction as a reward for his brave
and gallant behavior during the last campaign."[24]

In the decades following the end of the war, the Nottoways continued to buy time by selling reservation land though ever more
pinched by the change from food gathering to food growing. They
were too few in number to take any organized part in the American
Revolution, though the Nottoway chief fought and died in the
patriot ranks. By the beginning of the nineteenth century the tribal
inheritance had diminished to less than four thousand acres, the
arable portion of which was barely enough even for farming.[25]

But self-respect and self-identity remained. When they were
queried in 1808 as to whether they might be willing to sell more
land, the Nottoways announced that "the white people were already
as near them as they wished [them] to be," and declined selling anything. They also refused to have their children bound out as appren-
tices, giving as their reason that "an Indian . . . [was] never known
as an apprentice."[26]

Little besides their dignity remained. Trustees reported that the
tribe, whose cluster of small farms was now known as Simmons
Town, was without educational facilities and that the Indians practiced neither sobriety, industry, nor frugality.[27] Almost entirely illiterate, they seemed dependent on the good will of the trustees as
their only guarantee against fraud and unfairness in their dealings
with the white community.

In 1818 the Nottoways appealed to the General Assembly for the
right to sell the last of their lands except the few acres on which they
actually lived. Queen Edith Turner, along with Amy Woodson,
Fanny Bartlett, Henry Turner, Ellick Rogers, Jack Woodson, Solo-
mon Bartlett, and Nancy Turner, all of them illiterate, petitioned
that the two dozen or so members of the tribe were mostly either very
old or else infants too young to work. They held common title to
3,912 acres but could make use of very little of it and were in distress
for money and provisions.[28] The legislature in 1820 authorized sale
of about a quarter of the reservation, but a substantial part of the

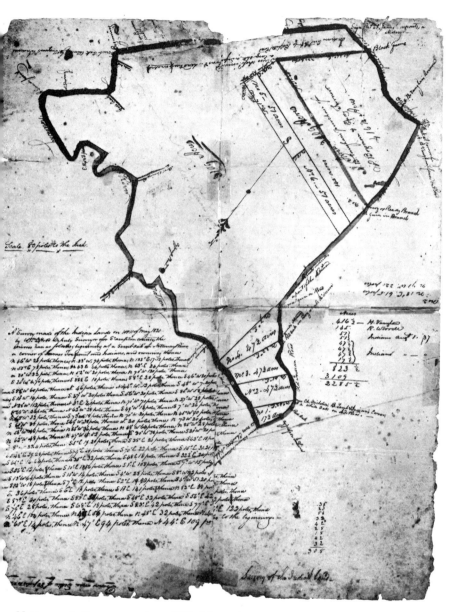

Nottoway Indian reservation, 1830. Map of reservation land shows tracts laid off for William G. Bozeman and other Nottoways following his petition to the Virginia legislature. (Southampton County Clerk's Office, Courtland, Va.; photograph by Colbert Howell)

proceeds had to be applied to the settlement of claims for goods advanced to the Nottoways on credit. With Edith Turner now seventy years of age, Littleton Schollar—the tribe's principal man— older still, another "totally blind," and Alexander Rogers lately convicted of murder (the tribe had borne the cost of his two trials), the situation was still darker than before.[29]

The Aborigine

It was at this crisis in Nottoway affairs that the state legislature in December 1823 was startled to receive from the hand of a member of the tribe a lengthy and incisive written analysis of the tribe's fundamental problems and a recommendation for how to solve them. The document was the work of a young man named William G. Bozeman who had left Virginia some years earlier, acquired by some means a formal education, and returned to try to improve his own lot and that of the fellow members of the tribe.

Unlike the humbly submissive appeals usually made by the Nottoways to the General Assembly, Bozeman's was the direct and forceful statement of a man who sought no charity and acknowledged no inferiority:

My forefathers help[ed] to achieve the independence of America, they enlisted under the banner of freedom, and went forth to battle against the hostile armies of King George 3. They fought, they toil'd, they bled, for that *liberty*, which the citizens of the U.S. now enjoy. My grandfather at that time was King of the aforesaid tribe of Aborigines, he fell in battle, contending for liberty, under the immortal WASHINGTON. . . . Will you now behold me an offspring of the then noble spirits, of the memorable Revolution, who by their confederated plan stood the test of British warfare and tyranny; they burst the fetters, and hurled them at their oppressors, and shouted they were free, the sound broke across the Atlantic and shook the fog wrapt island of Britain; and raised AMERICA to the first rank, among the nations of the Earth.[30]

Bozeman proceeded to analyze what he conceived to be the chief obstacle to the advancement of the Nottoways. It was, he asserted, communal ownership of their land, a circumstance that had the effect of stifling individual initiative for generation after generation and denying to the Indians political suffrage. "What is more disheartening to a man," asked Bozeman, "than to know that the labour of his hands [is] not to go to the children of his body? And when we know it will, with what energy of industry it animates man . . . for the happiness of his . . . children."[31]

The solution, then, Bozeman continued, was to permit him and others wishing to do so to have their proportionate parts of the reservation surveyed and granted to them in fee simple. Once this was done, individual owners would become zealous cultivators of their own soil and freedom of enterprise would insure that many would be able to emerge from their despondency and become productive citizens.

On February 23, 1824, the General Assembly passed an act allowing the trustees of the Nottoways either to provide Bozeman with tribal funds equal to the amount of his proportionate share of the reservation or to set apart for him a reservation tract of equal value which he would then own in fee simple. It was further enacted that any other member of the tribe seeking similar privileges was entitled to them, provided that the trustees were satisfied with the "good moral character" of such applicants. Bozeman, joined by the old queen, was allowed to select a tract on the road from Jerusalem to Belfield. The land they chose, probably with due deliberation, was considered to be "the most inferior" on the reservation.[32]

A remnant of the Nottoway reservation was still in existence in 1856 and probably for some years thereafter.[33] Elderly residents of Southampton in the 1960s could still recall that a few families of Nottoways were living at the close of the Civil War on the Kello farm on Nottoway River, four and a half miles above Courtland. They were said to have had a chapel or meetinghouse and to have formed a distinct community from the other races around them.[34] Families of Nottoway descendants have been reported living in the vicinity of Courtland and Norfolk in the twentieth century.[35]

A story that suggests the hardy persistence of Nottoway tradition is that passed down by Dr. W. B. Barham in 1928. Barham's tale concerned Old Mortality, called "the last of his tribe," who lived near Courtland in the antebellum period. It was the preoccupation of the old gentleman to visit the burial grounds of his people and mark their graves with stakes, crudely inscribed. As Barham explained,

Some years ago, . . . I sent [five of] the cedar stakes . . . to the Virginia Historical Society. They were collected from an old Indian burying ground south of the Nottoway river, . . . near Courtland. . . . In this section, now known as the Indian Wood, . . . lived a tribe of Indians, and some of them are to be found there now, though . . . the distinctive characteristic traits of the Indian have been lost. I remember, when a boy living in Jerusalem, now Courtland, having seen one or more full-blooded Indians, remnants of this tribe. From the best information I could gather at the time I sent the stakes . . ., they must have been placed at the graves in the closing years of the 18th century.[36]

One apparent reason the Nottoways held tenaciously to their identity and values was the transition initiated by William Bozeman from the communal to individual land ownership. In 1820 the Nottoways had appeared irremediably doomed to self-destruction, but they clung to shreds of their coherence for at least another half a century. Under the circumstances, this was a notable achievement and one that set the Nottoways apart from many other tribes.

Spadework

In recent decades some of the sites occupied by the Nottoways and earlier Indians in Southampton County have been investigated by amateur and professional archaeologists. A map drawn by Lewis R. Binford designates the locations surveyed by him in the course of his doctoral studies at the University of Michigan in the early 1960s. Site C-1, on the Richard Kello land four and a half miles north of Courtland, was identified by Binford almost certainly as that of Warekeck town, the old Weanock settlement of the 1650s.[37] This was also the site where the last Nottoways were said to have lived in the nineteenth century. The broken lines near the top and lower left indicate the bounds of the six-mile square laid off as part of the Nottoway reservation in 1705. Site C-20 is probably within the circle of reservation land that surrounded the Nottoway "great town." Indian material, including projectile points, pottery fragments, pieces of pipe, and so on, was found at all of the sites, though it repre-

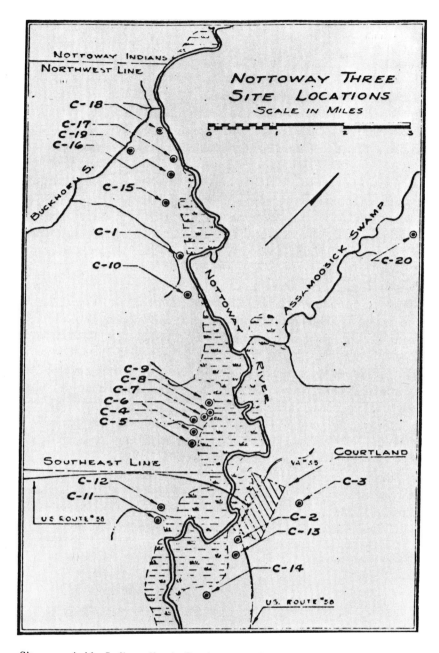

Sites occupied by Indian tribes in Southampton County. (From Lewis R. Binford, "Archaeological and Ethnohistorical Investigation of Cultural Diversity and Progressive Development among Aboriginal Cultures of Coastal Virginia and North Carolina" [Ph.D. diss., University of Michigan, 1964])

sented the relics not only of the Nottoways but several other tribes as well.

Binford's data suggest that sites C-1 and C-15 are the older ones inhabited by the Weanocks and earliest Nottoways. He found evidence that Courtland itself was inhabited by Nottoways within about a decade of the time it became the county seat of Southampton in 1753. The Indian settlements were all small and probably only seasonally inhabited by small family groups in what anthropologists call "dispersed hamlets" and small temporary camps.[38] It was by means of this constant shifting from one site to another within a restricted area that the Indians kept close to whatever food supply the woods and rivers afforded from one season to another.

Finally, Binford's study of the history of the Meherrins and Nottoways suggests a further possible explanation for the tenacious ability of the latter to retain their traditional mode of existence in the face of furious assaults. The evidence collected by Binford indicates that the Nottoways were ruled as a "tribal society" as opposed to the "chiefdoms" of the Powhatans, Nansemonds, and Chowans. The difference lay in the fact that the Nottoways were governed by a council of chief men while the other tribes were ruled autocratically.[39] More conservative and traditional in their councils than the coastal tribes, perhaps more deliberate and cautious in decision making, the Nottoways gradually adjusted to the European presence and survived while others failed.

Their destruction was inevitable, but the Nottoways refused to be hurried into oblivion. Maintaining their dignity and decorum almost to the last, they answered the summons of Fate in their own good time and in obedience to laws that were theirs alone.

2

The Borderland

Wyanoke Creek

Philip Ludwell had the tact not to bring it up in his journal of 1711, but the whole question of who owned this godforsaken frontier region sometimes seemed hardly worth settling. The trail from Nottoway Town down the east bank of the Nottoway River had to be negotiated through a soaking spring rain that lasted all day long. His party reached Richard Braswell's house near the river's mouth and crossed in Braswell's canoe, but one of the horses "tumbled out into the river" and another had to be swum over for want of space in the boat. It was ten miles more to John Dew's house on the Meherrin before the commissioners could dry themselves out, and the horses were so jaded that one had to be left behind when they set out again next morning. The trek southward from Dew's, conducted by a Meherrin Indian, was "a toylsome journey" across a weary succession of swamps and branches.[1] The Carolina commissioners finally made their appearance, but only in order to haggle interminably over technical details of the survey.

One difficulty succeeded another throughout the three weeks' ordeal. The Virginians, coming up the west side of the Chowan on May 21, were "well soused in a myery meadow" before reaching John Beverley's at the mouth of Meherrin. Here they lodged overnight in "a wretched Kennell of a Loghouse where we could hardly have our length and breadth." But this was a merry occasion compared with what they were to encounter a few days later. After pushing around the Dismal Swamp on May 26 in "2 old leaky canoes," the commissioners had to take their horses across "a terrible myery Pocoson." This led into "a very great marsh" where the horses had to be plunged "over head and ears . . . into the water" for a swim of half a mile. The party, "very wett, dirty and tired," arrived at Stephen Burgess's house where the whole family "was filled with the Itch." Assured that there was no place in the neighborhood that was not afflicted with the same malady, Ludwell and his company "made a virtue of necessity and lodged here all night."[2]

The greatest vexation continued to be the poor cooperation of the Carolina commissioners. The boundary between the colonies had been a source of mutual irritation for almost half a century, and both governments were anxious to settle it. The Virginians were satisfied that the border from Chowan River westward should begin at the mouth of what the Carolinians called Wiccacon Creek. The North Carolinians were equally sure that the line should proceed west from the mouth of Nottoway River, twenty miles north. Within the disputed area lay thousands of square miles of territory in which land-hungry pioneers were already starting to settle. Measurements with astrolabe and quadrant appeared to uphold the Virginia point of view, but the Carolinians, with a perversity born of a pork diet and a lawless society, refused to accept it.[3]

A critical question had to do with the location of "Wyanoke Creek," the branch of the Chowan from which the Carolina Charter of 1665 directed that the line westward should continue.[4] The Virginians identified it with Wiccacon Creek, but the Carolinians held that Wyanoke was an old name for the Nottoway River. The maps were discouragingly vague. Comberford's map of 1657 showed Wyanoke connecting with the Blackwater to form the Chowan. But Gascoyne's of 1682 and Hack's of 1684 identified Wiccacon Creek as the Nottoway. As late as 1718 Delisle's map labeled the Nottoway as the "Chowan" and Chowan as "Wyanoke."[5] The charts provided evidence both for those who argued that Isle of Wight County reached southwest to the lower Roanoke River and for those who insisted that the county terminated well north of that region.

Expert testimony furnished to the commissioners by a score of residents of the Nottoway-Chowan frontier in 1710 and 1711 clouded the issue still more thoroughly. Indian interpreter Henry Briggs, whose acquaintance with Nottoway River went back a quarter of a century, had never known it to be called Wyanoke, a strong argument for the Virginia claim. But Francis Toms, a Quaker who had known the Nottoway for almost half a century, was positive that it had been known until quite recently as Wyanoke. Robert Lawrence had lived for seven years west of Chowan in the 1660s and was sure that the name Wyanoke designated a creek several miles below the mouth of Meherrin River; Edward Smithwick, a resident of the same locality since 1663, knew "very well . . . that Nottoway, now called, was then called Wyanoke."[6]

The joint efforts of Virginia and North Carolina to resolve the problem in 1710 and 1711 were thwarted at every turn. Readings from Virginia's surveying instruments supported its claim to greater territory; readings from Carolina instruments contradicted the claim. When Ludwell filed his final report to Governor Spotswood,[7] it was clear that only one hope remained for settling the question. A costly joint surveying expedition would have to run the line all the way from the ocean to the mountains, and the sooner the better. It was chiefly owing to the Tuscarora Indian War, however, that the survey was to be delayed for another seventeen years.

The Blackwater Frontier

Exploration of the region between the Blackwater and Meherrin rivers probably began in the first years of the Jamestown settlement. As early as 1608, within a year after the seating of the James River colony, Captain John Smith began hearing reports that survivors of Sir Walter Raleigh's "Lost Colony" might still be living at Ocamahawan, an Indian town probably at the rapids of Roanoke River.[8] Ocamahawan lay some 120 miles southwest of Jamestown along a route that led across modern Southampton County. Proposals by the Virginia Company in 1609 called attention to the desirability of searching for the Lost Colonists as well as the importance of Ocamahawan as a center for trade with the southern Indians.[9]

Even before the end of 1608 Smith sent Michael Sicklemore and a party of explorers to visit the Chowanoke Indians and to make inquiries about the Roanoke colonists. Sicklemore returned without learning anything definite, and in 1610 Captain Samuel Argall led an expedition southward from Jamestown into "parts of Chowanock" east of Roanoke River. Still the mystery remained unsolved. In 1622 John Pory, secretary to the Jamestown Colony, took an expedition to the Chowan River "through great forests of Pynes 15 or 16 myle broad and above 60 mile long."[10] Any of these groups might have bypassed the present Southampton to the east, but it is likely that all of them passed through what was to become the eastern part of the county. In the meantime William Strachey's *Historie of Travaile into Virginia Britania,* ca. 1612, sparked renewed interest in Ocamahawan by passing along Indian reports of two-story stone houses there. The knowledge of how to build such houses had been learned, according to Strachey, from "those English who escaped the slaughter at Roanoke."[11]

Despite these and other intriguing rumors about the mysterious place on the Roanoke River, there is no evidence of an English visit to Ocamahawan prior to Edward Bland's arrival there in 1650.[12] Bland's route evidently skirted modern Southampton to the west, but English navigators were by that time probing beyond the Chowan and into its northern tributaries. The map prepared by London cartographer Nicholas Comberford in 1657 located "South Key" on the Blackwater and extended the courses of the Blackwater and Nottoway well beyond earlier charts.

The English settlements remained for three decades confined to the margins of the James River and the shores of Chesapeake Bay, leaving the interior country unknown except to an occasional explorer or intrepid trapper. By 1632, settlement to the south of the James was sufficiently extensive for the colonial government to order monthly courts held at Warrosquyoake, also known as Bennett's Welcome. Two years later, when the Virginia colony was divided into eight shires, one of these was Warrasquyoake, which by 1637 had come to be known as Isle of Wight County. Lying between Lawne's Creek and the vicinity of Chuckatuck Creek on the James, this county extended for an indefinite distance into the unexplored southwest through an area that included Southampton and several other future counties.[13]

For more than a century after the first tentative movements of the English into the southwestern interior, the organization of political subdivisions was preceded by those of the Church of England. Warrosquyoake Shire occupied the same boundaries as an Anglican parish formed in 1629, and a division of the parish in 1643 anticipated the subsequent partition of the county. That part of the county lying north of Pagan Creek was known after 1629 as Upper (later Warrosquyoake) Parish and the part to the south as Lower (later Newport) Parish. When these parishes were again partitioned in 1734, the portions west of the Blackwater, designated Nottoway Parish, comprised the area soon to become Southampton County.[14]

In spite of religious turmoil and civil war in England after 1641, the Anglicans remained on the leading edge of westward migration, zealously carving out new parishes though the established clergy were far too few to serve them adequately. A certain Thomas Davis (or Davies) took out a land grant on the east bank of Blackwater in 1645,[15] but sixty years more would pass before the colonial government agreed to allow white settlement on the western side. Throughout the latter half of the seventeenth century, the region west of the Blackwater was to remain the preserve of tributary Indians, the chief guarantee of security from hostile tribes still farther west.

As the seventeenth century drew to a close, the inability of the colonial regime to discourage much longer the demands of colonists to be allowed to take up land beyond the Blackwater was becoming apparent. Francis Howard, Baron Howard of Effingham, who became governor of Virginia in 1684, denied a request in the following year by the House of Burgesses to permit occupation of abandoned or Indian lands on the Blackwater. One Williamson, surveyor for Isle of Wight and Surry, was suspended in the spring of 1697 for allowing entries "on the South side of Black Water Swamp." As early as 1693 petitions began to appear protesting the ban on occupation of lands to the south and west of Blackwater.[16]

Spurred by illegal occupation of frontier land and the consequent difficulty in collecting quitrents, the Burgesses in 1705 established boundaries around tributary Indian tribes and threw open the trans-Blackwater region to settlement. In England, the Board of Trade in the next year sought to put limits on the size of grants awarded in the new area, but the Burgesses responded that only a few patents had yet been issued there, the largest of which was for a modest 4,500 acres. The governor's Council at the end of 1710 prohibited settlement between the Nottoway and Meherrin, but even this barrier was swept aside within a few years.[17] The rush of colonization westward, however, brought to a head the long-disputed issue over the boundary between Virginia and North Carolina.

The Tuscarora Indian War, which broke out in September 1711, demonstrated the growing importance to the English of the region west of Blackwater and Chowan and the value of the water route provided by these streams. During the five years of the war, this

route was a primary artery of trade and communication between
Virginia and North Carolina. In particular, the Blackwater wharf
at South Quay became the main point of contact between the governments of the two colonies.

Although "South Key" first appeared on colonial maps in 1657,
the overland route from this vicinity was probably well-established
long before European settlers arrived. An Indian king on the
Chowan in 1586 told Ralph Lane, governor of the first Roanoke
Colony, that his black pearls came from a great bay to the northeast. It could be reached, he said, by "going three days' journey in
a canoe up the river" and then passing "overland northeast to a
certain king's [Powhatan's?] country, whose province lies upon the
sea." It has been argued that Lane himself might have gone as far
north as South Quay while exploring the tributaries of Albemarle
Sound. [18]

By 1701 South Quay had become the site of a landing and trading post operated by John Cotton, later a member of North Carolina's Council. Cotton's landing, four miles south of the present
Franklin, came into prominence in 1711 as the point where North
Carolina received the supplies furnished by Virginia for levying war
against the Tuscaroras. It had also been proposed as a meeting site
for the Virginia and North Carolina boundary line commissioners
in 1711. As early as June of that year Edward Hyde, governor of
North Carolina, was pleading with Spotswood for all the assistance
Virginia could offer against the threat of conflict. Hyde promised
to "have a Sloop or Sloopes and Canoes" at South Quay to take on
whatever help in the form of men or materials that Virginia could
provide. Five months later Thomas Pollock, the new governor of
Carolina, applied to Spotswood for the delivery of spades, pans,
and hand grenades at "Mr. John Cotton's on Blackwater where
a Canoe will meet them." [19]

When the hard-pressed North Carolina government asked for a
meeting with Virginia officials to bargain for further help, South
Quay was chosen as the site for the conference. Hyde promised the
Virginia governor that he would come himself and bring along Tom
Blount, chief of a band of friendly Tuscaroras. But Spotswood,
arriving "in the dead of winter"—February 1712—was outraged to
find that Hyde had sent instead two agents, neither of whom had

authority to conclude agreements. Returning to Williamsburg, Spotswood reported to the General Assembly that North Carolina ought to be "mortgaged in order to carry on the war." But South Quay continued to serve as the shipping point for North Carolina supplies, and it was the route used by Mrs. Hyde when she visited Williamsburg in the spring of 1713.[20]

By the close of the Indian war in 1714, the lands west of the Blackwater and Chowan were occupied by hundreds of pioneer families who could not be certain of the validity of their grants. Not only did Virginia's claim still extend to Wiccacon Creek, but North Carolina was making grants as far up as the west side of Nottoway. What both sides claimed, neither could properly administer, and Spotswood learned that "loose and disorderly people" were flocking into the contested zone.[21] Both Spotswood and the new Carolina governor, Charles Eden, were now determined to bring the issue to some kind of resolution.

The Dividing-Line Survey

Governors Eden and Spotswood reached an accord in 1715 that set in motion the long-needed survey of their common border. A surveying party would be directed to start at Currituck Inlet at latitude 36°30′, as required by the Carolina Charter of 1665. If a line brought westward from that point reached Chowan River, the boundary would continue west from the mouth of Wiccacon Creek; if it reached Blackwater River, the line would resume from the mouth of Nottoway. But even now there was to be a lengthy delay as the agreement was reviewed by royal authorities on the other side of the ocean.[22]

While the London bureaucracy dallied, the trickle of settlers into the disputed region rose to a steady stream. The establishment of Fort Christanna on the Meherrin River in 1714 increased the traffic across the Blackwater-Nottoway region and emboldened colonists to push their settlements westward. In 1722 a group of settlers living "a grat Distance from whare Vessells comes for Tradeing," petitioned Spotswood's successor, Hugh Drysdale, to station customs officers on the Blackwater and Nottoway so that trading ships from the Chowan would be willing to venture northward. Another petition of the same year, citing the poor roads between the James and Meherrin rivers, appealed for a division of the Anglican parishes at the Blackwater.[23] But the colonial administration hesitated to create new districts whose dimensions would be subject to doubt and controversy.

The Spotswood-Eden agreement finally received the approval of Carolina's Lords Proprietors in 1724 and that of the English Privy Council in 1727. Accordingly, commissioners, chain bearers, and other personnel gathered at Currituck Inlet in the first days of March 1728 and set forth on March 7 on the trek that was to carry them to the Appalachian Mountains.[24]

Owing to the obstacles posed by running the line directly through the Dismal Swamp, it was April 2 before the surveyors reached the end of the first leg of their expedition—a mile and a half north of the mouth of the Blackwater: the mouth of the Nottoway would serve as the starting point for the remainder of the survey.

The dividing-line journey was fortunate to have as its chronicler the gifted grandee of Westover plantation, William Byrd. No expedition with Byrd in it could fail to be a first-rate adventure, and no fools or scoundrels could hope to avoid the censure of his caustic pen. Moreover, the notes kept by Byrd and other members of the party provide an intriguing glimpse of the region that in two more decades was to become the county of Southampton.

Having ferried across the Chowan River on April 2 near its confluence with the two Virginia streams, Byrd and his party pitched their tents that evening at an Indian old field half a mile west of the Nottoway's mouth. They had just settled down for a night of hard-earned rest when a great hallooing from the river announced the unwelcome arrival of two straggling commissioners, Virginia's Richard Fitz-William and Carolina's John Lovick. These two had gone off to Edenton a few days earlier and now returned with a dozen bottles of wine and as many of beer, a treat the others would have gladly forgone to be rid of the men. Quarrelsome and irresponsible, Lovick and Fitz-William were to desert the party again next day as the line was run past Valentine Braswell's house, a hundred yards inside Virginia, where they looked forward to "good chear" and, with luck, handsome daughters.[25]

The boundary was carried forward twelve miles on April 3, crossing two roads that connected Isle of Wight County with North Carolina. From James Williams's, two and a half miles up the Nottoway, and Dr. Jesse Brown's, five miles farther upstream, ran roads leading to Cheshire's Ferry on the Meherrin, a few miles below the present Murfreesboro. Within a quarter mile of the boundary, on the Virginia side, lay farms occupied by Braswell (1.7 miles west of Nottoway), Richard Williams (a mile and half farther west), John Barrett (five miles south of modern Newsoms), and George Jackson (two miles southeast of the present Boykins.) "Most of the Houses in this Part of the Country," wrote Byrd in his journal, "are Loghouses, covered over with Pine or Cypress Shingles . . . hung upon Laths with Peggs, and the doors too turn upon wooden Hinges, and have wooden Locks to secure them, so that the Building is finisht without Nails or other Iron-Work." [26]

The next night's rest, on the east bank of the tree-jammed Meherrin River, was again disturbed by the revelers Lovick and Fitz-William, who disappointed their colleagues by safely passing over the many sharp cypress knees along their route. But the line was next day continued, passing near Thomas Pitman's (two miles southwest of the present Branchville) and the Widow Allen's (a mile west of Pitman's). A third road, leading from Elias Brady's Meherrin ferry (three miles southeast of Branchville) to Mackinne's on the Roanoke, was crossed before the surveyors passed beyond the region later to become Southampton. On April 6, with hot weather approaching and snakes beginning to appear, the expedition was broken off to be resumed in September. Recording his "grief to part with that sweet temper'd" Fitz-William, Byrd turned northeast with his other Virginia companions and, during the next three days' travel, bisected the region that was to become Southampton County. [27]

After so many weeks in the wilderness, it was a relief for the travelers to reach Samuel Kindred's farm, probably in the neighborhood of what is now Newsoms, where a militia company was at drill on a Saturday afternoon. "There were Girls enough come to see this Martial appearance," Byrd wrote, "to form another Company, & Beauty's enough among them to make Officers of." A few miles farther west the party crossed the Nottoway at Bolton's Ferry and spent the night at the nearby plantation of Richard Parker, "an honest Planter, whose Labours were rewarded with Plenty." With no little regret, the surveyors next day took leave of Sally Parker, the planter's attractive daughter, and Molly Izzard, proclaimed by Byrd to be "the smartest Damsel in these Parts." After satisfying the curiosity of some of the commissioners at Nottoway Town (on the site of Courtland) that evening, the party reached the Blackwater bridge at Col. Henry Harrison's on the afternoon of April 8 and "congratulated one another" on their "Return into Christendome."[28]

Byrd's revealing description of his trip through the Blackwater and Nottoway country seems misleading only with respect to the state of religion there. Anglicans had erected a chapel in 1726 at the east end of what was afterward known as Middle Seacock Bridge (between Berlin and Zuni), and services were being held from time to time at William Blake's farm on Angelico Creek and other places in the region. Reverend Peter Fontaine, an Anglican parson who served as chaplain to the surveyors, christened two children at Kindred's and preached a sermon at Richard Parker's next day, but the Blackwater did not mark the bounds of Christendom any more than it did those of English settlement.[29]

Byrd described a region where a scant quarter century of settlement had already brought a network of roads, bridges, and ferries and a number of prosperous farms. The area probably had no schools, but a few doctors were included in the first generation of settlers and an organized military force insured the safety of the pioneer families. Although most of the homes were undoubtedly crude and small, a few handsome residences, such as Rose Hill on the Nottoway, were already beginning to rise, and an active maritime commerce was developing on the lower Nottoway and Blackwater. It was a country where a measure of abundance was, according to William Byrd, "the Constant Portion of the Industrious."[30]

Colonial Southampton

By the close of the 1720s the tide of western migration was carrying some settlers so far from the Isle of Wight courthouse (near modern

Smithfield) that attendance at court could mean five days of travel in each direction. The formation of Brunswick County west of the Meherrin in 1733 brought relief to the outermost settlements, but those between Nottoway and Meherrin were still remote from their administrative center. A petition of 1734 to the General Assembly called for the relocation of the courthouse to a point nearer the center of Isle of Wight. Two years later the legislature authorized the construction of a new court at Quinny's Bridge on the east bank of the Blackwater. This site (four and a half miles south of Zuni) was still too distant, and a petition of 1746 noted that justices of the peace in outlying areas rarely attended court more than six times a year. Many litigants, witnesses, and jurors had to "walk Thirty Miles," sleeping in the woods en route, and often could not find lodgings once they had reached Quinny's Bridge.[31]

The General Assembly yielded. By laws enacted in October 1748 and April 1749, the legislators divided Isle of Wight and designated a new county called Southampton to be erected within the existing confines of Nottoway Parish. Except for the addition in 1786 of what had been the southwestern tip of Nansemond County, the county lines have remained the same ever since.[32]

The new county is believed to have been named in honor of Henry Wriothesley, third earl of Southampton. The earl, who died in 1624, had been a swashbuckling associate of the earl of Essex and was almost executed by Queen Elizabeth for his involvement in Essex's conspiracy of 1601. Released from prison following the death of the queen in 1603, Southampton rose to great power and prestige under James I. He was especially active in promoting colonization and was founder and third secretary of the Virginia Company. Hampton Roads and other Virginia place-names had long since borne witness to the esteem in which his memory was held on this side of the Atlantic.[33]

The first court of Southampton County assembled on June 8, 1749, at the home of Mrs. Elizabeth Ricks, but all subsequent sessions were to be held at Flowers's Bridge, two miles east.[34] The August court commenced at the house of Exum Scott at the latter place, and work was soon afterward begun on public buildings on two acres nearby which were purchased from Mrs. Elizabeth Exum. The county's first courthouse, a frame structure measuring forty by

twenty-four feet, was completed in 1752 but had to be replaced
when it was burned, allegedly by an incendiary, in 1767. A prison,
together with pillory and whipping post, had also been completed before the end of 1751. The tavern license granted to Quaker
Exum Scott in 1749 probably gave the future town of Jerusalem its
initial business venture.[35]

The public affairs of Southampton Court in its earliest years
reflected the primary concerns of a community in transition from a
frontier to a more settled condition. Overseers were appointed for
maintaining the county's roads and bridges, and bounties were
established for the scalps of squirrels and the heads of crows. Sign-
posts were ordered for the principal crossroads, and inspectors were
appointed for Southampton's chief commercial exports—beef, pork,
flour, tar, and pitch. Anglican churchwardens, the designated
guardians of public and private morality, brought frequent actions
against unwed mothers and other offenders and were sued in turn
by the courts for failure to keep the chapels in good repair.[36]

The Negro slave bore the main burden of the rigors of frontier
justice in the criminal courts. For stealing a hog in 1762, Benjamin
Ruffin's Negro York received thirty-nine lashes. For the theft of a
horse in the same year, Albridgton Jones's Scipio was hanged. A
Negro picked up without a pass cheated white justice by refusing
to divulge his name and then setting fire to the jail and escaping.
A more ominous case was that of Joshua Harris's Tom and Samuel
Westbrook's Peter, charged in 1764 with giving poison in the form
of "medicine" to "sundry persons." The pair were found guilty and
ordered to have thirty-nine lashes each, Tom being burned on the
hand as well. An omen of things to come in Southampton was the
account presented to the court in January 1764 for "whipping 11
Negroes by Order of a justice on Suspicion of an insurrection" and
for maintaining twenty-five blacks in jail on the same charge.[37]

The 2,009 people listed in 1755 as subject to the tithe in Southampton represented a total population of about four thousand
whites and some two thousand Negro slaves. Except for a few whose
occupation was flour milling or coopering, virtually every family's
main employment was farming. Many of these, however, supplemented their income seasonally by collecting tar, pitch, and turpentine from the abundant pine forests. James Auld, a Maryland man

who passed through Southampton on horseback in March 1765, found the latter business flourishing. After crossing the Blackwater bridge at South Quay on March 5, Auld proceeded next day to the Nottoway through "piney Lands" with "Tarr and Tarr kilns plenty—which they cart to South Quay & being stored there by Mr. [Thomas] Fisher is carted by the owners to Suffolk Town at the head of Nansemond." The rivers, particularly at this season of the herring run, produced "Plenty of Fresh Water Fish." [38]

The leading men of Southampton were mostly large planters whose landed estates imposed upon them at least a moral responsibility for active public service. Benjamin Ruffin was appointed sheriff at the first court in 1749 but was soon superseded by Samuel Blow. Thomas Clark was the first constable, and Richard Kello, owner of a gristmill, served as clerk of the court throughout the county's entire colonial period. Robert Jones, his merit certified by a commission from the president and masters of the College of William and Mary, was named first surveyor of the county. [39]

The names of Joseph Gray and Thomas Jarrell loom as those of early Southampton's most conspicuous leaders. Jarrell, with Etheldred Taylor, was elected to the House of Burgesses from Southampton in 1752 after having served as major in the county militia [40] and churchwarden since before 1749. [41] Gray, a native of Surry County, had been a burgess from Isle of Wight for thirteen years before the formation of Southampton and his election to the House from the new county for the years 1754–58 and 1762–69. Colonel of the county's first militia regiment, churchwarden for both Isle of Wight and, later, Southampton, sheriff of the latter in 1751–52, and justice of the peace, Gray was a figure of prominence in all phases of the life of the developing community. [42]

The principal institution of the county, aside from its court, was the Anglican church. Nottoway Parish was subdivided in 1762, the part west of Nottoway River becoming St. Luke's Parish. Besides Seacock Chapel, which had stood since 1726, the eastern (Nottoway) parish by now had a second chapel near Nottoway Swamp (three and a half miles east of Courtland) and a third at Flowers's Bridge. The only church building in St. Luke's at the time of its creation was the chapel finished in 1734 at William Blake's plantation (two miles northeast of Capron), but the edifice afterwards known as

Vick's Old Church was completed around 1768 a mile or so east
of the present Newsoms. The construction of the main church
(O'Berry's), in the fork of the Blackwater and Nottoway rivers,
about the same time marked the greatest extension of the Church
of England in colonial Southampton.[43]

The Anglicans were never able to provide properly for their outlying congregations, and the Nottoway settlers seem to have relied
for almost half a century on the occasional visits of ministers settled
farther east. Reverend Thomas Burges, however, was apparently
living in Southampton at the time the county was formed and seems
to have remained there until moving to Halifax, North Carolina,
in 1759. Reverend William Agar, whose presence in the colony was
precipitated by "some family crisis" in England, seems to have
served briefly in Southampton before his appointment to a profes-
sorship in mathematics at William and Mary in 1767. St. Luke's
Parish was fortunate to acquire a resident minister around 1763,
Rev. George Gurley, who was to remain a permanent resident and
sire a distinguished family of Anglican and Protestant Episcopal
clergymen.[44] Reverend Henry John Burges was briefly settled in
Nottoway Parish on the eve of the American Revolution.[45]

The Quakers of colonial Southampton constituted a large part of
the population of the county from its earliest days of settlement,
though only one meeting, that established at Black Creek, near Sedley, in the 1760s, is known to have existed before the Revolution.
The Baptists, awakened by the missionary work of John Meglamre
in the last decade before the Revolution, inaugurated their first
Southampton congregation at Mill Swamp in the summer of 1774
and another at South Quay that autumn.[46] The vitality of these
groups contrasted glaringly with the waning energies of the Church
of England, whose very name tied its destiny to that of the distant
monarchy.

The only formal educational institution known to have existed in
Southampton during the colonial era was the boarding school
operated at Broadwater by Samuel Nelson. His advertisement in
the *Virginia Gazette* in 1771 boasted that the school offered Latin,
Greek, and French along with geography and astronomy.[47] No
doubt many of the wealthier planters had the services of tutors by
this time or else sent their sons away to schools at Williamsburg

and elsewhere for their literary culture. Reading law with a licensed attorney or serving as apprentice to an established physician was the normal route into the learned professions, but for the majority of Southampton's youth the most serviceable education was still experience in the practical affairs of everyday life.

No longer a borderland by the 1770s, Southampton had become a settled community, in most respects well integrated into the mainstream of seaboard life. With no towns worthy of the name, however, lying athwart no thoroughfare of colonial commerce, the outlook of its citizens remained narrow and provincial. But then, quite unexpectedly, the events of the Revolution were to thrust Southampton briefly into the vortex of cosmopolitan concerns and make the county the very portal through which the Continental Army was to receive a large measure of its sustenance. Few interior populations were to be quite so jolted from their normal pursuits by the war as those of the lower Blackwater and Nottoway.

3

The Tale of the Spanish Cannons

The Row Galleys

For an arrangement thrown together in such a thoroughly unbusinesslike way, the building of the row galleys got off to a notably quick and smooth beginning. Superintendent Christopher Calvert fixed upon South Quay as the site for the construction and had his workmen assembled there by August 1776. Ox teams and crews of sawyers were sent into the woods in search of stout timber. Tar and pitch were available locally in any amount needed, and nails, iron, canvas, and other supplies could always be scrounged from somewhere in the Tidewater country. By the end of the summer the hull of the *Caswell* was already taking recognizable shape, and prospects seemed good for an early launch.[1]

Willis Wilson, a seasoned merchant captain from Portsmouth, was appointed to command of the *Caswell* (named for the first governor of the state of North Carolina) in September and directed to lose no time in recruiting a full crew for his vessel. Benjamin Franklin, Silas Deane, and Arthur Lee were authorized by the Continental Congress to contract with a European foundry for the casting of cannon from Swedish steel.[2]

In the first weeks of 1777, the Virginia Navy Board directed the purchase of forty-two bolts of cloth for the galley's sails, together with sail needles and twine. By early spring, the Board had also seen to the purchase of six time glasses, a log line, four speaking trumpets, and other gear. In the face of critical shortages, the Board located cartridge paper, lead, cutlasses, small arms, and other munitions for the *Caswell*. The procurement of flour, pork, bacon, and a ton of grease betokened a vessel in the last stage of readiness for encounters with the Navy of King George.[3]

The first year of construction ended and the second began with the *Caswell* still high on the scaffolding at South Quay and the *General Washington* apparently not yet started. A Virginia agent went to Edenton to receive materials North Carolina had agreed to furnish and found there only a little sailcloth and a couple of anchors.

The workers at South Quay grumbled about their wages and talked of quitting unless they got more money. Every few weeks seemed to bring a new alarm·over British penetration into the Tidewater backcountry and fresh levies on the dwindling manpower of Nansemond and Southampton counties. There was no word from Europe about the cannon, and a wide-ranging search turned up only three guns at Hatteras. These were shipped to South Quay, but they would not go far toward the armament of two 16-gun galleys.[4]

The lesson seemed clear even before 1778 began with the galleys still not ready: North Carolina and Virginia should never have become partners in this enterprise. It was true that both states stood to gain from the protection of Ocracoke Inlet against British warships. The closing of major Atlantic ports by blockade had redirected a great part of the overseas American trade to places like Edenton and South Quay which were beyond the reach of British men-of-war. But experienced businessmen knew from the start that the states would regret having no written contract to spell out mutual obligations. Those old enough to recall the boundary-line turmoil in the early years of the century wondered much that the two were attempting such a joint effort at all. If it took over half a century, with the Carolina Charter of 1665 in front of them, to settle a question of latitude, the likelihood of fidelity to a verbal agreement seemed altogether utopian.

Everything seemed to work against the plan. The North Carolinians thought their commitment was to outfit two vessels built by the Virginians. The Virginians understood that each state would build and equip an equivalent force. North Carolina authorities could neither beg, borrow, nor buy the equipment they were obligated to furnish. No cannon could be procured from the northern states, and South Carolina, in spite of appeals from the Continental Congress, could spare but little ordnance from its own defense.[5]

Pressed repeatedly by inspectors from the Navy Board, Superintendent Calvert pushed the work on the *Caswell* and got the keel laid for the *General Washington*. The former, launched and sent down to Edenton in the fall of 1777 while two British brigs were ravaging Ocracoke, was still seven months short of being seaworthy. But the

Caswell appeared, nevertheless, to be a splendid sailer. Seventy-five feet long and ten feet deep amidships, the galley had twenty-four rowports and six gunports on each side.[6] With her shallow draft and lateen sail, she could make headway in the shoalest sailing waters and even in a dead calm. In rivers and enclosed bodies of water the *Caswell* represented the ultimate in naval architecture for speed and maneuverability. At her station on Ocracoke Bar she would discourage enemy privateers and warships from the kind of havoc they had played with coastal shipping during the first three years of the war.

During the late spring of 1778 the *Caswell* lay at Edenton taking on such stores as fishhooks, sailcloth, blankets, clothing, and flour. She appears to have taken up her station in July, however, with only a part of the guns she was designed to carry. The *General Washington,* evidently launched in July, was not yet ready for sea duty and had still less prospect of a full complement of cannon once she was commissioned.[7] On the whole, it appeared that the Royal Navy would have little to fear from boats of such limited firepower.

And then Providence, as was her way in the English war, intervened once again on behalf of the beleaguered patriots. The *Caswell* had probably been on station at Ocracoke only a few days when Captain William Boritz arrived there in the *Sacre Coeur de Jesus* with forty-five new cannon for the patriot army and navy. Twenty-four and eighteen pounders, they had been acquired by Franklin, Deane, and Lee from the Rey and Brandenburg foundry in Spain and were to be paid for in Virginia and North Carolina tobacco, the former receiving twenty-two of the guns and the latter the rest.[8] Suddenly, the defense of Ocracoke and the thousands of miles of waterways to which it gave access seemed once more a feasible proposition. The *Caswell* and the *Washington* could ride out to meet the enemy in dignity and style, and the long war looked once again as if it could be won by the Americans after all.

The Safety Committee

The firing of the first shots at Concord Bridge in the spring of 1775 had found Southampton County organized for resistance to the crown, though most other Virginia counties were well ahead of it in this respect. A gathering at the courthouse on March 9, the initial meeting of Southampton's Council of Safety, resulted in the formation of a committee of correspondence to assist in gathering relief supplies for the patriots of blockaded Boston. Edwin Gray, son of the colonial legislator Thomas Gray and for the past six years himself a delegate to the House of Burgesses, was made chairman of the Committee of Safety and a member of the committee of correspondence. Serving with him on the latter body were Henry Taylor, his colleague in the House, along with Benjamin Ruffin, Jr., Thomas Edmunds, and Rev. George Gurley. Their duty was to work with similar committees in Surry, Sussex, Prince Edward, Dinwiddie, and Brunswick in gathering the supplies and forwarding them to Boston.[9] The drive would also serve the useful purpose of separating once and for all the earnest patriots from the conniving friends of the English monarch.

At meetings of the Committee of Safety in April, the members registered their approval of the call for defense of the colony issued from Richmond in March by the second Virginia Convention and scheduled an election for April 17 to choose a delegate to the "provincial congress." Henry Taylor and Edwin Gray were elected.[10] Each member of the committee was obligated to pay £10 toward providing lead and powder for the county militia, and a canvass of the county was called for to raise further contributions. By early fall the command of the county's seven militia companies had been vested in Captains John Taylor, Joshua Nicholson, John Rogers, William Blunt, Jesse Whitehead, Nathan Barnes, and Richard Blow.[11]

The alacrity of the Safety Committee was not universally shared in Southampton, and Edwin Gray and Henry Taylor had to be reimbursed by the committee when a subscription for funds to help send Virginia's delegates to the Continental Congress fell short by £20. But the receipt of commissions by James Ridley and Benjamin Blunt to serve as colonel and major, respectively, completed the county's militia organization in November. Captain Henry Taylor was successful in recruiting a company of "minute men," and the committee convened at Hay's Store in St. Luke's Parish to review the new company and hear oaths of allegiance by "36 able bodied men." In February 1776 a company of regulars was raised and placed under the command of Capt. Thomas Ridley, with Richard Blow and Albridgton Jones as lieutenants and Timothy Thorpe as ensign.[12]

Although there was apparently little outright hostility to the patriot cause in Southampton, various bits of evidence indicate a want of real fervor as yet among a great many inhabitants. Perhaps it owed something to the presence of a large and influential population of pacifist Quakers, but the mildness of the regime of the Committee of Safety seems noteworthy. While Nansemond's Safety Committee was publicly castigating Parson John Agnew for lack of patriotism, its Southampton counterpart was up to nothing more incendiary than summoning some merrymakers for "gaming at . . . John Scotts" in violation of the Continental Association. No action against the miscreants is recorded, however, in this, the only occasion in which the committee pondered exercise of its punitive power in the fifteen months for which minutes exist. The refusal of several citizens to accept proffered public offices is recorded in the minutes, but the committee appears to have taken an indulgent view of such things when they occurred.[13]

Whatever the sentiments of its citizens might have been, Southampton provided a full measure of its sons to the defense of the state. A sizable proportion of the county's 1,200 white males over sixteen years old saw service in the patriot cause, as did many of its slave and free Negro men, who numbered about a thousand. Owing to the frequency of alarms in the Hampton Roads area, many of the able-bodied men were called away as often as half a dozen times or more in the seven years of the war.[14] Lord Dunmore's activities around Norfolk, climaxed by the destruction of the city in January 1776, drew levies from Southampton, including Henry Taylor's minutemen, who occupied a station at Suffolk for a while during the winter. When the company was discharged in March of that year, it was replaced at Suffolk by Thomas Ridley's regulars.[15]

Despite the uneasy situation beyond its eastern boundaries, marked by Redcoat landings at Norfolk in May 1779 and October 1780 and by the occasional depredations of tory guerrillas near the Dismal Swamp, Southampton experienced the war only vicariously during the first six years of hostilities. Indeed, there were some on the lower reaches of the Nottoway and Blackwater rivers who probably shared the view of the inhabitants of Edenton and "wished peace away"[16] owing to the booming commerce that the times had brought to wharves unaccustomed to the rapacious demands of a nation at war.

The Haven

A commerce of modest proportions had been conducted at South Quay since the time of John Cotton in the first years of the eighteenth century, but it was the enterprise of Thomas Fisher that made it the leading river port of the Tidewater interior. By 1757, and perhaps earlier, Fisher, from Isle of Wight County, was engaged in trade at his South Quay warehouse. After his marriage around 1762, he was in partnership with his father-in-law, Dr. Henning Tembte of Nansemond. Besides their store and other facilities at the Blackwater wharf, Tembte and Fisher also owned the schooner *Dolphin*, built for them on the Nansemond River in 1763. This vessel traded as far away as the island of Saint Christopher, evidently carrying naval stores and agricultural produce on her outward voyages and returning with brown sugar, rum, coffee, molasses, and other products from the West Indies.[17] The firm's role as a conduit for tar bound overland to the Nansemond was noted in the preceding chapter.

A description of the South Quay establishment, published in the *Virginia Gazette* in 1769, indicates that Fisher lived in a 32-by-24-foot frame dwelling with four rooms and a brick cellar. Besides outhouses and "a young thriving orchard," there was a store and two new warehouses, each one measuring 30 by 20 feet, with 10-foot-wide sheds on all sides and "nine feet of water up to the warehouses." The site was considered especially important for the storage of pork, tobacco, and other products en route from the Roanoke and other rivers in North Carolina to those rivers tributary to Hampton Roads.[18]

By 1777, though Tembte and Fisher were both dead, the South Quay facilities had attained major significance in the Virginia economy. Operated by partners Benjamin Baker and Richard

Blow, the mercantile establishment became the nexus of a thriving trade carried on by small coasting vessels and, in some instances, transatlantic carriers. The pages of the *Virginia Gazette* in 1777 mention the presence at South Quay of the schooners *Westover* and *Friend Will*, lately from the West Indies, and the *Good Intent*, having imported loaf sugar, coffee, bottle corks, cotton and wool carding, sail canvas, rum, wine, and cloth.[19]

The existence of the log of the schooner *Conclusion*, of Newburyport, Massachusetts, allows us an inside glimpse of the trade of the lower Blackwater for a period of over eight months in 1778. The *Conclusion*, towed through a heavy rain by its own boat crew, reached South Quay at 1:30 in the morning on February 1. The vessel had run aground two or three times after leaving Wyanoke, at the North Carolina line, and was required to tie up at some trees instead of the wharf at South Quay landing, perhaps because available berths had already been taken.[20] The business of the next several weeks had to do mainly with careening the ship so as to pay the hull with turpentine and oil, painting, making candles, and from time to time, stowing a few precious hogsheads of tobacco.

Having expected to embark for Spain within about six weeks, the crew and officers of the *Conclusion* were disappointed to find that very little tobacco was on hand and that a long wait would be necessary before enough was brought in to make a payload. A single hogshead on February 28 was followed by two more on March 1 and an additional four on March 14, drawing from the keeper of the log the gloomy observation: "ye god only knows when we shall have 4 More for I Dont."[21] Spring passed into summer and summer into fall with the *Conclusion* lying dead in the water at South Quay and still not enough tobacco to fill its hold.

The onset of hot weather was torture for the pale New Englanders, who spent much time getting the schooner "in under the treas to keep the Sun from burning our Skin" and "covering our Ship with Pine boughs to keep the sun from burning her up." Mid-July brought a roaring freshet that carried away the South Quay Bridge and overflowed the low-lying fields, destroying much corn. But more vessels arrived, apparently undaunted by the news of slow trade on the Blackwater, including Captain "McFealeamey's" schooner from Cap-Français, and that of Captain Turner from

Saint Eustatius. One vessel left in June for Holland, and there were others venturing from time to time upriver to search for cargoes at smaller landings. Periodic reports were heard of "brittish Vessels . . . cruseing off Ocrocoak and have chased Several Vessels a Shore" or "Inglish Crusers" at Ocracoke Bar which had seized "6 Vessels and Run 5 on Shoar." The news that a French fleet had arrived on the coast in June and taken five British ships was a cause for general rejoicing. [22]

Not until the second week of October did the *Conclusion* receive its final loads of tobacco, perhaps delayed by the shortage of labor to harvest and haul it, and make ready for departure downriver. In company with the sloop *Saratoga,* the ship left South Quay on October 14, sent a party ashore four miles down the river to buy provisions, and reached Edenton in the early afternoon of October 16. [23] It was a good beginning in waters where ships could be idled for weeks by the absence of wind or by a sluggish current, but the *Conclusion*'s mission had been in vain. A few days after passing Ocracoke Bar she was run down by a British warship and sent to England under a prize crew. The *Esther*, which had put out from South Quay on February 19, was also taken by the British shortly after leaving the American coast. [24] Somehow, the row galleys did not seem to be achieving their purpose.

The Boritz Guns

Not least among the frustrations of the Revolutionary governments in Virginia and North Carolina in this period was their inability to provide adequate protection for the merchant vessels using their ports. Notwithstanding the commissioning of the *Caswell* and the *General Washington* and the arrival of the Boritz cannon, the enemy seemed to grow increasingly bolder in its forays along the Capes and Outer Banks. The curious history of the Boritz guns, in fact, pointed up the obstacles to cooperation between Virginia and North Carolina authorities and a disturbing want of efficiency in the councils responsible for coordinating the patriot war effort.

Upon reaching Edenton in July, 1778, Captain Boritz had promptly written to Congress for authority to deliver the guns. To this request he received no reply at all for some three months, his ship and crew standing idle at Edenton at considerable cost to himself and the North Carolina government. In October an agent finally arrived from Virginia with the authorization, and Boritz, unloading the North Carolina share of the cannon at Edenton, set sail up the Chowan with the remainder. After depositing the Virginia guns at South Quay and picking up Virginia tobacco in payment for them, Boritz returned to Edenton and began the negotiations with Carolina authorities which were to result in his being paid for the rest of the cannon and his own expenses—at the end of 1784.[25]

In the meantime, the guns had been dealt with in the most extraordinary manner by both state governments. Whether any of the cannon actually saw service in the war is an open question. North Carolina officials in December 1778 ordered eight of them taken on the *Caswell* for delivery to Fort Hancock, an earthwork on the Outer Banks. Captain Wilson was directed to take from the others at Edenton any that might be suitable for use on the galley. But a Virginia officer reported in 1797 that he had lately seen "about 30 exceeding fine cannon of 18,s and 24,s" at Edenton, evidently the entire North Carolina consignment. The Edenton guns had to be thrown into the bay during threats of a British attack before the end of 1781. They were subsequently salvaged but served the community in the years that followed only for occasional salutes on the Fourth of July.[26] Spiked by federal troops in 1862, some of the ill-fated guns still remain as decorative relics at Edenton and on the grounds of the state Capitol in Raleigh.[27]

The South Quay guns had a scarcely less inglorious career. Seven of them were moved laboriously to Suffolk in 1780 on fourteen-horse wagons with crews of workmen shoring up bridges along the route as they proceeded. With Lord Cornwallis moving north toward Virginia in the spring of 1781, the other guns remained idle while the Virginia War Office puzzled over the problem that "the people" in the South Quay neighborhood seemed "not well affected" and might react adversely to impressments aimed at moving the cannon. Governor Thomas Jefferson proposed that they be moved on flats down to some point where it might be easier to get them overland to the James, but the month of August found only three "on the road from South Quay to Milner's," near Suffolk. All were finally moved to the Nansemond in the closing weeks of 1781, too late for the seige at Yorktown.[28]

Equally depressing had been the service of the two row galleys. Captain Wilson found it impossible to get a full crew for the *Caswell* at the state allowance of half a dollar a day but managed to enroll 145 when a bill was introduced in the North Carolina legislature to raise the pay to $20 a month. The last wages earned by the crew before the galley's bottom rotted out and she sank in the spring of 1779 were paid to their heirs in 1803. The *General Washington*, commanded by Goodrich Boush of Norfolk, went into service at the end of 1778 but, like the *Caswell,* appears to have accomplished little, if anything, in the defense of the coasts or of trade.[29]

H.M.S. *Ariel,* stationed off the North Carolina coast by the British in May 1778, took six merchant vessels in her first month there and caused two others to be burned. In July, North Carolina newspapers reported that "the cruizers are yet very troublesome on our coast, having lately cut several vessels and small craft out of Roanoke and Currituck Inlets." Governor Richard Caswell learned in November that the "coast is much infested at this time with the enemy which are constantly landing men and plundering," and enemy privateers entered Currituck Inlet that month to capture and set fire to two Carolina ships. A disgruntled Governor Patrick Henry wrote to Caswell in February 1779 to wonder if North Carolina did not feel obligated to reimburse Virginia "in some considerable degree" for "the great expenditures incurred" in the construction and equipping of the galleys but evidently received no answer to his letter. When North Carolina rejected a Virginia offer to sell the ships, the Virginia General Assembly issued orders that they be dismantled and disposed of for whatever compensation they would bring.[30] So ended the voyages of the *Caswell* and *General Washington.*

The coup de grace had not yet been delivered. Lord Cornwallis, moving in a wide arc up from North Carolina and then south along the James in the summer of 1781, was creating pandemonium throughout central and southeastern Virginia. Mary Fisher, widow of Thomas Fisher, was still living at South Quay when Cornwallis approached the Virginia border in the spring, and she shared the general apprehension that the Blackwater commerce would be a

Governor's Palace in Williamsburg. Sketch inside cover
of Southampton County Will Book, vol. 3, pt. 1, shows
palace at the time of the Revolutionary War. Does the
artist's name (Kello?) appear in the chimney smoke?
(Clerk's Office, Courtland, Va.; photograph by Colbert
Howell)

key objective of the British army. A letter from her to Southampton
Clerk of Court Samuel Kello in March implored his services in
marrying her daughter Tembte Fisher to Redmond Hackett even
though Tembte was legally a resident of Nansemond. In view of
the situation, Mrs. Fisher had "thought it prudent to Remove my
Daughter from this public place to a friends house one Mr. Hardy
Cobbs in So. Hampton where she will live untill . . . the Enemy's
Departure."[31]

The blow fell on July 16. Tarleton's cavalry, seven hundred strong
and one of the most feared fighting units in the British army, galloped into South Quay and "destroyed Houses in which were a considerable Quantity of private Stores," including rum, tobacco,
sugar, ship rigging, and other valuable property. A detachment
sent on farther down the Blackwater ravaged warehouses at Wyanoke and Maney's ferries on the upper Chowan, burning at the

latter place a large quantity of supplies recently impressed from Baker and Blow at South Quay by Maj. Hardy Murfree. When they retreated toward Suffolk on July 19, the British left South Quay a smoldering ruin.[32]

But the destruction of South Quay was not the end of its significance as a shipping point. Thomas Blount, a member of a prominent North Carolina mercantile family, wrote from there in September 1781 to inform his brother that "a very extensive trade is carried on here. Tobacco comes down in great quantities for which Salt is given at the rate of 1 Bushl p Cwt. . . . Colo Baker's family are all well."[33] In fact, a final little drama of the war was to be acted out at South Quay in the early part of the following year.

Dr. Robert Lenox was a Scot of Bertie County, North Carolina, who had gotten himself into difficulties with the government of that state in 1777 for his reluctance to subscribe to the oath of allegiance to the patriot cause. Compelled to leave the state in 1779, Lenox left his family behind to try to hold title to his considerable property in land and slaves. He was granted permission to return to North Carolina in 1781, but he arrived at Edenton in February 1782 with a cargo of illegal goods, including blankets, hats, silks, axes, adzes, ginger, nutmeg, porter, rum, and ivory-handled knives and forks. Two privateers, one of them Virginian, seized possession of Lenox's ship, the *Three Friends,* and sailed it to South Quay where the odds were stronger that the vessel would be condemned and its ownership vested in the captors. The incident led to recriminations between Governors Burke of North Carolina and Harrison of Virginia but was finally smoothed over so that the privateers were able to auction off the vessel and cargo and divide the profits.[34]

South Quay continued to play a part in the economic fortunes of the adjacent country for some years to come, though its vitality does not seem to have returned even to that of the years immediately preceding the war. A petition to the General Assembly in late 1784, signed by 121 persons, many of them farmers and businessmen of the surrounding counties of Virginia and North Carolina, called for revival of the customs depot there. The petition pointed out that the place had formerly had warehouses sufficient "to contain all the tobacco which went with great safety" to its markets. Since 1781 the proprietors had rebuilt the warehouses so that they were "not sufficient to contain 600 hogsheads." Thomas Browne was later appointed collector of the port, but exports from South Quay in 1791 were down to less than $900 a year, the lowest of any port in Virginia. The decline of the facility continued and the place appears to have been abandoned, at least for commercial purposes, within another few years.[35] Not the British army but the changing patterns of commerce had been responsible for South Quay's demise.

The Peace

The signing of the peace treaty with England in 1783 brought to Southampton a tranquillity that was not altogether welcome. The giddy boom-time in the last years of the war had given some people a taste for quick riches and a life-style that could not be maintained there in normal times. Some, no doubt, were lured away to the coastal cities in the hope of finding opportunities to continue the pursuits that the war had stimulated. Others headed west to take up bounty lands earned for service in the war. Among those who remained, however, the impact of the flush times during the war soon manifested itself in a spirit of improvement, an effort to bring a new vitality to the county's businesses and institutions.

Some such spirit had already given rise to Southampton's most ambitious eighteenth-century educational enterprise, Millfield Academy. Reverend Henry John Burges, an Anglican minister who settled in Southampton about the beginning of the Revolutionary War, opened a school at his home (between present Berlin and Ivor) and soon gained a wide reputation for the excellence of his instruction. His most celebrated student was William Henry Harrison, the future president, who attended Burges's school in the mid-1780s. Burges, a son of Rev. Thomas Burges, was born in 1744, probably in what is now Southampton, ordained in London in 1768, and had preached and taught in Isle of Wight County before the Revolution. He was a member of Isle of Wight's Safety Committee at the outbreak of the war and spent some time as a prisoner of the British after he was captured in 1779.[36]

When the General Assembly in 1790 authorized Francis Boykin, Benjamin Blunt, and others to raise £300 by lottery toward the erection of an academy, Burges and his wife deeded two acres of land for the erection of both Millfield Chapel (Episcopal) and Millfield Academy.[37] The progressive impulse also gave rise to the act passed in 1790 for clearing Blackwater River to make it navigable from Broadwater to points farther up the river. The addition of South Quay and the lower Nansemond to Southampton County in 1786 and talk of a canal to connect Albemarle Sound with Hampton Roads seemed to augur well for the commercial prospects of the region as well as the educational ones.[38]

But the capstone of the postwar progressive movement was the establishment of Southampton's first town at what had been known as Southampton Court House, in 1791. Petitioners, including Samuel Kello, Benjamin Ruffin, John T. Blow, Benjamin Edwards, and Josiah Vick, declared to the legislature that the site was "an eligible situation for the reception of all kinds of produce." Inhabitants of the vicinity, however, had always been required to carry their goods a considerable distance to the nearest markets. The General Assembly agreed to the laying off of town lots on ten acres of land belonging to Joseph and William Scott and decreed that the new town should be known as Jerusalem.[39]

Not unrelated to the fresh outlook for the material prospects of the county was the new vigor of its religious institutions. Reverend George Gurley resigned his rectorship in St. Luke's in 1793 but left his son and assistant, Joseph Gurley, to carry on his work among the Episcopalians.[40] Colonel Thomas Ridley, returning from a distinguished career in the Continental Army, became a vestryman in St. Luke's Parish, raising hopes for the rise of a new Episcopal organization from the ruins of the Anglican. The Baptists, gaining rapidly in the optimistic atmosphere of the new republic, founded a new congregation in 1786 at Black Creek, near modern Ivor, where Rev. John Dupree had first preached fourteen years earlier. Hebron Church, on Flat Swamp, first known as Sturgeon's Meeting House and later as Meherrin Church, was organized in 1788 with John Meglamre as its first pastor.[41]

Methodists drew their inspiration from their itinerant ministers, whose periodic visits were becoming more frequent by the time of the Revolution. Francis Asbury, greatest of the itinerants, preached in Southampton on a number of occasions in the 1780s and, very likely, for some years afterward. His journal observes that he "beheld the power of God manifested in several lively meetings" here in June 1788. He had attended Methodist services at Nottoway Chapel as early as the spring of 1780.[42] Within a few decades, Methodism would become a major force in the life of Southampton's people, spurred on mightily by the influence of the Great Revival.

The forces of moral reform in Southampton faced a formidable challenge. The region's excellent apple and peach brandy, the fondness of many of its inhabitants for horse racing[43] and gambling probably brought about the relapse of many a pious convert. Captain James Wilkinson of Millbrook plantation on the Meherrin in 1790 paid 100,000 pounds of tobacco—at forty shillings per hundred pounds—for the studhorse Medley, which had been imported from England in 1784.[44] By the century's end there were to be many other celebrated thoroughbreds on the farms of Southampton.

The lower orders of Southampton society found their sporting entertainment in less expensive pursuits, including boxing and cockfighting. Elkanah Watson, visiting Southampton from his Chowan River plantation in August 1787, witnessed and described a raucous cockfight which he attended in company with a Mr. Wright, "a great planter" of the county. "We reach'd the ground," says Watson,

about 10 0'C. . . . the roads alive with carriages. . . . Several scattering houses form a spacious square opposite to a bridge, in the centre of which was a large Cockpit, surrounded by many gentele people intermixt with the gouging gentry. Very beautiful Cocks were produc'd with long sharp steele pointed gafts firmly fixt over their natural spurs—the moment they were dropt, betts run high. . . . they step'd round with great pride— & conscious dignity approaching nearer & nearer at length, they spontaneously flew at each other at the same instant with a rude shock—the fatal & cruel gafts hove up into their bodies. . . . I was soon sickened with the scene for which I had no taste and retired under the shade of a large willow, where I was much more entertain'd in witnessing a *voluntary* battle between a wasp, and a spider.

I was really astonish'd in withdrawing from the crowd to Notice men of respectability—some—giving countenance to this ignorant & barbarous sport, so abhorent to every sentiment of humanity.[45]

The first federal census of Southampton County, conducted in 1790, found a total of 12,864 inhabitants. The white population, now amounting to 6,312, had lately been overtaken by the combined totals of slaves, free Negroes, and Indians, who numbered 6,552.[46] Many white families, including especially some of the Quakers, owned no slaves, but some planters were beginning to put together great plantations worked by large gangs of Negro laborers. The slave code had not yet developed into quite the iron system it was to become, but already the first stirrings of black revolt were being heard on the island of Santo Domingo and slave owners read with apprehension of the successes of slave armies against their white overlords in the West Indies. It was food for much thought in a county where blacks increasingly outnumbered their white masters.

4

Incident at Black Creek

A Preacher's View

Whatever hopes the Protestants held out for Southampton County appeared to have died even before the old century ended. Reverend David Barrow, removing to Kentucky in 1798, complained of "the present deadness and coldness of religion" in and about Southampton. The Great Revival swept over Virginia and much of North Carolina in 1801 and 1802, but Rev. Lorenzo Dow, passing through Jerusalem in April 1804, pronounced that village "a place of much wickedness." Although Dow had preached a sermon in the courthouse, nobody had asked him either to eat or drink, "which is the greatest inhospitality," he lamented, that "I had met with for some time." Theophilus Gates, preaching the first sermon of his career in Southampton in March 1810, was disappointed to encounter a congregation that was "filled with amazement" by his impassioned discourse, one member having actually "left his seat, got into his carriage and road away" while Gates was speaking. Next day, in northern Hertford County, he was consoled to find his listeners "uncommonly attentive" and "more pious than any I had met with since I left Maryland."[1]

Piety, indeed, seemed to be confined below the North Carolina line in this vicinity. Reverend John Early, a Methodist itinerant, conducted services at a North Carolina site known as Boykins' Camp Meeting in July 1812 and experienced what he called "the greatest disorder I ever saw at a meeting, for the Camp Meeting was near the line of Virginia and the Virginians came over and a number behaved like ludicrous fellows . . . the magistrates punished several, though we had several pistols presented at the magistrates."[2]

Contributing to Southampton's reputation for wickedness and irreligion was the fondness of so many of its inhabitants for spirituous liquors, especially in the form of the county's celebrated apple and peach brandy. Virtually every farm between the Blackwater and Meherrin had its orchard and distillery; and brandy, as a native observed, "was the principal source of revenue" for many South-amptonians. Congressman Edwin Gray's plantation in 1814 boasted an appurtenance comprised of five stills with capacities of 140, 141, 149, 174, and 177 gallons, respectively. A visitor to the county around 1810 was entertained by a well-to-do planter whose morning invariably began with a toddy of apple brandy, and the same drink preceded every meal. The only medicine in use on this plantation was a mixture of brandy laced with sugar or honey, and the visitor was assured that "no doctor [had] ever been called, professionally, to see anyone at the place."[3]

Almost equally pernicious, in the view of some, was Southamp-ton's enthusiasm for horse racing and horse breeding. Races were being held at Jerusalem at the opening of the nineteenth century but may have lapsed for a few years prior to the formation of the Jerusalem Jockey Club in the autumn of 1830. Club President William B. Goodwyn and Secretary Alexander P. Peete announced in October that the races beginning on November 9 would include a $100 sweepstakes for colts and fillies in a one-mile heat and purses of from $150 to $500 for horses, mares, and geldings in heats of one, two, and three miles. There was another racing season in May, so scheduled as to coordinate with those in Lawrenceville and Norfolk in order that sportsmen might attend all three in succession.[4]

The outstanding horse breeder in Southampton was Capt. Thomas Gray (brother of Edwin) of Round Hill (between modern Vicksville and Berlin). Gray's stables at one time or another included eighteen thoroughbred horses, from Pegasus, certified in 1814, to Terpsichore, certified in 1823. Levi Rochelle's ten pedigreed studs, Maj. Thomas Ridley's eight, Benjamin Cobb's seven, and Jeremiah Cobb's three ranked them among Southampton's leading breeders, who also included Congressman George Booth Cary, William Blow, Joseph Ruffin, and Benjamin Blunt, among others. Many of their horses were descended from the illustrious stallion Sir Archie, owned by William Amis in Northampton County, and very likely several fortunes could trace either their beginning or end to the risky investments made by Southampton's gentlemen of the turf in prime horseflesh.[5]

It was not exactly dissoluteness with which the Southamptonian of the time could typically be charged as much as a certain joie de

vivre that set worldly pleasures ahead of spiritual ones. There was
a gambler's mentality abroad in the land, and the penchant sometimes took surprising turns, as when Mrs. Nancy Hill, aged seventy,
in 1827 took for her husband Master Howell Francis, a lad of sixteen.[6] Men of the pulpit labored earnestly against the natural instincts and proclivities of their Southampton brethren, but the odds
they could offer were not sufficiently attractive to summon forth
very many wagers. The mighty wind of the Great Revival, it
appeared, had blown past Southampton County without so much
as stirring a leaf or bending a twig.

But the root evil in Southampton and its environs was understood by Rev. David Barrow of Black Creek Church to be neither
liquor nor horses but money, and this cause, in turn, was the main
prop to the institution of slavery, the most inexcusable of all man's
sins against his fellow man. A native of Brunswick County where he
was born in 1753, Barrow had spent twenty-four years as a Baptist
minister in Southampton and adjacent counties before delivering
his published attack on the slave system in 1798.[7] The occasion
of his outburst was his decision to move from Virginia to Kentucky,
and it was through the medium of a circular letter to his friends
and other interested persons that he sought to explain his reasons
for leaving his congregations.

The main reason, Barrow indicated, was that he could no longer
support his family properly "in a poor country, without falling into
the line of speculation, or that of holding slaves." The latter alterna-
tive was even more repugnant than the former, the writer having set
free his slaves in 1784, ten years after becoming a preacher.[8]

The grounds for Barrow's opposition to slavery were both political
and religious; in brief, he was convinced that the institution of
slavery was inconsistent with the republican form of government
and with the revealed word of God. With Thomas Jefferson, he
affirmed "the natural equality of man" and the principle that
liberty was "the inalienable privilege of all complexions, shapes,
and sizes of men." No human being, he contended, could legiti-
mately be bound "in person, or property, but by laws of his own
making or those of his representatives fairly chosen." Those who
maintained that slavery was not evil when enforced by kind masters
seemed to forget, observed Barrow, that slaves in such cases were

still liable at any time to become the property of some heir or successor who might well be cruel, and against such a fate the slave had no legal recourse. Not only was slavery opposed to the principles of good government, however; it was equally contrary "to the laws of God and nature."[9] If, therefore, the writer must depend in part on farming for his family's support, then let his field of enterprise be in Kentucky or some other place where slaves were not needed in order to glean from the soil a decent living.

Though he left no champion of equal boldness and talent to carry on his antislavery crusade in Tidewater, it was clear that Barrow spoke not for himself alone. Within the circuit of his ministry were several Quaker communities which had been denouncing slavery as an evil since the close of the Revoluntionary War. More recently, similar notions had been voiced by some of the Methodists, among whom it was well known that Charles Wesley himself had been a determined enemy of human servitude. Black Creek Church, as well as other Baptist congregations under Barrow's influence, had a clear majority at this time in favor of abolition.

The enemies of David Barrow no doubt rejoiced at his departure from Virginia, and Black Creek Church would soon enough settle into a less demanding role than that of spearheading the antislavery vanguard. But the questions raised by Barrow would not lie still. Within a decade the departed minister would issue a more forceful indictment of the slave system than that of 1798, and in 1825, the ghost of David Barrow was to return to haunt the Black Creek congregation by forcing on them once again the necessity of consulting their consciences on the terrible unanswered questions he had raised.

Nottoway Depot

During the second decade of the nineteenth century, enterprising people of the Tidewater interior exerted themselves again to try to reduce some of the obstacles that restricted the commercial opportunities of their region. Those who lived on the lower Blackwater enjoyed the benefits of a tight but adequate ship channel, though Ocracoke Bar and its treacherous seven-foot-deep passage still limited severely the size of boats that could reach the Chowan and its tributaries. But the navigation of the Nottoway was an adventure through minefields of submerged cypress knees and fallen timbers, and the Meherrin above Murfreesboro was simply not to be negotiated except by flatboats and canoes.

A consequence of these difficulties was that the farmers and businessmen of the Albemarle-Tidewater region paid considerably more for everything they imported and received proportionately less for the goods they exported than almost any others along the eastern seaboard. A gathering of interested people from throughout the region assembled at Murfreesboro in 1830 to propose the opening of Roanoke Inlet through the Outer Banks barricade as a form of relief to their distress. They approved a report which contended that they could command no more than $25 a thousand for their pipe staves, for example, while at Suffolk, which had free and unimpeded access to the ocean, the same produce brought $40 per thousand. Staves, shingles, and other lumber products brought a third less in profits to this region, a circumstance tending to discourage industry and handicap farming.[10]

As gloomy as the outlook appeared, a series of developments reaching back to about 1811 had been working their way toward a solution of sorts and greater economic progress for the affected areas. The Meherrin River Navigation Company was incorporated in that year for the purpose of clearing the river from Murfreesboro north to the Lower Falls, several miles inside Virginia.[11] But it was on the Nottoway that the greatest signs of enterprise were to be seen.

In December 1817 Clements Rochelle, owner of Brown's Ferry, a Nottoway crossing eight miles below Jerusalem, petitioned the General Assembly for a town at the site. He pointed out that this was the highest point of navigation on the river for oceangoing vessels and that the adjacent country abounded in lumber, naval stores, and "articles of heavy transportation." There were fisheries in the vicinity that would add much to the commerce of the Nottoway, and the river might be cleared for as much as seventy miles farther up to accommodate smaller craft. These and other prospects seemed promising for the rise of "a prosperous and flourishing town." The new town, named for incumbent President James Monroe, was incorporated in 1818, and a new petition before the year's end requested permission to add fifty more acres in view of "the rapidly increasing demand for property in the said town, in consequence of the commercial advantages which it presents."[12]

Monroe had a post office by 1819, but its history was to be surprisingly brief. By a deed of 1824, most of the land comprising the place was conveyed by Tyler Edwards to John Marchant of Worcester, Massachusetts, reserving lots owned by Hardy Cross, Zebediah Washington, John Thomas, and others along Jack's Street, Catherine Street, Washington Street, Rochelle Alley, and so on.[13] Such a speculative transaction suggest that Monroe may already have begun to decline, and the town appears, indeed, to have been all but abandoned even before the coming of the Portsmouth and Roanoke Railroad rerouted its traffic along other channels in 1835. The problem for Monroe may have been the costs involved in attempting to maintain the Nottoway's shallow and twisting channel intact despite the freshets that periodically threw up fresh sandbars or laid down intricate new patterns of logs and debris as discouragements to ship captains.

A single circumstance, however, had given the town of Monroe its permanent footnote-niche in the history books: the birth there on December 1, 1826, of William Mahone, who was destined for a remarkable career of personal achievement and integrity, as Confederate general and United States senator, on fields darkened by corruption and defeat. His father, Fielding Jordan Mahone, was locally celebrated as a mathematician and English scholar, but William may have owed his warlike propensities to a kinsman whose Irish heritage manifested itself in occasional donnybrooks. A Murfreesboro physician, himself a Catholic Irishman, in January 1825 made an entry in his diary about having been called to visit a certain Joe Williams, "who says he was stab'd & shot by P. Mahone of Munroe—as I dislike cases of the kind, knowing that if he died I should have to attend S.Ampton court for some time—directed him to another Doctor." The Mahones lived in a large old brick home built by the Brown family, who had furnished the county with several generations of reputable physicians.[14]

Sons and Stepsons

That Southampton was no longer characterized by the insularity of its formative years was reflected by the growing numbers of its sons who were going forth in the opening years of the nineteenth century to careers of usefulness in other spheres. Edwin Gray, son and namesake of a noted Southampton legislator of the previous century, served seven terms in Congress before his retirement in 1813, and John Cowper Gray of Jerusalem briefly filled a congressional vacancy during the 1820–1821 legislative term.[15] Two Southampton natives, James Turner and William Miller, occupied the governor's office of North Carolina, the first from 1802 to 1805, the second from 1814 to 1817. Turner also served two subsequent terms in the United States Senate, and Miller was a state legislator before his appointment in 1825 as chargé d'affaires to Guatemala. Biographers have been challenged, however, to discover anything of particular merit in the careers of either man. Turner died in 1824, Miller in 1825.[16]

The leading citizen of Southampton in these years was not a native of the county: he was John Young Mason of Greensville County, sometime resident of Fortsville plantation in western Southampton. Following a brilliant career as a student at the University of North Carolina, Mason in 1819 earned his license to practice law in Virginia. He was elected in 1823 as Southampton's representative to the House of Delegates and three years later to the state Senate. Elected in 1831 to Congress, he distinguished himself as a stalwart Jacksonian, and it was he who introduced the bill calling for recognition of the independence of Texas. Following appointment in 1841 as a United States District Court judge, he was selected by President John Tyler for the position of secretary of the navy, an office he continued to hold under James K. Polk, Tyler's successor and old friend from Mason's college days.[17]

Mason returned to the Virginia legislature in 1850 where, "[f]at, ruddy, and . . . pleasant speaking," as a Richmond paper described him, gray-haired since before he was thirty, he seemed to have been turned permanently out to pasture. After campaigning strenuously for Franklin Pierce, however, Mason was in 1853 named minister plenipotentiary to France and was associated in the following year

James Turner. Governor of North Carolina, 1802–5, Turner was born in Southampton on December 20, 1766, but his family moved to Warren County, N.C., in 1770. Chosen to fill a vacancy in the U.S. Senate in 1805, he remained in Congress until 1816. (N.C. Division of Archives and History, Raleigh)

William Miller. A Southampton native who was North Carolina's governor, 1814–17, Miller was also a state senator and U.S. chargé d'affaires to Guatemala. (N.C. Division of Archives and History, Raleigh)

with the ministers to England and Spain in drawing up the so-called Ostend Manifesto. By this secret but flamboyantly worded document, the three ministers called on Secretary of State William Marcy to undertake to purchase Cuba from Spain or, failing that, "the wresting it from Spain if we have the power." It was a symbol of the age of Manifest Destiny, but when the document was leaked to the public, northern opinion suspected a southern plot to create a Caribbean slave empire. An embarrassed administration summarily rejected the scheme, and Mason, suffering a stroke of apoplexy at the legation in Paris, died there in October 1859. He was buried at Richmond, and his family retired to Fortsville.[18]

John Y. Mason. Born in Greensville County
in 1799, Mason lived much of his adult
life in Southampton. He was a state legislator, congressman, district court judge,
secretary of the navy, attorney general,
and framer of the Ostend Manifesto.
(Reproduced through courtesy of the
Virginia Historical Society)

The Unsparing Rod

The advance of Southampton's sons and stepsons upon the stage of
national affairs indicated the progress, among other things, of
educational facilities within the county and a stronger inclination
on the part of the planters to insure, if possible, the higher education
of at least one son. Legislation enacted by Virginia in 1818 led to the
appointment of the county's first Board of School Commissioners,
including Dr. Goodwyn and James Rochelle of the horse-fancying
fraternity, Dr. Carr Bowers (a prominent Baptist layman), magis-
trate Jeremiah Cobb, and eleven others. With a limited budget
derived from the state Literary Fund, it was their responsibility to

assist, where feasible, in the construction of schoolhouses and to provide partial salaries for teachers. Schools aided by the commissioners included those of John R. Williams near Newsoms, William D. Hood near Vicksville, and James W. Murfee of Murfee's Depot. By 1831 there were also some sixteen other small schools scattered about the county which received some part of their funds through the school commission.[19]

The regimen of these spartan institutions, perhaps not quite so severe as in earlier times, was nevertheless demanding, at least with respect to discipline. W. O. Denegre was an old man living in Minnesota when he recalled his school years under Schoolmaster Hood in the 1830s. The teacher he remembered as "a Tartar—of fierce and ungovernable passions, fiery and impulsive and more than willing on any occasion to use the hickory on us, boys or girls." A frequent victim of Hood's ire was Master William Rawlings, "a holy terror" even in Denegre's eyes, who remained superbly unintimidated by the four or five hickory sticks that hung at all times from nails along the wall. The only check on Hood's temper was the occasional intervention of an irate father large enough to cast his shadow over the Vicksville tyrant.[20]

If schoolmasters tolerated little unruliness from their charges, the school commissioners were not less vigilant about the devotion of teachers to their duty. The commissioners were quick to discover in 1832, for example, that Brookes R. Trezevant, who conducted a school near Jerusalem, had become quite stupefyingly enamored of Rachel Godwin. Trezevant, though described by one of his pupils as "a competent Latin schollar and a very excellent teacher," unwisely tried to attend to the young lady "and school at the same time," and had to be "very prudently dismissed" by the commission. But Brookes was married to Rachel on Christmas Day following and, with a regularity unhinted in his professional life, fathered by her ten children.[21]

Elliott L. Story, one of Trezevant's students, began his school years in 1829 under Israel Gillette near Nottoway Chapel in an era when students had not yet surrendered the "turning out" ritual whereby they sometimes won for themselves an early start on a vacation. Story, as a teacher himself in 1838, was able to resist rather a feeble effort of the kind, wherein students would attempt physically to overpower the teacher and require him to declare an early beginning to Christmas vacation or some other holiday. Story's own philosophy of discipline, shaped by his experiences under Gillette, Trezevant, Joseph Pretlow, Thomas W. Joyner, and other schoolmasters, was later encapsulated in his journal in these terms: "When a caution fails to render the little urchin tractable to duty, when a well understood and severe look, fails to bend the larger lad to that which conduces to his own future good, more decisive must be the look and language and the caution must be exchanged for the compulsive power of the rod although so repugnant to the feelings of the doctor, and patient."[22]

At Elliott Story's own Blackwater Free School the regular academic routine included morning lessons in reading, writing, ciphering, spelling, and geography. After an hour's "dinner" or "play-time," students returned for recitations until 5 P.M. in all of the morning lessons plus American history. It was the teacher's responsibility to assign each student to a class appropriate to his ability and former training and to draw up and enforce all rules and regulations. Friday was an especially busy day, involving recitations of weekly lessons and the study of tables of arithmetic, rules of punctuation, abbreviations, and so on. Not until he had been teaching for several years did Story introduce composition in writing as part of the curriculum. "No school to which I ever went," he explained, "did the teacher require any of the students to write compositions of their own. . . . I now consider it one of the most useful exercises in which the students engage."[23]

Because nearly all lessons were learned by rote and repetition, regularity of attendance on the part of both pupil and teacher seemed a critical concern. "I am . . . disgusted," Story wrote, "with the way that most of the children are sent to school . . . staying at home a week and coming a week, staying at home a day and coming a day, and thus knowing but little more at the year's end than they did when they began." As for himself, there was "more necessity of regularity in teaching school than almost any thing else, and besides when a teacher takes a day the students are apt to take more and thus a day's absence may confuse . . . the whole week."[24] With scarcely five years of formal schooling of his own, Elliott Story and others like him were performing a major service in raising the sights of Southampton's citizens to an enlarged appreciation of the world in which they lived.

Trampling Out the Vintage

Although the Great Revival that opened the nineteenth century had little immediate effect upon Southampton, the first thirty years of the new century saw a gradual broadening and deepening of religion across the county's landscape. Formation of the Portsmouth Association in 1791 laid the foundation for a disciplined growth among the Baptists, though Tucker Swamp was the only new congregation formed in Southampton during the next forty years. Methodists enjoyed a more encouraging growth, so that by the 1830s they had churches at Mount Horeb and Barnes's in the southeastern part of the county, at Peete's and Applewhite's in the west, and Clarksbury (originally Turner's) in the central part. Members of the Christian church, an offshoot of Methodism, organized Barrett's and Union congregations and enjoyed an active associa-

Clarksbury Meeting House. Reverend Joshua Leigh drew this architectural plan for the church building in 1837. The church was erected according to Leigh's specifications. (Southampton County Historical Society; photograph by Colbert Howell)

tion under Rev. Burwell Barrett, his son James, and other Christian
leaders. The leading religious spokesmen in Southampton included
Rev. Robert Murrell, the "soldier preacher" at Hebron Baptist
Church for thirty-seven years, and Rev. Simon Murfee, minister
at South Quay Baptist Church before his removal to Nansemond
County.[25]

The slow growth of active church membership in Southampton
owed much to the zeal of dedicated men and women who often
worked tirelessly to win over the unconsecrated to a faith in the
Lord Jesus. But it also owed something to the sacrifice of fundamental moral issues to superficial ones. Following David Barrow's
departure in 1798, churchmen tended to concern themselves with
such questions as whether it was more godly to sprinkle or immerse
and ritual fulminations against sins of the flesh. The question of
slavery was put to rest, and ministers learned to reconcile themselves to slaveowning, perhaps even to invest in a few slaves of their
own.

The history of Black Creek Church bore solemn witness to the
Protestant retreat from the slave question. In 1786, when David
Barrow raised with Black Creek the question of whether it was "a
righteous thing for a christian to hold or Cause any of the Human
race to be held in slavery," the answer he received was an unequiv-
ocal negative. There was even strong sentiment at Black Creek to the
effect that it was immoral to hire slaves from a slaveowner. But the
issues that concerned Black Creek after Barrow's removal to Kentucky ran more along the lines of whether it was acceptable for
Elizabeth Fowler to have a child only four months after her marriage.[26] If Black Creek could set aside the slave question so readily,
it was clear where sister congregations must stand on the matter.

And so the situation remained until the memorable fourth Sunday in December 1825. On that morning Rev. Jonathan Lankford,
a member of the church for more than twenty-five years and its minister for the past seven, startled his congregation with an announcement that he "could not, nor would not administer the ordinances
of the gospel to the Church any longer—because a Part of the church
were slave-holders." It appeared that a sizable minority were owners
of slaves, so largely had the character of its membership changed
since the time of David Barrow.[27]

A church committee was appointed to inquire into Lankford's behavior, and its findings were presented to the church in December 1827. The committee had ascertained that Rev. Mr. Lankford had, "through the vain influence of Improper impressions, yielded too much to the delusion of Satan, and thereby lost sight of the duties of the Gospel, has been actuated in this case, by self interested and improper motives, That his [real] object has been, to split the Church asunder, in order to Promote, in some way or other, his own selfish views and purposes."[22] In fact, Lankford had already been expelled from the congregation in 1826, after which he invited nonslaveholding members to join him in leaving. None did. It seemed to the committee ungrateful on the part of the errant pastor that he had "waxed fatt and kicked" the very church which had been the means of "raising him from the very depths of his Poverty." He must not, in any case, be allowed to exercise control of the congregation "on an important question, over which they considered he had no cognizance further than as regarded his own conscience."[28]

David Barrow, in all likelihood the indirect instrument of Jonathan Lankford's downfall, had been in a Kentucky grave for twelve years. But in 1808 he had issued a pamphlet with the self-explanatory title *Involuntary, Unmerited, Perpetual, Absolute, Hereditary Slavery, Examined; on the Principles of Nature, Reason, Justice, Policy, and Scripture.* To those who argued that the Scriptures enjoined upon slaves the duty to obey their masters, Barrow replied that this was not the same as justifying the condition of slavery. To those who pleaded that slavery appeared to exist through the foreknowledge of God, that He had permitted and not abolished it, wherefore He must have decreed it, the author replied that this argument would "justify all the abominations that have ever infested our world." In response to all who cited the curse evoked by Ham's mocking of his father's nakedness, Barrow observed that the punishment seemed ill-suited to the crime and that the prophecy of doom was made not against Africa but Canaan. To those, finally, who held that slavery gained its legitimacy from its acceptance by those who had "obtained forgiveness . . . through our Lord Jesus Christ," Barrow offered a reminder of those who, though confessing candidly their sins, "have again fallen asleep."[29]

It was the fifth paragraph on page 41 of the pamphlet that might have commanded the attention of those who could not be swayed by exegeses of the Scriptures. "Upon the whole," Barrow wrote, "I do most sincerely pity (as well as blame) those poor Christians, and others, who are involved in the fashionable sin of holding slaves, who must feel at times the scourges of conscience on the occasion, and foresee the bitter consequences which do, and will in future attend it: yet will plead for, and hug the evil."[30]

As it was with David Barrow's ringing indictment of slavery in 1808, the Bible was to serve as the text for a still more notable opponent of slavery, also professing a Baptist ministry, who would deliver his blow against the institution in the summer of 1831. At Black Creek Church, the congregation would gather for regular services on the fourth Sunday in September of that year and the entry for the day in the minute book would be a model of pious circumspection: "It is agreed," wrote the secretary, "that the sacrament be Postponed in consequence of the unpleasant feeling the white brethren have towards the black brethren."[31] The occasion, in fact, for the postponement of the sacrament was the murder nearby of more than a hundred human beings, white and black.

5

Element of Surprise

The Precursers

The Negro revolt of October 1799 came, as usual, as a shocking surprise. People recalled, of course, the plot uncovered at Richmond in the summer of 1793 and the conspiracy in Petersburg a month later and the threats from the Negroes in Norfolk and Portsmouth that fall and the poison murders by slaves in neighboring Hertford County in 1794.[1] But these things always seemed to catch the whites off their guard and to come at places and times when they were least expected. And it was certainly possible to persuade oneself that the trouble in 1799 would never have occurred if the slave buyers had not unluckily chosen to direct their course through Southampton County instead of some other way.

This latest outbreak among the Negroes had taken place on the evening of October 15 on the high road from Broadwater to Jerusalem. Slave dealers Joshua Butte and Harris Spears had just purchased from William Boykin and Ben Drew some likely looking Negroes and added them to the slave gang they were driving toward Georgia. According to the testimony of Jeffry and Lydia, two members of the slave coffle, Butte and Spears had been set upon by several of the slaves armed "with sticks knives and pistols." Both white men had been killed and then robbed of $30 in silver by their assailants. The culprits were identified as Hatter Isaac, Old Sam, Jerry, Isaac, and Young Sam. The court, after weighing the testimony, handed down convictions against the first four, all of whom were sentenced to hang on November 25, and against Young Sam, who, pleading benefit of clergy because of his youth, was given thirty-nine lashes, branded on the hand, and released.[2]

In the late summer of 1800 all of Virginia was thrown into a frenzy of bewilderment when word leaked out that Gabriel Prosser, a Henrico County black, had been prevented from leading an army of hundreds of slaves in storming Richmond, seizing the arsenal, and burning the city. A network of agents had reportedly enlisted large numbers of slaves from as far away as Petersburg. They were found to have planned to kill all the whites with the exception of Quakers, Methodists, and Frenchmen and to crown Prosser as king of Virginia when their victory was complete.[3] Southampton magistrates sent out patrols to "visit all Negro quarters and places suspected of entertaining unlawful assemblies &c.,"[4] but no evidence of sinister designs could be found among the county's black inhabitants.

Despite mysterious reports of unrest among the blacks around Petersburg in November 1801, followed by the discovery of slave conspiracies in Nottoway, York, Accomack, and Powhatan counties,[5] Southampton whites were again startled to learn in early February 1802 that the serpent of rebellion was now coiled within their own jurisdiction. The news came in the form of a terrifying message said to have been found lying in the road near Barrow's Store and detailing a conspiracy which was "that precisely by which they succeeded in St. Domingo and enveloped that whole colony in flames in an hour on the same night, and murdered thousands of whites."[6] The message was signed "J.L." and addressed to "the Representative of the lower Company." It spoke menacingly of "intelligence from all parts that our intentions have successfully spread . . . and meets with unanimous approval among our fellow sufferers." The writer boasted that "we shall certainly succeed without difficulty if our scheme is not betrayed before hand as there is but one in a family to know of it until the time is actually arrived, I do not apprehend much danger of that, & as [for] the poor sort that has no blacks if any such should escape I doubt not but the general conflagration of Horses, fodder stacks &c. will strike such a damp on their spirits that they will not only be willing to acknowledge liberty & equality but [be] glad to purchase their lives at any price."[7]

A postscript reference to the "Representative of the Roanoke Company" appeared to indicate that the plot might extend well into the Roanoke River valley in Virginia and North Carolina. There was little doubt that the note exposed "a plan now on foot," as one slave owner saw it, "by the blacks for the execution of the whites."[8] The suspicion gathered strength from the simultaneous detection of a plot in Brunswick County[9] and then a great rash of reports of the same kind from Nelson, Orange, Augusta,[10] and several North Carolina counties. No one seems to have been charged with responsibility for the Southampton letter, but the murder of William Summerell by slaves in early February created much consternation over whether the crime might be only the protruding tip of a massive conspiracy.

Testimony in the Summerell murder case showed that the victim, overseer on James Wilkinson's Meherrin River farm, was so thoroughly despised by his Negroes that some had talked among themselves about poisoning him—a few, indeed, were "raving for it." In the spring of 1801 a slave named George had proposed a subscription to purchase some poison, and a quarter dollar each was contributed by Hercules, Henry, and Big Anthony. With this, George procured some scorpions' heads, but the plan miscarried when George's wife, fearing they were meant for her, destroyed them.

A new plan was concocted and took effect on Monday, February 8, 1802, as Summerell was crossing the Meherrin in a boat from the Greensville side to Southampton. He was within about fifteen feet of the Southampton shore when Hercules fired a gun at him from the brush, the charge striking Summerell in the breast. Assisted by a fellow slave named Aaron, Hercules scrambled out to the boat, and the two Negroes pounded the overseer with large sticks until they were sure he was dead. Then they buried the corpse under some logs in a mud flat and left to help themselves to meat and brandy stored in Wilkinson's cellar and smokehouse.

The county court convicted Henry, George, and Hercules, all of whom were hanged. Evidence suggested it had been an isolated incident, but the murder of three whites and the execution of six slaves in a space of less than eighteen months had frayed the nerves of Southampton's citizenry. In July, Dick Claud was brought to trial for the attempted murder of his master, Joshua Claud. The evidence of witnesses was conclusive, and Dick was swung off on Friday, August 13. Five weeks later, two more were hanged for the murder of a fellow slave.[11]

The late spring of 1802 had, in the meantime, been a mournful period of insurrection panics, trials, convictions, and executions throughout Virginia and eastern North Carolina. In April there was a wave of terror in Halifax, Amelia, and Charlotte counties, the discovery of an alleged Negro plot to burn Norfolk, and spates

of alarm in Hanover, Middlesex, Pittsylvania, Lunenburg,[12] Campbell, and King and Queen counties.[13] Early May brought the revelation of still another plot to burn Richmond and then a catastrophic
outburst in all the North Carolina counties bordering the Virginia
Tidewater.[14] At least thirty alleged conspirators were executed in
the two states before the crisis ended in late June.[15]

A Nansemond County resident, writing in June to Governor
Monroe, confessed his dismay over the latest disturbances, coming,
as they did, "just as the citizens of this county . . . were in some
measure relieved from apprehension of danger."[16] The whole thing,
it seems, had burst upon the whites as a baffling and demoralizing
surprise.

The "Blue Lizard"

Through the eyes of a black boy growing up as a slave on a Southampton County farm in the early nineteenth century, the institution
of slavery was less a matter of corporal brutality (though there was
that, too) than of acute personal insecurity and physical squalor.
Fed Moore would remember in later years old lady Betty Moore,
his owner, as a bespectacled and snuff-sniffing crone who carried
about with her a blue-painted cowhide, "dangling at her side like
[English] ladies . . . wear their scissors." The instrument was known
among the slaves as the "blue lizard."[17]

Fed's mother Nancy belonged to old Widow Moore, but Joe, his
father, lived with a planter named Binford in Northampton County,
North Carolina. Joe was the son of an Ebo who was "stolen from
Africa," and although Fed never remembered seeing his father but
once, he recalled that he was "very black." Later, when Binford
moved farther away from Southampton, Nancy abandoned hope
of ever seeing him again and took another husband. This was Lamb
Collier, a slave on a plantation adjoining the widow's. To the three
children she had by Joe were now to be added three more by Lamb,
all of whom, with Nancy's niece Annikie and at least three of her
children, lived in Nancy's cabin.

The living quarters of the ten or more people comprising Nancy's
family was a two-room log structure with a mud floor, thatched roof,

and walls of wattle and daub. "Our sleeping place," the only furniture, Fed remembered as having been "made by driving a forked stake into the floor, which served to support a cross-piece of wood, one end of it resting in the crotch, the other against the shingle that formed the wall. A plank or two across, over the top, completed the bed-room arrangements, with the exception of another plank on which we laid straw or cotton-pickings, and over that a blanket."

Every morning old lady Moore would call the black children up to the "big house" and have each of them take a dose of garlic and rue "to keep us 'wholesome' . . . and make us 'grow likely for market.'" When the draught was swallowed, each child had to run around the big sycamore in the yard, making, if possible, a progress rapid enough to keep the "blue lizard" securely in its case. "She liked to see her people constantly employed," Fed related, "and would make us all set to work at night, after our day's labour was over, picking the seed out of cotton."

Fed's own responsibility as a small boy was mainly that of keeping watch over his younger brother during the day while his mother worked in the fields. Until they reached the age of twelve or thirteen, all of the slave children went naked, with sometimes an old shirt to wear in case they were called up to the big house or sent on an errand by the widow. At puberty, boys began receiving their yearly allotment of two pairs of thin cotton pants and two cotton shirts, the girls receiving two petticoats and a shirt similar to those of the boys. Such clothing, "made of the lowest quality material," according to Fed, was almost always ragged and useless within a short time, "even for the purpose of the barest decency."

A traumatic event for Fed and his family in these early years came one autumn (probably around 1805) when, the last of Widow Moore's daughters having married, it came time to divide the estate according to directions in her late husband's will. All the slaves were collected under the great sycamore and parceled out by the executors among the widow and daughters, Fed and his mother being assigned to James Davis, a son-in-law who lived in Northampton County. "It was a heart-rending scene," as Fed recalled; "there was so much crying and wailing," as Nancy's other children were delivered to new owners. "I really thought my mother would have died of grief at being obliged to leave her . . . children, her mother, and relations behind."

Next morning Fed, his mother, and other Negroes belonging to Davis's portion set out on foot along the road to Northampton County, forty-five miles distant. Along the way they subsisted on johnnycake, hoecake, and water, camping that night by a woods and sleeping in the wagons or on piles of leaves around a campfire. Urged on at times by Davis's whip or, alternatively, by a promise of black-eyed peas, bacon rinds, and hard cider at journey's end, the coffle reached Davis's farm next afternoon. Here Fed fell quickly into the eighteen-hour-a-day regimen of hard work that was to be his lot for the next year and a half. Sold away from his mother at the age of ten to a Georgia slave buyer, he spent many years in the cotton fields of the deep South before finally escaping to freedom. He was living in London in 1855 when he related the memoirs that became a book entitled *Slave Life in Georgia,* a stinging indictment of the slave system and those who supported it.

Not many found permanent escape possible from this squalid existence, but many tried it and by a variety of means, legal as well as illegal. The most enterprising of the runaways, even if they failed to reach free territory and remain, sometimes managed to exist for years at a stretch by hiding out in woods and swamps and stealing food from orchards and smokehouses. A notable example was Bob Ricks, a slave of a Southampton farmer, who in 1824 helped form a notorious gang of fugitives that raided along the Carolina-Virginia border.

It appears that Ricks and a fellow fugitive recruited their own outlaw band by contriving to rescue seventeen slaves from a coffle passing through North Carolina en route to Georgia. For months afterward the gang plundered farms in Southampton, Sussex, Gates, and Nansemond and were accused of the murder in Gates County of Elisha Cross. In June 1824 four of Bob's confederates made their way to Petersburg, procured forged papers identifying them as free Negroes, and attempted to secure passage northward on board a ship. The captain became suspicious and had them arrested by Petersburg police, but Bob Ricks, presumably, was able to continue his fugitive existence along the backways of the Tidewater

Anthony W. Gardner. This Southampton
native became president of the Republic
of Liberia, 1879–83. He was also vice-
president, legislator, and signer of Liberia's
Declaration of Independence. (Reprinted,
by permission of Fountainhead Publishers,
Inc., from C. Abayomi Cassell, *Liberia:
History of the First African Republic*)

country. Mr. Womble's Tom was another Southampton runaway
whose exploits became a topic of editorial complaint in the 1820s.[18]

By Virginia law any slave manumitted by his owner was required
to leave the state after a certain period of months, a rule that sometimes worked hardships on those affected by it. Anthony Blunt,
freed by the will of his master, Benjamin Blunt, Sr., in 1826, appealed to the legislature for the right to remain in Southampton,
citing the fact that he was past sixty years of age and, evidently,
rapidly approaching a time when he would no longer be able to fend
for himself. The petition was rejected.[19]

Others, mostly members of Southampton's free Negro community, were able to secure the sponsorship of the American Colonization Society (ACS) in seeking emigration to Africa. The colonization

scheme enjoyed moderate popularity among the whites of the region in the mid-1820s when a chapter of the ACS was established at nearby Murfreesboro, North Carolina, and ACS agents paid several visits to the area.[20] Thirteen Southampton blacks named Clarke left for Liberia on the schooner *Cyrus,* from Norfolk, in 1824, and fifteen named Brown and Davis on the *Hunter* in the year following. After a lull of several years, a total of forty-two more obtained passage in 1830 aboard the *Valador* and *Montgomery.*[21] But the free black population of the county, frequently enlarged by manumissions performed by Quaker, Methodist, and other slave owners, was growing much faster than those of either slaves or whites. For most, Africa held out little prospect of a better life and the ACS created little interest among black people—at least before the autumn of 1831.

Among the last to leave for Liberia on the eve of the slave rebellion was a free black family named Gardner, which took passage from Norfolk on the *Valador* on January 11, 1831. Anthony W. Gardner, at that time eleven years old, was to obtain an education in the schools of Liberia during the 1830s and serve three terms as the eighth president of the Republic of Liberia between 1879 and 1883. The Southampton native also served for sixteen consecutive years in the National Legislature, four years as vice-president of the republic, and as a member of the convention which drafted Liberia's constitution in 1846. Prior to his death in 1886 he was the last surviving signer of his nation's Declaration of Independence.[22]

The most dramatic and controversial attempt at legal escape from slavery was that made in behalf of a black man named Sam Blow, a slave of Southampton planter Peter Blow. Sam Blow, or, as he was later to style himself, Dred Scott, was born near Edom, in the Shenandoah Valley, in 1809.[23] He was reared, however, partly on Blow's 860 acres of farmed-out land at Gum Branch, some seven or eight miles northeast of the locality in which Nat Turner resided.[24] Following particularly poor crop years in 1814 and 1815, Peter Blow in 1816 moved with his family and slaves to Huntsville, Alabama, and, in 1823, to Saint Louis.

While Blow took charge of a boardinghouse, Sam was hired out as a house servant and his brothers Luke and William as stevedores. In 1829 Sam was married to a young woman belonging to a neighbor of the Blows, but she was sold away to Arkansas a few months later. Sam ran away not long after this, but he was caught, whipped and returned to his owner. It was about that time that he began to use the name of Dred Scott in place of the name he had carried since birth.

Peter Blow soon died, and Dred was sold to an ill-tempered army surgeon named John Emerson, who took his servant along with him to various army posts, including Fort Snelling, near Minneapolis. Although he was now living on free soil, no issue was raised about Dred's status, and he was married around 1836 to Harriet, a girl of fifteen, who belonged to Major Louis Talifiaro. Their first child, Eliza, was born on a Mississippi riverboat in 1838 as Emerson, having purchased Harriet, was en route back to Saint Louis.

Not long after returning to Saint Louis, Dred Scott proposed to Dr. Emerson that he be permitted to purchase his freedom along with that of his wife and child. The doctor refused and hired out Dred instead to an army captain who carried him to Texas where he remained until Dred contracted malaria in 1845 and was returned to Saint Louis. Upon recovering, Dred petitioned the Circuit Court of Saint Louis for his freedom, citing that he had lived for several years in the state of Illinois and the Minnesota Territory, neither of which recognized slavery. While the case pended, his second daughter, Lizzie, was born in 1846. The court granted Dred's petition, but the matter was appealed to the Missouri Supreme Court where the decision was overturned.[25]

Five of Peter Blow's children, all of them opponents of any further extension of slavery, joined with Dred in helping to bring his case before the United States Supreme Court. To the amazement of slavery's opponents north and south, the high court, in its ruling in 1857, held not only that Dred was not free by virtue of having lived in free territory but that the Missouri Compromise of 1820 had been unconstitutional. It was the position of Chief Justice Roger B. Taney that slaves were no different from any other property protected by the "due process" clause of the Federal Constitution. Laws aimed at restricting the extension of slavery into free states and territories all seemed to be in jeopardy. The Dred Scott decision had the effect of rousing abolitionist tempers to white heat and bringing on the crisis resulting in secession and civil war four years later.

Although the test case involving Dred Scott had ominously backfired, Dred was purchased and given his freedom later in 1857 by Peter Blow, Jr., Stephen Blow, and other children of Peter Blow. Dred took a job as a porter at the Theron Barnum Hotel in Saint Louis but became ill in the winter and died on September 17, 1858, of tuberculosis. His funeral expenses were paid by his fellow Southamptonian, Henry Blow.[26] By a means as unwitting as Nat Turner's had been deliberate, Dred Scott had contributed to the destruction of the institution of slavery in the United States.

Dred Scott. Under the name Sam Blow, Scott lived for several years in Southampton before moving west and gaining celebrity as the principal in the famous slavery case. (Original in the possession of the Missouri Historical Society, St. Louis)

The Omen

On Saturday, August 13, 1831, residents along the entire eastern seaboard of the United States awoke to a morning sun that seemed to be in its last stages of extinction. Its pale, silvery light, changing as the day progressed to an eerie blue, was somewhat like that accompanying an eclipse, and it was possible to stare directly into it for any length of time without discomfort. Those who did stare observed a black spot on the sun's surface a little to the lower right of center.[27] The beamless light was such that it gave "an unusually ghastly appearance to the countenances of persons," and "the great orb of light," wrote a New York witness, "seemed to have left the skies, and to hang in our own atmosphere, suspended like a balloon at no very great distance from the earth."[28]

At sunset—6:30 P.M.—the western sky began to turn into a "curtain of vermilion," the light increasing for some time after sunset and remaining visible until around 8 P.M., and, on Manhattan Island, giving the impression of a huge fire burning in Newark. The moon during the evening gave off a sickly green color, thought one viewer, "like the inside of a good citron melon."[29]

Newspaper editors everywhere commented extensively on the solar phenomena. The occasion was described by a Charleston, South Carolina, journalist as providing "the most extraordinary optical appearances that have ever fallen under our observation."[30] In Fredericksburg, Virginia, it was "a spectacle, altogether such as we have never seen before."[31] Savants and amateur astronomers offered a wealth of explanations, mostly having to do with an unusually large amount of vapor in the atmosphere, but some editors wondered aloud if it might not be unwise to call so much attention to the events. "We know our patrons are too much enlightened to harbor [superstitious] sentiments," wrote the proprietor of a journal in Raleigh, North Carolina, "but this paper may fall into the hands of others for whom we cannot vouch."[32]

The note of caution concerned that class of persons who, "adhering to the absurd predictions of the ancient Astrologers, view such events as ominous of some direful catastrophe—think that the world is coming to an end, or a bloody war" is near. There were those, another noted, who "take it for granted that war is at hand."[33]

And, on a remote farm in the southeastern part of Southampton County, the celestial wonders were observed by a black field hand who, as he afterwards confessed, saw in them the signal that "determined me not to wait longer."[34]

Catalyst

Nat Turner was born in Southampton County on October 2, 1800, in the midst of the panic over Gabriel Prosser's plot and two days before the Southampton magistrates ordered out the county's patrols in response to the Richmond disturbance. Bred to a strongly religious cast of mind, he had, about the year 1827, undergone an intense spiritual experience which he shared first with a somewhat dissolute local white man named Etheldred T. Brantley.[35] The two applied together for baptism at a local church, and when this was refused, Nat gave out that they would publicly baptize themselves. He was said to have announced that on the appointed day "a dove would be seen to descend from Heaven and perch on his head." Onlookers gathered for the event and watched as the two entered the water together, where they were "baptized by the Spirit," though no dove appeared.[36]

Long interested in signs and portents, Nat now became a serious student of such things and became convinced that they held for him a special and profoundly significant meaning. The solar eclipse of February 1831 was a signal, he felt, that he "should rise and prepare" himself. Before that had come a "loud noise in the heavens," on May 12, 1828, and an admonition from "the Spirit" that "the time was fast approaching when the first should be last and the last should be first."[37] From these and other mystical occurrences, including personal visitations from "the Spirit," Nat came to feel that he had been chosen by God to take the lead in liberating the black people from bondage.

In the late summer of 1831, Nat had been for not quite two years the servant of a rural carriage maker named Joseph Travis, who owned a small farm a little west of Cross Keys community.[38] Nat's legal owner was a boy named Putnam Moore, a stepson of Travis who, in October 1829, had married Moore's mother.[39] Before that,

Nat Turner. This sketch, reputedly executed by William Ernest Braxton, may have been copied from the portrait of Nat accompanying T. R. Gray's edition of the *Confessions of Nat Turner* in 1831. (The Associated Publishers, Inc.)

Nat had had three previous owners: Thomas Moore, who died in 1828; Samuel Turner, dead since 1822; and Benjamin Turner, Samuel's father, whose death had occurred in 1810.[40] The farms of all three men were within an area of a few square miles, so that the various changes of residence had meant for Nat little interruption of the relationships he had known since boyhood and probably little alteration in the round of chores and activities that circumscribed his life. He had probably never been more than a few miles from his birthplace. His labor was hard, but the crops of corn and cotton that formed the staples of Southampton County probably did not demand of him the brutal work that hundreds of thousands of slaves farther south were forced routinely to endure.[41]

There is no indication from available records that Nat's masters were notably cruel to their slaves in general or to him in particular, though one was reported to have whipped him in 1826 for declaring that the slaves should be free and one day would be. He had run away from an overseer, probably shortly after the death of Samuel

Turner, but he returned voluntarily after about thirty days.[42] The breakup of the slave family of Thomas Moore at the beginning of 1830 may have separated Nat from his wife, but Giles Reese, her new master, lived near the Travis place and Nat would presumably have been able to see her often. Hark, a fellow slave whom Nat had known for many years, was sold at that time to Travis, and Sam, also a slave of Thomas Moore's estate, may have been conveyed to Nathaniel Francis, another nearby farmer.[43] But Joseph Travis had come to live at the house of his new wife and Nat was not required to leave the farm.[44]

Soon after the eclipse in February, Nat began to make the arrangements that seemed to be demanded of him by the spiritual powers now directing his thoughts. In the early spring he revealed his intentions to four of his fellow slaves in whom he placed the greatest confidence. These were Hark Travis, Nelson Edwards, Henry Porter, and Sam Francis, all of them slaves on farms in the immediate vicinity of one another. By about the beginning of the summer of 1831 the five men had settled upon a plan to launch the revolt on the Fourth of July.[45] As the Fourth fell on Monday, there would be a holiday preceding, on which to make final preparations, and many of the whites could be expected to be absent from home for much of the day on Monday, attending local celebrations.[46]

In the last days before July 4, Nat grew ill from tension and worry and was forced to postpone the date of the initial assault. But he had recovered by August 13 when the blue sun with the black spot on its surface appeared in the heavens and showed him that the time to strike was now certainly arrived. The plotters fixed upon Sunday, August 21, as the most suitable day.[47] Many white families were planning to attend a camp meeting in neighboring Gates County,[48] and the Travises themselves would be away from home all day attending religious services. On Saturday, Nat held a conference with Hark and Henry, and the three agreed to prepare a banquet next day at Cabin Pond, a dank and secluded area near the Travis home,[49] for those who would launch the uprising. Once the conspirators were all assembled, a final plan would be adopted and put into execution.

Next morning Hark caught and killed a pig, which he carried to the designated site, and Henry brought some brandy, probably lately distilled by his master, Richard Porter. Sam and Nelson soon arrived, as did Will Francis, another of Nathaniel Francis's slaves, and Jack Reese. Nat, arriving late, as was his policy, was not surprised to find Jack among them, he being "only a tool in the hands of Hark," the husband of Jack's sister. But the leader had not anticipated the presence of Will Francis and asked him how he came to be there. Will responded that "his life was worth no more than the others, and his liberty [was] as dear to him" as theirs.[50] The plot would be laid, therefore, by seven men whose loyalty to one another seemed certain.

The conspirators, lingering for several hours over the fresh brandy and the roasting pig, resolved that the attack would begin that night at the Travis house. On the question of whether any whites should be spared once the slaughter began, Nat gave it as his opinion that both sexes and all ages must be destroyed until their force had grown large enough and their weapons powerful enough to exercise lenity toward noncombatants and, perhaps, the slaveless poor.[51]

Having remained at Cabin Pond until "two hours into the night," (probably between 10 and 11 P.M.), the seven walked through the woods together to the Travis home. Travis's slave Austin and a boy named Moses greeted them there, the former agreeing at once to take part in the assault. All but Nat went to the cider press to drink, and the group appears to have passed several hours in and about the kitchen dependency before finally resolving to get on with the business they came for.[52] The loss of a substantial part of the night, however, had already denied to them a large measure of the terror they could hope to generate in the hours ahead. Only Nat's absolute conviction that he acted at the behest of a fostering deity gave the plot substance and the chance of success.

Joseph Travis and his wife Sally, with their infant child, Travis's apprentice Joel Westbrook, and Sally's son Putnam Moore had been away from home most of the day and did not return until after dark. They are believed to have gone fourteen miles southeast to worship services at Barnes's Meeting House, a Methodist church near the North Carolina line.[53] The sermon they heard was evidently preached by Rev. George W. Powell, an uncle of Mrs. Travis, perhaps assisted by young Richard Whitehead. Powell subsequently stated that on August 21 he "preached to many that were afterwards murdered, and besought them, with all the sincerity of my soul, to make their peace with God, before it was too late."[54]

The preacher's counsel was neither offered nor received as a warning of imminent danger. Many in the congregation may have known something of the flaming call to action by black abolitionist David Walker in his pamphlet of 1829 and the insurrection trial at Richmond that August,[55] of the threats of black revolt at New Bern and elsewhere in North Carolina at the end of 1830,[56] of the implacable new assault on slavery by a Boston journal known as the *Liberator*, and so on. But the Barnes's Chapel worshipers were taken wholly by surprise by the terrible events of the night that followed Powell's earnest admonition.

6

The Southampton Rebellion

The Solvent

Hark Travis had started toward the front door with his broadax when he was stopped short by the tense whispers behind him. There was another fevered conference while the plotters calculated the consequences of axes slamming against stout oaken doors and doomed victims screaming their agony onto the stillness of the summer night. It would not do to launch the business by rousing the neighborhood to a sense of its peril. The midnight silence was a useful ally and ought to be enlisted in the service of the plan.

The downstairs windows were bolted, but a partially opened one on the second floor offered silent access to the very bedsides of the family. Nat Turner directed Hark to fetch a ladder and place it beside the chimney, its upper end touching the window ledge. There was a painful wait while Nat cautiously ascended the ladder and raised the window far enough to permit entry. But now he disappeared into the room and, moments later, unbarred the front door for the seven men huddled on the porch.

Even now there was a taut moment of indecision. After removing the three muskets from the racks inside, Nat proposed that someone other than himself should strike the first blow. But not even the raging spirit of Will Francis could be harnessed to the awesome responsibility; Nat must affirm his resolution by delivering the first stroke himself. The leader beckoned to Will to follow him and once more entered the house.[1]

Gliding up the staircase, Nat paused beside the bed only long enough to estimate the arc of the blade toward the pillow before swinging his hatchet at the sleeping figure. Joseph Travis, his head grazed by the errant blow, still had another instant of mortality in which to leap from bed and shout his wife's name. But Will Francis, his last doubt banished in the echo of the cry, laid Travis open with another blow. In two more rapid swings he killed Mrs. Travis and both of the sleeping boys in the other bed before any of them could awake to an awareness of the attack.[2] The rest of the insurgents scrambled up the steps to find that the blade of Will Francis had accomplished for them in three strokes what two centuries of debate had not.

Abruptly transformed from a field hand into a general, Nat Turner searched his recollection for clues as to what he must do next. He joined in a scavenging search for weapons that produced some powder, a fourth gun, and several unserviceable muskets, but half his force must still venture out against the enemy with axes and grubbing hoes.[3] Moses Moore, a slave boy of the household, was impressed into the ranks,[4] and Nat led his men out to the barn where he lined them up in a caricature of military dress. He improvised a series of drills such as he had often seen performed by the Southampton militia and instructed the group in coordinated movements until each man appeared to understand what was expected. It was probably past 3 A.M. when he finally set them off at a quick march toward the farm of Salathiel Francis, bachelor brother of Sally Travis, perhaps six hundred yards away.[5]

The company took several horses as they left Travis's but had not proceeded far when someone realized that not all of the members of the Travis family had been accounted for. Somehow overlooked in the upstairs darkness had been the sleeping form of Mrs. Travis's infant child in its cradle. Nat sent Henry Porter and Will Francis back to the house, and they returned shortly to report that the deed was done.

Leading his men into Francis's yard, Nat sent Sam and Will Francis, slaves of Salathiel's brother Nathaniel, to the front door of the one-room structure. They knocked loudly and heard Francis ask who was there. Sam identified himself and said that he had a letter for him from Nathaniel Francis.[16] When Salathiel opened the door, the two men snatched him forward into the yard, raining blows until the lifeless body slumped between them.

Whether the rebels gained any recruits from among the seven slaves of Salathiel Francis is not known,[7] but a few more firearms and horses were added to the small stock collected at Travis's. More hastily now, and with less pretense of military formation, Nat reassembled his force and set them off toward the next substantial farm, two miles distant. Mrs. Piety Reese had gone to bed on Sunday evening without barring her door and was spared the horror of awakening to witness the blow that killed her. Her son William had only time to call out "Who is there?" before he too was slain. A nearly grown Negro boy of Mrs. Reese's was enlisted before the rebels left for their next destination. [8]

Despite a hurried pace, it was nearly 6:30 and sunrise before Nat and his men could cover the mile between the farms of Piety Reese and Elizabeth Turner. Hartwell Peebles, overseer for Mrs. Turner, was already at work at the brandy still and three of the raiders— Henry Porter, Austin Travis, and Sam Francis—veered off to deal with him. Nat led the rest on to the "great house" and saw the front door open briefly and slam shut as his men came into the yard. Will Francis dismounted on the run and split the door with a blow of his axe. In the room just beyond, transfixed in disbelieving terror, stood Mrs. Turner, Nat's former owner, and Mrs. Sarah Newsome, a sister of Joseph Travis. [9] Will immediately struck down Mrs. Turner while Nat, seizing Mrs. Newsome by a hand, began striking her about the head with the dull blade of a sword. Again it was Will who delivered the mortal blow. In the meantime Hartwell Peebles, shot down by Austin Travis, had died near the still. [10]

Joined by three of Mrs. Turner's Negroes—Davy, Jordan, and Sam [11]—the insurgents rounded up more horses and weapons for further forays. The next destination was Caty Whitehead's farm, but Nat sought greater effect by dividing his followers into two groups. The nine men with horses or mules were ordered to proceed directly to Whitehead's, while the six on foot were sent through a by-way to Henry Bryant's farm before rejoining the others at the Whitehead place. The foot soldiers were soon able to report that they had killed Bryant, his wife Sally, child, and mother-in-law.

Nat's cavalry sped from Turner's to the Whitehead farm at a head-long gallop, thundering down the lane toward the latter dwelling to find Mrs. Whitehead's son Richard at work with some of his slaves in the cotton patch. Will Francis, pausing beside the lane fence, demanded that the young man come to him and, when he reached the fence, struck his head from his shoulders with his axe. [12]

Nat Turner, leading the main body of his horsemen toward the house, was almost in the yard when a figure darting around the garden caught his attention. It took only a few seconds of pursuit to find that it was a frightened servant girl, but Nat turned back to the house to discover the killing far advanced. Three of Mrs. Whitehead's daughters and a grandson were dead, and the old lady herself was being dragged from the house by Will Francis. As Nat rode up, Will all but decapitated Mrs. Whitehead with a heavy blow of his broadaxe. Moments later Nat caught sight of the fourth daughter, Margaret, crouched in a corner formed by a projecting cellar cap and a chimney. The girl ran when she realized she had been discovered, but Nat easily overtook her and, after several blows with his sword, finally killed her by striking her head with a fence rail.

While the ransacking of the farm proceeded, two more recruits joined the rebel army. Joe Turner, a slave of John Clark Turner, and Nat, property of James and Elizabeth Turner, had been hunting raccoons nearby when they heard the shouts and screams from Whitehead's. Joe, who lived a mile off, was especially concerned because his wife lived at the Whitehead farm.[13] Already armed and mounted, they were welcome additions to the growing rebel force.

With two dozen armed cavalrymen at his command, Nat Turner now had enough speed and firepower to overcome any kind of resistance he might expect to find on the farms of this thinly settled region. More than twenty whites were dead and waves of alarm must soon be rippling across the countryside. In the panic and confusion that would follow lay the only real hope for the success of his ragged farmhands. For it was not the white people who were the enemy so much as the system of organization and social discipline that regulated their lives. Terror was the only feasible solvent of the sinews of control that held the Negro in bondage, and chaos among the whites was more to be desired than throngs of eager recruits.

Alarum

As Nat regrouped his men at Whitehead's around 7:30 A.M., word of his uprising had not yet spread to the surrounding farms or habitations. Even at the vortex of the ravaged neighborhood, white families and their slaves were beginning the day's work with no hint of the events of the past hours. But the first news of the revolt was already moving along the country lanes and would reach several farmhouses within the next hour.

Perhaps the first white person, apart from the victims themselves, to learn of the disturbance was John R. Williams, a schoolteacher known as "Choctaw" for his long hair worn Indian-fashion. Williams, who lived on a neighboring farm, was attracted toward Whitehead's by the noise of the assault and arrived there to find the house and yard littered with corpses. Returning toward his own home, Williams was met by one of his Negroes who informed him that the rebels had visited his farm in his absence and murdered his wife Louisa and their child. It was "Choctaw" Williams who, several frantic hours later, brought the first news of the rebellion to Murfreesboro, North Carolina, some twelve miles south.[14]

Nathaniel Francis, whose farm stood only a mile or so northwest of Whitehead's, was another who received early warning. Francis was at work around 8 A.M. when a slave boy of Travis's is said to have rushed into the field and blurted out that all the whites were dead at his master's farm. The deaths had apparently been discovered only after daybreak on Monday and the informant could give no account of who was responsible or why. Francis was not inclined to credit the story but told his wife and mother that he thought he should ride over and make sure that his sister, Sally Travis, and her family were unharmed.[15] He would have his proof within the next half hour.

Jordan Barnes, another white farmer of the vicinity, was at work in his field in the early morning when Jack Reese, a slave he had hired from Joseph W. Reese, informed him of the killings at Whitehead's. Jack, with Barnes's permission, had left a few days earlier for a visit to the Reese farm and had fallen in with Nat Turner and the plotters on the eve of the rebellion. Having grown ill on Sunday evening, Jack tried to quit the enterprise even before it began. Only the imprecations of Hark Travis, who had considerable influence over him, had induced him to join. But Jack, continuing ill, had been of little service to the cause and used his first opportunity during the pandemonium at Whitehead's to desert. His story to Barnes was that he had been told of the killings by one of Whitehead's Negroes.[16]

Several Southampton households received their first reports of
the uprising from two of Mrs. Whitehead's servants who spent a
frustrating day of indecision trailing along in the wake of the rebels.
Jack and Andrew, in company with Tom Whitehead, had fled the
farm at the first appearance of the insurgents.[17] The first two returned to the house not long afterward and were told by other slaves
that the rebels had left orders for these two to follow and join the
uprising. Neither had much heart for it, but the gory evidence about
them suggested that it would be unwise to defy the command. Plac-
ing blankets across the back of the only horse left,[18] they mounted
it together and set out along Nat Turner's route.

When they reached Richard Porter's farm around 9 A.M., Jack
and Andrew learned from Venus, a Porter slave, that the rebels
had passed that way, just missing the Porter family who fled ahead
of them. On reaching the house of Thomas Haithcock, a free Negro,
the two men told him of their doubts and asked what he thought
they should do. At his own trial later on, Haithcock's wife and stepdaughter agreed that he advised the two men that they must do as
the rebels demanded. Asking that they wait for him, Haithcock
had something to eat and then rode off with them in search of the
insurgents. After hours of futile pursuit, Jack and Andrew in the
late afternoon turned themselves in to James Powell, a white farmer.
Finding them "very humble," Powell escorted the pair to Cross
Keys and turned them over to authorities. Haithcock, however, had
apparently not abandoned hope of enlisting in the rebellion.[19]

In spite of these vagrant reports, several hours were to pass before
the alarm became general in Southampton. Nat Turner and his
lieutenants could count on panic and slow communications to
retard the buildup of organized resistance in the rear, but speed was
their chief asset on the road ahead. If they could outdistance the
flight of the alarm along the line of march, a great army might yet
be collected before any pitched battles occurred. Some of his men
were treating each raid as an occasion for alcoholic revelry, but Nat,
firing his cohorts with visions of victory and freedom, struggled
against indiscipline and held his force intact.

Before leaving the Whitehead farm Nat divided his followers into
two detachments of a dozen or so men each. The most reliable men
were positioned at the head of each group and ordered to gallop

with all possible speed toward each new destination. Since silence was no longer necessary, a great whooping and shouting would precede each successive attack. The orders may also have included an injunction to spare no embellishment of gruesome butchery in the execution of victims. Such tactics would not only prevent escapes but add measurably to the panic that would paralyze resistance.[20]

Apogee

While Nat led one column north toward Richard Porter's, the second moved west toward Trajan Doyel's with orders to rejoin the first at Nathaniel Francis's. Doyel was overtaken on the road a few minutes later and instantly killed. Joe and Davy Turner, members of this detachment, also visited the Elisha Atkins farm between 8 and 9 A.M. but found there only a servant who said that the family had fled. Davy proposed that they break into the house and look for guns and ammunition, but Joe objected that they had plenty and must not tarry. One of Atkins's slaves was induced to leave with them, but the man is said to have slipped away and returned soon afterward.[21]

In the meantime the first detachment stopped briefly at Porter's to find that the whites had been forewarned and were gone. Jacob, Moses, and Daniel, slaves of the proprietor, and Aaron, owned by Richard Porter's ward, Jesse J. Porter,[22] were enrolled, but Nat was disappointed to learn that the alarm was moving ahead of his columns. Hurrying his men toward Francis's, he doubled back alone to rally his second force. He came up with it as it was leaving Howell Harris's, but here too the whites had fled. Urging all possible haste, the rebel leader pushed forward in the hope of overtaking the alarm and forging ahead of it again.

The first detachment ravaged and plundered the Francis farm at a breakneck pace, cutting down three whites even before reaching the house itself. Little John L. Brown, three-year-old orphaned nephew of Francis, ran forward to ask for a ride on a horse and was decapitated. His eight-year-old brother Samuel, witnessing the scene from the barnyard, broke for the woods but was run down and killed.[23] Henry Doyel, overseer and still operator, ran from the house where he had gone to warn Mrs. Francis and was shot dead in his tracks.[24]

Servants reported that Nathaniel Francis had gone to the Travis place, to which he had been followed by his mother, and the apparent escape of Lavinia Francis, his nineteen-year-old wife. But Lavinia, some eight months pregnant, had been hidden by her servant Nelson as the insurgents burst in. Several of the rebels entered the closet where she was hiding, but a hurried search failed to detect her under a pile of blankets and clothes. The farm, however, yielded more guns and horses, and three of Francis's slaves— Nathan, Tom, and Davy—were lined up and marched away in the train of the flying vanguard.[25] Dred, another of Francis's Negroes, needed no such coercion before casting his lot with the fate of the rebellion.[26]

Racing northeastward, the first detachment struck the Peter Edwards farm, where again the whites had received enough notice to escape. Several new recruits, including Sam, Austin, and Jim Edwards,[27] were enrolled as the detachment remounted rapidly and moved off toward J. Thomas Barrow's. Their haste this time was rewarded, for Barrow, though apprized of the danger, had refused to believe it and thus "fell a victim to his own incredulity."[28]

The raid on Barrow's gave rise to a scene of martyrdom that would be enshrined in white legend down through the years. Barrow fired his musket through a window at the first rider to approach the house and then rushed to an adjacent room for his rifle. As the rebels broke down the front door, Barrow ordered his wife to flee and cracked the stock of his gun over the first assailant to reach him.[29] While her husband struggled, Mrs. Barrow ran out, only to be caught and held by her servant girl Lucy. But another slave woman came to her aid, and Mrs. Barrow somehow made good her escape. Her husband was killed, but his stout resistance was said to have led the rebels to declare that they hoped they would neet "no more Tom Barrows" in the course of their march.[30] A few moments later they killed George Vaughan, Mrs. Barrow's brother, whom they met as he returned to the Barrow farm from a morning fox hunt.[31]

The rebels left Barrow's only minutes ahead of Nat Turner who, scrambling forward with his first detachment, bypassed the Francis farm and arrived too late at Peter Edwards's. When he finally overtook the first group at Capt. Newit Harris's a little past 10 A.M., he was informed that here again the white family had escaped injury due to advance warning.[32]

Nat rode into the Harris yard amid a chorus of shouts and huzzahs from his elated ranks, now amounting to some forty men.[33] But the rebel chieftain probably shared little of the high spirit of his followers. Even his charging vanguard had not been able to overtake the spreading alarm. The flames of terror and disorder among the whites could be kept raging only by the fuel of indiscriminate slaughter. Without the disorder, the hundreds of black recruits needed for victory would not find the heart to trust their lives to the cause. As Nat evaluated his situation at Harris's, he may have recognized that the offensive phase of his campaign had failed to attain the momentum necessary to sustain it. It remained to find some stronghold where he might fight off the enemies soon to attack him and seek to rally the uncommitted slaves of the countryside to support the rebellion.

Directing his army eastward from Harris's along the Barrow road, Nat struck off toward the intersection of that route with the road from Cross Keys to Jerusalem. A dramatic descent on the county seat, with the seizure of sizable stores of munitions, food, and other supplies, would sustain the morale of his troops and give to all blacks who heard of it a surge of hope that deliverance was possible at last. Or so it may have seemed in the desperation born of Nat Turner's growing awareness of the disaster that loomed ahead.

Perihelion

Three miles west of Newit Harris's, Nat's flying advanced guard swooped down on the farm of Levi Waller, which was to be the scene of the most devastating raid of the uprising. Waller was at work at his still around 10 A.M. when information was brought to him that the rebels were nearby.[34] The erratic behavior of the man in the next half hour forms a bizarre footnote to a day of astonishing events.

A quarter mile distant from Waller's still was a boarding school where the teacher, William Crocker, was apparently supervising a recess period. Waller, whose own youngest children were at the school, sent his son Thomas to summon teacher and pupils to the dwelling for protection. Crocker arrived with the children to find Waller busily engaged at the still and was advised by him to proceed to the house and load the guns. When Crocker rushed back a short time later to report that the rebels were in sight, he found Waller still engrossed in the brandy works. Both men, however, now sought whatever safety they could find, Waller falling among some weeds in a corner of the garden. His flight was observed by Dred Francis and other rebel horsemen who, coming near the fence, failed to detect him in his concealment. Waller subsequently attributed his luck to the rebels' attention being diverted by another, who proved to be his Negro blacksmith, Alfred.[35]

While the slaughter at his house progressed, Waller was able to make his way from the garden to a swamp some distance farther away, but he had now become severely unhinged. After a brief interval he returned to a spot among some currant bushes within sixty yards of the house. Here, a bemused spectator, Waller was near enough to identify Daniel and Aaron Porter and Sam Francis as they entered the house where his wife was killed and emerged with Sam carrying Mrs. Waller's scissors.[36] He saw his own Negro, Davy Waller, appear on the scene, change into clean clothes, drink with the raiders, and ride off with them "in great glee," and was later able to recount the role of Nelson Edwards in knocking out the brains of a member of the Waller family with a musket. "This man," it was reported a week later, "is now raving distracted—he goes about saying how they killed them!! and then shakes his sides and laughs!!!"[37]

Waller's derangement, however, was only temporary. As an invaluable witness in the insurrection trials, he testified that he returned to the house after the rebels left and found the bodies of his wife and the ten schoolchildren stacked in a grisly pile inside. He was evidently too distracted, however, to notice that one of the children, though gravely wounded, was not dead.[38] He also overlooked twelve-year-old Clarinda Jones, who had taken refuge in the dirt chimney of a log-house dependency while her sister Lucinda was being killed. Some hours later, Waller was to confirm the doleful tidings of rebellion at the town of Murfreesboro.[39]

From Waller's the insurgents pressed eastward to the William Williams farm three miles farther along the route to Jerusalem. Here they fell upon Williams and two boys, Miles and Henry Johnson, at work in a fodder field.[40] Mrs. Williams witnessed the execution of these three from the house and managed to run some distance before being caught by one of the rebels, who placed her behind him on his horse and brought her back to the point where her husband's body lay. She was ordered to lie down beside the corpse and, when she did so, was shot to death.

Shortly before noon the insurgents reached the farm of Jacob Williams, uncle of William Williams, a short distance farther east. Williams had gone to the woods to measure some timber, but Edwin Drewry, overseer on a nearby farm, had arrived a few minutes earlier and was loading corn with the help of a Negro slave when he glanced up and exclaimed: "Lord, who is that coming?"[41] Moments later he was run down and shot while other rebels went to the dwelling and killed his wife and three children. At overseer Caswell Worrell's house nearby, Mrs. Worrell and her child were also killed.

A quarter mile northwest the raiders, joined by Jacob Williams's slave Nelson,[42] struck the home of Mrs. Rebecca Vaughan. Mrs. Vaughan, standing on her porch, saw the "great dust in the distance" and asked a female servant what it could mean. She ran inside the house when she recognized the danger, but the rebels dismounted in her yard and surrounded the house, aiming their guns at the doors and windows. The frightened woman appeared at a window pleading to purchase her life with all of her possessions but was immediately shot. Ann Eliza Vaughan, eighteen-year-old niece of Mrs. Vaughan, rushed from upstairs to be met and slain by Marmaduke, a stalwart rebel.[43] Arthur, Mrs. Vaughan's fifteen-year-old son, believed to have thought his brother had returned from Jerusalem, ran up from the stillhouse to investigate and was shot as he came over the fence. Moses Barrow, a slave of Tom Barrow, was recruited near the Vaughan farm, to which he had been sent, as he later testified, "to see what the news was."[44]

Reaching the intersection of the Cross Keys–Jerusalem highway, Nat wheeled his hurtling column to the northeast in the direction of the county seat, four miles distant. Half a mile farther along, the insurgents came to the lane gate of James W. Parker's farm. Nat was anxious to move quickly along to Jerusalem, but some of his men insisted that they could raise able recruits from among Parker's Negroes. While Nat and several others kept lookout at the gate, the main force headed across a cornfield toward the house, half a mile distant. It was this untimely division of the rebel force that would bring the rebellion to premature collapse.

Nat fidgeted for some minutes at the gate, grew impatient of the delay, and rode off alone toward the house to spur his men along. He had collected them and started back toward the road when a party of whites was seen approaching from that direction, where they had just surprised and routed the group left at the gate. Nat ordered his men to halt and began forming them in a horizontal line for a charge. The critical moment of the rebellion was at hand.

The white patrol had ridden out from Jerusalem late in the morning, shortly after receiving an express from the afflicted area. Notice had been forwarded to militiamen throughout the county, "but such was the confusion and delay," as one report described it, that it would be Tuesday evening before an effective muster could be held at Jerusalem. The whites picked up the trail of the insurgents at Waller's and, led by Captains Alexander Peete and James Bryant, continued in pursuit of the rebels. On catching sight of Nat's main force, Peete ordered the eighteen men to hold their fire until the blacks were within thirty paces.[45] Both sides were armed mostly with "fowling pieces," and this, with the showers that wet some of their powder,[46] meant that shots exchanged at any greater distance must necessarily be futile.

A more decisive battle at Parker's appears to have been prevented by one of those accidents of war that mock the ingenuity of the finest tacticians. One of Peete's troopers was a young attorney from Jerusalem named James Strange French, who is said to have experienced some difficulty in procuring a mount on which to join the party. The others had already left town when innkeeper Henry B. Vaughan offered French the use of a colt that had not been broken. Saddling the unruly animal, French soon caught up with the patrol. As the two sides faced one another across the no-man's-land at Parker's field, the neighing of the horses caused the colt to start, accidentally discharging its rider's gun. The colt bolted toward the rebels, carrying the startled French headlong toward Nat Turner's line for some distance before he could bring the animal under control and wheel about.[47]

The disturbance created by French's colt sent about half of Peete's company into disordered retreat. Nat Turner, noting the disintegration of the enemy line, ordered his own force to charge and was within fifty yards of those whites still holding their ground when they, too, firing once, joined the retreat. In the next hectic seconds several whites were overrun and struck from their horses (including one Pope, who was injured),[48] the rest galloping across the top of a small hill and momentarily out of sight on the far side. Reaching the crest of the hill himself, Nat found that the whites had unwittingly rushed into the midst of a second patrol, which had just arrived from Jerusalem. In that instant the scale of advantage tilted sharply from the black side to the white.

The unexpected sight of the first white party pausing to reload and being bolstered by a second threw Nat's recruits into a fatal disorder. Several of the foremost rebels, plunging into the fusillade of the whites, were injured, and Hark Travis's horse was shot from beneath him. Nat managed to grab the reins of another horse and hold it until Hark ran up, but the rebel cavalry was now hopelessly scattered. Summoning those within earshot, Nat ordered a retreat and turned away from the advancing whites.[49]

Eclipse

With no more than twenty of his men, Nat outdistanced his pursuers and made his way into a little-used private road. Calculating that the whites would expect him to reappear at some point along the highway, he hoped to pass undetected to Cypress Bridge, three miles below Jerusalem, and strike at the town from that direction. He also hoped to pick up some of his stragglers from Parker's field, but two of his men who caught up with him informed him that the remainder of the force had simply disappeared. Most would probably return to the farms from which they came and try to persuade skeptical masters that they had been dragooned into marching with the rebels.

Reviewing his predicament, Nat concluded that his only chance of success lay in rebuilding his band before making another attempt on Jerusalem. But reinforcements could probably be found only in the vicinity where he had influence, and this meant that he must make a further foray through the area west of Cross Keys. In the waning hope of some miracle of divine intervention, Nat wearily led his followers back toward his old neighborhood.[50]

Weakened and demoralized, the rebels lurched forward from one deserted farm to the next, drafting a few additional recruits but finding little else of value. The abandoned farms of Jacob Williams, Mrs. John Thomas, Spencer, and others stood eerily silent in the twilight, gloomy reminders of lost opportunities during the day.[51] Crossing the Barrow road in early evening, Nat made his way a short distance along the Belfield road before seeking rest at Buckhorn, a farm owned by Maj. Thomas Ridley. The proprietor lived a little way to the east, but several of his Negroes were here, and Nat was able to persuade four to join him, bringing his strength back up to nearly forty. Two of these, Curtis and Stephen Ridley, agreed to set out on mules for Newsom's and Allen's quarters near Monroe to enlist more men.[52] After posting sentinels, Nat lay down for his first rest in many hours.

But even rest was to elude the dejected rebels. Nat had been asleep but a brief time when he was roused by shouts and commotion among his men. One of his sentinels had mistakenly given an alarm that they were about to be attacked and some were already mounted for resistance or flight. After considerable difficulty, order was restored and Nat sent scouts to reconnoiter the area. No enemy was found, but the scouts, returning at a noisy gallop, generated new panic among the uneasy rebels and scattered them irretrievably into the surrounding darkness. When calm returned, Nat found that half his force had deserted. More in despair than hope, he gave up thought of further rest and led his remaining men toward Dr. Simon Blunt's, a mile distant, the nearest place offering the prospect of reinforcement.[53]

It was the grayest moments of early dawn when the rebels broke open the gate at the head of Blunt's lane and started for the house, about eighty yards away. Shadrach Futrell, Blunt's overseer, was standing beside the porch when he saw the rebels coming through the gate. Signaling their approach, Futrell ducked into the house and took his position in the ambush awaiting the rebels. Crouched behind window sills and doors were gouty old Dr. Blunt, his fifteen-year-old son Simon, neighbor Drewry W. Fitzhugh, two other white youths, and some of Blunt's and Fitzhugh's Negroes. They were armed with several guns and a variety of less formidable weapons.[54]

As the insurgents raced down the lane, Mrs. Blunt thrust her youngest child into the arms of Mary, her servant girl, and told her to try to escape. In company with several other slave women, Mary started across the garden with the child, but Moses Barrow, first of the raiders to reach the yard, caught sight of them. Flinging down his gun and dismounting, Moses yelped, "Oh God damn you have I got you," and, despite a game leg, leaped the garden fence in ardent pursuit of the women. He had gone only a few steps when Hark Travis, firing a gun to determine whether anyone was in the house, was answered by a musket ball. Hark and several others were shot from their mounts in the succession of blasts that followed, and Nat, whirling his horse about, fled back up the lane with the remnant of his cavalry. The wounded Hark was taken prisoner, along with Moses Barrow, who was found a little later hiding in the garden. One of the rebels lay dead near the house.[55]

In company with Will Francis and others, Nat doubled back toward Newit Harris's, raided the day before, but arrived there to find a group of armed white men. Amid a hail of fire, the rebels scattered for cover, Nat and two of his men taking shelter in a woods to await darkness.[56] Believing that he had been deserted by the rest of his band, the rebel general now gave up any idea of quick recovery and turned his thoughts to a plan for reclaiming fugitive cohorts.

It was unfortunate for Nat that he was unable to make contact later in the day with one or both of two groups still carrying the banner of rebellion across the Southampton countryside. One of these was a small force that appears to have emerged independently under the leadership of William "Billy" Artis, a tall, light-skinned free Negro.[57] Artis, with his wife Cherry and two boys, had appeared around noon on Tuesday at the farm of the late Benjamin Blunt and solicited slaves Ben and Luke Blunt to join him in revolt. Luke declined, but Ben joined and was still with them in midafternoon when they passed the place again in company with Thomas Haithcock and a third boy. Luke later testified that he saw Artis on the second occasion at a distance, flourishing his hat and shouting that "he would cut his way, he would kill and cripple as he went." Haithcock and four boys were said to have come by Peter Edwards's farm on Tuesday morning and told the Negroes there that "Gen'l Nat would be there on Wednesday or Thursday and Mr. Edwards had 4 likely boys that he would take with them."[58] Nat, they stated, had had a fight with the whites at Parker's and was on his way to Belfield.

The second rebel force still in the field after Nat went into hiding consisted of the remnant of the men who were with him after leaving Dr. Blunt's. Will Francis and perhaps others had been killed in the encounter at Newit Harris's, but enough remained to talk boldly among themselves about returning to Blunt's on Tuesday night and seeking revenge for the ambush they had suffered there. This group seems to have split up by nightfall but not before creating fresh alarms in the vicinity of Dr. Blunt's farm.

Late in the afternoon on Tuesday a Negro boy belonging to Thomas Ridley reported to the garrison at Blunt's that he "had seen the banditti after they had been repulsed . . . , that they told him whilst he was in company with them that they . . . would return there . . . (Tuesday) evening and . . . see whether [Blunt] and his company could keep them out of his house."[59] Upon receipt of the report, Drew Fitzhugh immediately sent an express to Jerusalem for help and organized the Blunt defenders for resistance to renewed assault. Captain Peete arrived some hours later from Jerusalem with ten men and remained until daylight brought to the embattled plantation a sense of greater security. An unfortunate accident, however, marred the otherwise successful reinforcement of the Blunt farm.

The Blunt and Fitzhugh slaves had been entrusted during the night with arms and stationed near the front door of the house. Just before dawn broke on Wednesday morning, an alarm was raised, and in the confusion of the moment, a trooper of Peete's named Harris shot and killed a Negro belonging to Mrs. Thomas Fitzhugh. The dead man, considered to be "likely . . . and of good character," had been visiting his wife at Blunt's when the rebellion broke out. A petition for compensation from the state for his life noted that "alarms of this nature were frequent at Dr. Blunt's and at other places during the excitement . . . produced in the neighborhood."[60]

Pandemic

News of the insurrection crept outward from the fiery center during Monday and Tuesday at an astonishingly feeble pace. At Murfrees-boro, a village within fourteen miles of the outbreak, no warning seems to have come until around midday on Monday, some ten hours after the first attack and four hours after the earliest alarm.[61] At Halifax, North Carolina, within thirty miles of the Travis farm, the first warning arrived in late afternoon. Richmond was sixty miles away but heard nothing until 3 A.M. on Tuesday.[62] Suffolk, Norfolk, Edenton, and other places within forty to sixty miles knew nothing of the revolt before daybreak or later on Tuesday. In no direction does the news appear to have progressed at a rate exceeding about three miles per hour from 8 o'clock Monday morning. The slow pace may have reflected the tendency of each community to look first to its own safety before broadcasting the alarm.

Virtually every community within a hundred miles was thrown into paroxysms of panic by the report. A group of whites already assembled for mutual protection at a Hertford County farmhouse a few miles south of Cross Keys learned from a "well-dressed and sober" man, riding up at great speed in the rain, that the rebels were approaching from Boon's Bridge, a mile and half away. In the thirty minutes it took to contradict the report, a witness later recalled the "immediate cries of the women, as to what they should do," and the "frantic distress depicted on every face."[63] At Jerusalem, where four hundred women and children had gone for safety, a harried writer told a Richmond newspaper that "every house, room and corner . . . is full of women and children, driven from home, who had to take to the woods, until they could get to this place. We are worn out with fatigue." From a farm five miles east, a woman wrote relatives in Richmond that some two hundred women, mostly from west of the Nottoway River, had been packed into Vick's Tavern and Bivins's at Jerusalem, her own family having slept out "in a thick cluster of pines, with a blanket each, and a pallet for the children."[64]

At Murfreesboro an express from Northampton, characterized by a resident as "a lily-livered boy," brought news that the rebels were within eight miles of town. A patrol promptly went out and found the report false, but farmer Thomas Weston, an elderly resident of the town, came out on his porch to learn the cause of the excitement and dropped dead when he heard it. There were reports of two other deaths nearby from the same cause. A Murfreesboro witness told of "fear . . . in every face, women pale and terror-stricken, children crying for protection, men fearful and full of foreboding."[65]

At a farmhouse in the Gumberry section of Northampton, a few miles south of Cross Keys, a thirteen-year-old boy later recalled how "all the women and children were put into the largest room. . . . The door was securely fastened by putting chairs against the back on the inside. The gun I loaded myself putting in a double charge of powder and shot so as to kill several at one fire. . . . Besides this we had an axe in the room. . . . We had a boy stationed out as a sort of picket with a horn to blow in case he heard any noise, so that we might be ready for the fight."[66]

Authorities at Halifax, North Carolina, called out all able-bodied white men and converted the courthouse into a depot for arms and ammunition. At Belfield, in Greensville County, a company of guards and an artillery piece were in position at the Meherrin River by dusk on Monday. A nearly indecipherable note from Col. James Trezevant at Jerusalem alerted Petersburg officials at midnight Monday although failing to cite the locality of the trouble or the number of Negroes thought to be involved. Governor John Floyd received the same note at dawn on Tuesday.[67]

Militia companies poured into Southampton during Tuesday and Wednesday, including the Richmond Dragoons and Lafayette Artillery, three companies of infantry and some sailors from Norfolk, volunteer cavalry from Portsmouth, a troop of horse from Prince George, and others. The Halifax Blues, a company of twenty-five cavalry, arrived too late to see any important action but contrived to suffer two casualties before reaching the Virginia line. At a bivouac on Wednesday night at Absalom P. Smith's in Northampton County, the clatter of an approaching express rider caused a brief panic among the Blues. One of the company awoke in the midst of the confusion, glimpsed a man "with his right hand raised as if in the act of stabbing one of the Blues," and fired his musket. Militiaman Shepherd Lee, a native Virginian, was wounded in the leg by the blast and D. Turner in the shoulder. Lee unwisely accompanied the unit to Cross Keys and died from loss of blood at Jackson, North Carolina, while returning on Thursday.[68]

A busy center of militia activity was Richard Darder located midway between Jerusalem and Cross Keys. Sixty ᴠ. North Carolinians, evidently from Northampton and commandᴇᴜ by one Sherrod, spent a night at Darden's and helped to drink off some of the "3 Barrels of Spirits," including some "very old brandy & Wine," for which Darden later billed the General Assembly. Another sixty to eighty Norfolk troopers stopped at Darden's en route to and from Cross Keys and reduced his stock by ten to twenty pounds of chewing tobacco, bread, several large middlings of bacon, and liquor, which the proprietor "had no time to measure . . . as it was Catch as you could until They got it." Since "Richd. Darden's," in the words of the proud innkeeper, "was the place to stop to git some Refreshments," a continual stream of smaller parties also made free with his provisions during the period of the disturbance.[69] Some measure of the excesses of the militia, no less than those of the blacks, may perhaps be set down to the influence of alcoholic drink.

The Avengers

"It has been nothing but kill, kill! murder, murder! . . . I never supposed human beings could be capable of such barbarity, much less did I ever expect to be in the midst of, and to witness such scenes!" O. M. Smith was a young man from New Hampshire who was living at William Harrison's in Littletown, Sussex County, some nine miles from the scenes of violence, when he described the revolt for his parents on August 29. By this time, the last fugitives had been trapped within a wooded area where the militia "have been for four days and four nights hunting them out and killing them, like so many wolves!" Some twenty blacks had been killed by this time and twenty-three or twenty-four others taken captive, "of whom 10 or 12 have been tantalized to death, in trying to make them divulge the plot, but not one word of information can be extorted from any of them, they will stand with a red hot iron burning their flesh until they die!!"[70]

While Smith's account is probably somewhat overdrawn, the mop-up of fugitives was unquestionably accompanied by scenes of shocking brutality. Hertford County's militia mustered at Murfreesboro at midday on Tuesday and detailed a hundred men to march to Cross Keys. The cavalry contingent, led by Col. Charles Spiers, reached Cross Keys at sunset, but Ens. S. Jordan Wheeler's infantry arrived only on Wednesday morning. The handful of houses making up the settlement were packed to the rafters with between 1,500 and 2,000 women and children, with some 200 men on guard.[71] Despite the acute distress of the citizens, a Southampton militia officer assured the Carolinians that the danger was past, all but five or six of the rebels having been killed or captured.[72] But the arrival of the infantry next morning, followed by a parade intended for the restoration of tranquillity, prompted suggestions that a joint foray proceed into the surrounding country in search of Nat Turner, Will Artis, and others. The party that set out, continually enlarged by volunteers, was soon split into two groups, one of which appears to have had an uneventful tour. The activities of the second, however, would remain a sore point of controversy for many weeks.

The second party, commanded by Col. Elisha H. Sharpe of Hertford, and including four Southampton men, encountered Richard Porter, apparently on his way to Cross Keys with three Negroes who had confessed to him their complicity in the revolt. These three— Jacob, Moses, and Aaron—were taken into custody by the patrol along with an unidentified boy, perhaps Daniel Porter. When they reached Whitehead's the patrol viewed a grotesque panorama of bodies lying about the yard "chopped to pieces" and "trees, fences and house tops covered with buzzards preying on the carcases." While the men contemplated the spectacle, a Negro of Mrs. Whitehead's (said to have been a preacher) appeared and began to tell of his impressment and harsh treatment by the insurgents. But the Southampton men in the group, including Drew Bittle, Clifton Harrison, and Charles Fuller, identified him as having been among the rebels at Parker's field on Monday, whereupon, according to later reports, the whole company emptied their guns into him. It was probably this unfortunate individual whom O. M. Smith had in mind when he described how a rebel, "a Methodist minister among his black brethren," had been tortured to death. "They burnt him with red hot irons—cut off his ears and nose—stabbed him, cut his hamstrings, stuck him like a hog, and at last cut off his head, and spiked it on the whipping post for a spectacle and a warning to other negroes!!!!"[73]

The enraged whites now elected to execute the three Negro men of Porter's without further ceremony. The three were marched into a field and shot, having first been relieved of $23 in cash and a gold watch. Colonel Sharpe, observing that the party "might as well be paid for their trouble as not," proposed a division of the spoils, counselling that nothing should be said about it to the rest of the Hertford militia. The division of the property, rather than its return to white owners, was publicly castigated by fifteen of the troopers when it became known some weeks later. The Negro boy was delivered to authorities at Cross Keys.[74]

Other militia and vigilante units acted with equal disregard of technical niceties. A North Carolina paper reported the case of three slaves who were recruited into the revolt at a Southampton farm on Monday, returned to enroll others on Tuesday, and were "seized by the balance of the Negroes, tied and delivered over to the militia, and by them instantly dispatched." On Monday afternoon, the party under Captain Peete ran down Alfred Waller, a thirty-year-old blacksmith of Levi Waller. Because the captors did not have, in Peete's words, "an opportunity to secure him otherwise he was disabled by cutting the larger tendon just above the heel in each leg." When Alfred was found next day by a troop of Greensville Dragoons, he was near death and considered unlikely to live long enough to stand trial. The whites thereupon tied him to a tree and shot him "as a beneficial example to other Insurgents." An incident reported by O. M. Smith concerned a slave who was sent on an errand to a neighbor's, was seen by militia who supposed him to be "an enemy fleeing," and was shot dead, as was the horse he was riding.[75]

The mop-up of fugitive rebels continued for several days. Reports that an insurgent leader, taken on Tuesday evening, had made a full confession and then been "publicly shot and his head hoisted on a pole," probably concerned the fate of Henry Porter, one of Nat's original conspirators. A similar fate awaited Nelson Edwards, who was spotted on Wednesday in the orchard at his master's farm, escaped, but was shot next day. It was reported from Cross Keys on August 26 that "Gen. Nelson's" head was on display there and that a doctor assigned to the militia was to bring the trophy to Norfolk. Joseph Joiner, one of Nelson's assassins, paid the dead man the compliment of saying that he "was about thirty five years

of age, was uncommonly likely, and worth at least $400, and had
he been mine, I would not have taken $500 for him."[76] Jim, another
of Peter Edwards's Negroes, was brought by his master to Cross Keys
and turned over to the same Captain Joiner with a request that he
be kept until he could be tried. Joiner tied him "and placed him
against the side of the house, when a party rushed up and shot him—
he fell dead at my feet." A party visiting Edwards's house on Wednesday came upon Austin Edwards "standing in the yard by himself
perfectly defenseless" and instantly shot him down.[77]

Still other rebels were relentlessly sought out in the days following. Sam Edwards was taken on Tuesday night when a patrol found
him hiding under a house at his master's farm. Davy Waller was
captured on Thursday night, and Dred Francis surrendered to his
master on Saturday. Billy Artis, reported to have been wounded four
days earlier, was found dead on September 2, believed to have taken
his own life.[78] Marmaduke, reputed slayer of Miss Vaughan, evidently died in Jerusalem jail before the trials began; editor John
Hampden Pleasants of the Richmond *Whig*, who saw him there
on August 26, commented that Marmaduke "might have been a
hero, judging from the magnanimity with which he bore his suffer-
ings." A rebel named Tom, said to have made a confession though
"desperately wounded and about to die," was another whose death
may have cheated the gallows.[79]

Stories of massive homicide by white patrols, multiplying for
weeks after the uprising, were often no less exaggerated than early
rumors of the scope of the rebellion. A letter from Belfield on August
24 spoke of only three or four blacks killed in skirmishes in Southampton on Tuesday and a message from Cross Keys next day raised
the toll to but "10 to 15."[80] General Richard Eppes, writing from
Jerusalem on Thursday, gave the number so far killed as fifteen,
and a Norfolk man, who left Jerusalem on Saturday, reported
thirty-eight killed up to that time. Next day a directive from Jerusalem "headquarters" forbade any further killing of blacks lest
important evidence and valuable property be squandered. A week
later Postmaster Trezevant cited only twenty-two as having been
slain "without law," probably not counting those killed in skirmishes. The Richmond *Whig* on September 3 complained of instances in which some had been killed without trial and "under

circumstances of great barbarity." Editor Pleasants had heard in Southampton of between twenty-five and forty such deaths and had spoken to one individual who claimed credit for ten to fifteen of them.[81]

Rumors, perhaps in part designed for the intimidation of blacks everywhere, continually increased the figures. A Northampton preacher heard that "many negroes are killed every day," and a Halifax merchant spoke darkly of "Negroes . . . taken in different directions, and executed" daily. The Washington, D.C. *Globe* was told that "about 50 or 100 negroes had been killed and still the companies are in pursuit of the remainder." A North Carolina paper set the number of dead Negroes at 270.[82] But the total of blacks killed in suppressing the revolt in all likelihood fell below 50. There were, in addition, isolated instances of Negroes killed in adjoining counties. A slave from the Ahoskie section of Hertford County, coming through Murfreesboro on August 24 with a pass from his master, was shot in the street, after which his head was severed and placed on a pole at the corner by William Rea's store.[83] Benjamin W. Britt, of nearby Riddicksville, North Carolina related to a Connecticut acquaintance later that he "shot a black on that occasion, for the crime of disobeying Mr. Britt's imperative 'Stop!' "[84]

Roving patrols were able on Tuesday and Wednesday to trim down the more frenetic stories of carnage among the whites. Clarinda Jones, after spending a night alone in a swamp at Waller's was found safe on Tuesday by a white party visiting the farm.[85] Members of this or another group also found among the corpses at Waller's a small child not yet dead. She was placed in some shade as the patrol left in hot pursuit of rebels but, apparently receiving no further attention for some hours, died next day.[86] Lavinia Francis, who had been hidden by her slaves, and Mrs. Barrow, were also soon located. At Whitehead's, where Harriet Whitehead had saved herself by hiding between a bed and mat in the same room where one of her sisters was killed, a slave named Hubbard led her to a hiding place in the woods.[87] An overseer by the name of Balmer, or Barham, may have been found alive at Piety Reese's after having been attacked by the rebels there and left for dead.[88] Mr. and Mrs. James Story, two daughters of Francis Felts, Mrs. Trajan Doyel and child, and Jacob Williams were others who were found after initially having been

listed among the victims.[89] A letter from Southampton on August
31 stated that "many heretofore supposed to be murdered, were
secreted in the woods, and have been searched up." The death toll
among the whites was finally fixed at fifty-five.[90]

It remained to track down the author of the rebellion, the wiliest
fugitive of them all. Nat Turner's wife, a slave of Giles Reese,[91] was
lashed into cooperating with the whites and revealed to them a
cache of documents thought to represent Nat's ruminations before
the revolt. These included what some took to be a list of names,
some symbols such as a crucifix and sun, various figures (6,000,
30,000, 80,000, etc.), an apparent map of the county, and certain
"hieroglyphic characters" said to have been inscribed in either
blood or pokeberry juice.[92] O. M. Smith reported that "a written
plan of the insurrection, containing the order in which they were
to take us, [was] found on one of the generals!"[93] But the documents
gave as little clue to the whereabouts of the black prophet as they
did to the secret thoughts that had loosed the lightning of revolt
on Southampton County. As long as Nat Turner remained free,
Southampton's white community was not.

Requiem for a God-fearing Man

Counsel for the Defense

"Should my son Thomas R. Gray . . . bring any claim against my estate whatsoever it is my desire that the portion . . . bequeathed to my Grand Daughter Ellen Douglas Gray may be equally divided between my son Edwin and my Daughter Ann Gray." There was really no question at all about it, then: Capt. Thomas Gray must have stretched himself out and died in the second week of September precisely in order to spite his son. The young man was not only cut entirely out of the will,[1] but his father's death had come at the most damaging moment possible, at the height of the insurrection trials. As a result—one the old man undoubtedly foresaw and relished—Thomas Ruffin Gray of the Southampton Bar had gone the whole period from September 7 to October 18, when over half the cases were heard, without a single assignment.

Moreover, it must have seemed clear to the young attorney that the court's prejudice had operated against him even before his father's death. While William C. Parker was handling seven cases in that first week of trials and the upstart French no less than nine, Gray had been given only four and the court had convicted every man he defended. A docket of almost forty cases had gained him $50—less expenses—or a dollar a day for the period of his involvement.[2] It was too bad there was no God whose wrath could be called down on rascal magistrates and faithless fathers or a hell where they might go for an eternity of contrition. For Thomas R. Gray of Round Hill there was no consolation in having played a role in one of the most significant events in American history. His ruin was even more complete now than it had been before Nat Turner launched his hatchet at Travis's cranium.

Despite an atmosphere still bordering on hysteria in and about Jerusalem,[3] the trials and executions were handled with admirable efficiency and dispatch. Daniel Porter, on Levi Waller's testimony that he had seen Daniel among the rebels at his own house, was convicted on the last day of August and hanged six days later. Jack and

Andrew Whitehead, whose crime amounted to several hours of uncertainty over what to do, were found guilty on September 1 and were recommended for executive clemency and sold out of the state. September 2 and 3, the harshest days in the history of Southampton court, resulted in the death penalty being handed down for Moses Barrow, Davy Turner, Curtis and Stephen Ridley, Sam Francis, Hark Travis, Nelson Williams, Davy Waller, and James and Elizabeth Turner's Nat. Isaac Charlton, convicted for indiscreet behavior in the presence of Nancy Parsons on the day the revolt began, was transported.[4]

With the immediate need for admonitory examples having been met, the court settled down on Monday, September 5, to sober consideration of the merits of each case. Dred Francis, Nathan Blunt, and Jack Reese were condemned to death, though the sentence of the last-named was commuted to transportation. Nathan, Tom, and Davy Francis, along with Hardy and Isham Edwards, were found guilty and transported. Half a dozen subsequent cases brought no convictions, but Joe Turner and Lucy Barrow received the death penalty on September 19 and Frank Parker and Jim and Isaac Champion on September 22, the latter three on the testimony of fellow slaves that they had vented some seditious sentiments. (Frank Parker's sentence was commuted to transportation.) The convictions of Sam Edwards on October 17 and Moses Moore (commuted to transportation) the next day concluded the work of the court for the time being, with only the fate of Ben Blunt and the four free Negroes still to be decided. Of the twenty-seven convicted so far, only fourteen had actually ridden with Nat Turner's company.[5]

His small and unsuccessful part in the litigation that focused the attention of a large portion of the world on Jerusalem courthouse that autumn brought only further humiliation for Thomas R. Gray. His financial collapse, accompanied by the death of his young wife,[6] had come about only since 1829 when, as owner of eight hundred acres of farmland and twenty-one Negro slaves, he had been one of Southampton's more prosperous and promising planters. The 1830 tax listings, showing his slave gang reduced to seventeen, was a warning signal for the catastrophic year 1831, which left him with only one Negro and a little over three hundred acres. But the worst was yet to come, for the 1832 listings would record his ownership of neither land nor slaves, his sole item of taxable property being a horse.[7] He had been practicing law for only eight months at the time of the Southampton rebellion.[8]

Even his little girl was a source of anxiety. As designated heiress to a third of her grandfather's estate, Ellen Douglas Gray might come before long into considerable property, but for the time being her father could scarcely find the means for her support. With no established reputation as a lawyer, no consideration from the Southampton magistrates, and no property whatever, he faced the prospect of having his daughter assigned to a guardian and, should worse befall, perhaps his own imprisonment for the debts he could not pay.

At the nadir of his troubles in the fall of 1831, fortune thrust before Thomas R. Gray a sudden and dazzling prospect of salvation. On the morning of Sunday, October 30, Benjamin Phipps, an obscure dirt farmer of the Cross Keys neighborhood, stumbled upon Nat Turner hiding in a small cave in the woods and took him prisoner. The rebel leader was brought early next afternoon to Jerusalem jail, and Gray applied for and received permission from the jailer to interview the prisoner and make a formal record of his statement.[9] Parker was assigned to Nat's defense, but a nation waiting eagerly for a clear picture of Nat Turner's character and motives could now have its curiosity gratified, and the credit—and royalties—would belong exclusively to Thomas R. Gray.

The Fugitive

Although he had several times been reported seen or even captured as far away as Washington, D.C., and Fincastle, Virginia, Nat revealed to his captors that he had not left the vicinity of the insurrection. Instead, he had gone into hiding on August 23 with two of his men, Jacob Porter and James and Elizabeth Turner's Nat, that night dispatching them to search for Hark or Henry or others of his most reliable lieutenants who might be hiding in the neighborhood where the revolt began. But the pair had not returned, and the rebel general realized by Wednesday evening that no further hope remained of keeping the rebellion alive.[10] Patrols were swarming across woods and fields in quest of the last fugitives and had no doubt seized nearly all of them.

After gathering some provisions at the deserted Travis farm on August 25, Nat had spent his first six weeks hiding nearby in a hole under a pile of fence rails. Patrols appeared and reappeared in the vicinity so frequently that he was unable to venture out except for a few minutes each night for water. By early October, however, the patrols had thinned out sufficiently for him to roam about at night, and he had even been able to eavesdrop at various farmhouses.[11]

Two weeks of nocturnal freedom, with Nat returning each night just before daybreak to his makeshift cave, ended on October 15 through an unlucky accident—a dog being attracted to the hideout by the smell of some meat Nat had there. Nat returned from an evening ramble to find the dog emerging from the hole, and the same animal returned two nights later. This time the dog accompanied two Negroes on a night's hunt (so much had security loosened) and barked as it neared Nat's cave. When the fugitive identified himself to the two men, both immediately fled and Nat realized that they would probably betray his hiding place, which they did.[12] A report from Petersburg boasted that between five and six hundred men had located the cave, finding in it "a pistol, and a ham of bacon"[13] and a stick with forty-one notches in it, believed to represent the number of days he had spent there.[14] But Nat himself was gone.

Even now Nat was able to avoid discovery for another two weeks, this time by hollowing out a space for himself under two adjacent fodder stacks in a field on Nathaniel Francis's farm. Again, he was reduced to foraging only in the late hours of night, but he obtained two bacon hams and enough sweet potatoes to sustain him, if necessary, through a lengthy seige. On Wednesday, October 28, however, Francis came riding through the field, saw the rebel leader, and fired a pistol charge at him, twelve pellets passing through Nat's hat as he fled barefooted toward the woods. A new hiding place on the same farm, a cave fashioned under the top of a fallen pine tree, proved futile; around noon on Sunday, October 30, young Benjamin Phipps, whose farm was nearby, noticed some brush stacked in a peculiar way around the treetop, removed some of it, and saw Nat underneath.[15] Phipps ordered Nat to hand out his sword and then to lie on the ground so that his arms could be tied.[16] Aware that the area was full of armed searchers, suffering from the effects of cold on his ragged body and shoeless feet, Nat surrendered quietly.

Phipps and others led Nat off to Peter Edwards's farm where he would spend the night before being taken next day to Jerusalem. During the afternoon and evening, however, he was taken from place to place around the neighborhood, "several females" having "expressed a curiosity to see him." Next morning, as he was escorted to Jerusalem, the news of his capture spread and brought to town a large number of curious people. "The firing and rejoicing was so great," wrote one enthusiastic Southampton witness, "as very soon to collect a large concourse . . . from the surrounding country, who joined in the general expressions of joy."[17] There was some inclination among members of the crowd to lynch him, so that it was "with difficulty he could be conveyed alive" to the jail. Though not markedly abused, the prisoner appeared to one observer "dejected, emaciated and ragged" from his seventy-day ordeal. After an hour and a half of questioning by magistrates James Trezevant and William C. Parker, he was locked in chains behind the bars where he was to spend his last days. Phipps, hero of the hour among the whites, had earned exclusive claim to the $500 reward offered by the state plus another $600 that had been put up by individuals.[18]

The Confession

The Southampton jail was a depressing tomb of a place with four "apartments," each sixteen feet square and lacking either a stove or fireplace. A committee examining the structure in June pronounced it "clean & aired" though not "duely whitewashed." The place was secured by a single lock, and the only bed at that time had no blanket or covering. In the steaming August week before the trials opened, the jail had held up to fifty prisoners at a time.[19] But the work of the court had gone far to relieve the congestion by late October, so that there remained only Sam Edwards, scheduled to die on November 4; Moses Moore, awaiting transportation; and Ben Blunt and the four free Negroes, all of whom had been remanded for trial by the superior court.[20]

Thomas R. Gray could not have failed to acquire substantial information about Nat Turner's life and ambitions even before their first interview, and may, indeed, have had a manuscript already in an advanced stage of preparation. Besides the details gathered about him from others during September and October, Nat had furnished a lengthy confession on the preceding evening. Norfolk readers of the *American Beacon* had learned on November 2 that the captive "evinced great intelligence and shrewdness of intellect, answering every question clearly and distinctly, and without confusion or prevarication." He had conceived the enterprise, revealed it to his cohorts "a few days before, and then only 5 or 6 in number!" He had been actuated, he claimed, by "a revelation."

In a letter of November 1 from Southampton, a correspondent of the *Richmond Enquirer* reported that the prisoner told "with great candour" of "the operations of his mind for many years past; of the signs he saw; the spirits he conversed with; of his prayers, fastings and watchings, and of his supernatural powers and gifts, in curing diseases, controlling the weather, etc." The "idea of emancipating the blacks [had] entered his mind" about a year before, but it was August 21 when he "rendezvoused in a field near Travis's" with his fellow plotters. It had been Nat himself who entered an upper window of his master's house, opened the outer door, and struck the first blow at Travis.[21]

Other informants passed on additional details gleaned from the same interview on October 31—how Nat claimed to be able to "command the thunder and can thunder when he pleases; that he was in the way of his duty; that he can read it upon the leaves of the trees, &c."[22] It was learned that he claimed to be able to "produce a drought or a rain, by the efficacy of prayer," that he was "induced to believe that he could succeed in conquering the county of Southampton . . . as the white people did in the revolution,"[23] that "the *dark appearance of the sun*" had been the signal for him to begin. From the moment when "he struck his master . . ., who called on his wife" and "received the fatal blow from one of [Nat's] associates" to the details of his flight and capture, Nat had already made his confession, and Gray was undoubtedly among the fascinated audience who first listened to it.[24] "He does not hesitate to say," one witness concluded, that "if his time were to go over again, he must necessarily act in the same way." He had intended, he remarked, "to lie by till better times arrived."[25]

It remained to make a full transcript for the court record, but Gray had other purposes in mind besides. By encouraging Nat to dwell upon his early life and development into manhood, the interviewer could flesh out a portrayal that would not fail to intrigue thousands of Americans. An inexpensive pamphlet might serve admirably to gratify public curiosity as well as calm the fears of those who wondered if the Southampton rebellion might only foreshadow a terrible conflict in which white and black races would resolve by savage violence the agonizing problem of their permanent relationship.

In three days of intermittent sessions from November 1 through November 3, Gray sat in the jail with the shackled rebel leader, listening to his account, occasionally interjecting questions, from time to time taking unobtrusive notes. The result was in many respects the most remarkable document produced by two and a half centuries of American slavery.

While more than half of the five thousand words or so that comprise the confession relate to already well-publicized circumstances of the raids on various farms, it is the first two thousand of these that give the account its depth and vitality. Here the prisoner related his early awareness of abilities and a destiny that set him apart from ordinary men—the infant utterances that gave rise to speculation that he might be a prophet, the assurance of his parents that certain marks on his head and chest confirmed it, the indications of great intelligence and keen powers of observation. Bred to such a conviction, he had, in his words, "wrapped myself in mystery" and "studiously avoided mixing in society" in order to preserve the aura of superiority that seemed to surround him.[26]

It was in turning strongly to religion in early manhood that Nat, according to his confession, began the transition from mere mystic to insurgent. A series of encounters with "the Spirit" strengthened his belief that he "was ordained for some great purpose in the hands of the Almighty," but some years passed before he made the connection between his "great purpose" and remarks by others in his childhood that he had "too much sense" ever to "be of service to anyone as a slave." After a subsequent vision of "white spirits and

black spirits engaged in battle," the critical phase of his psychological preparation began on May 12, 1828, when he was told that
Christ had now "laid down the yoke he had borne for the sins of
men" and that Nat must "take it on and fight against the Serpent,
for the time was fast approaching when the first should be last and
the last should be first." Commanded to await "the first sign"
before taking any action, Nat interpreted an eclipse in February
1831 as the warning to prepare himself and the solar phenomenon
of August 13 as the signal to strike.[27]

Thomas R. Gray, in a fury of expository zeal, dashed off his final
draft of the document, added a preface, made a copy for the court,
and was conferring with printers in Richmond within four days of
his last meeting with Nat Turner. After finding on November 7
that the presses in Richmond "were so occupied with other matters"
that the first edition he wanted—"about 50,000 copies"—could not
be handled there, he sped on to Washington for a copyright (issued
on November 10) and within ten days had his first copies run off
by a printer in Baltimore.[28] They were on sale at Washington, D.C.,
by November 22 at twenty-five cents a copy, representing a potential gross of $12,500 and a handsome royalty for the author. Nat
Turner, condemned by the Southampton court on November 5,
had been hanged at Jerusalem on November 11.[29]

Even though Gray's preface promises that Nat's confession is
offered "without comment," the publication contains various personal asides and remarks that bear overtly upon his own estimation
of the rebel general. The introduction treats of "a gloomy fanatic"
with a "dark, bewildered, and overwrought mind . . . endeavoring to
grapple with things beyond its reach." But Gray's concluding
impressions, subtended to Nat's statement, describe in moving terms
a subject with "a mind capable of attaining any thing," one who,
"for natural intelligence and quickness of apprehension, is surpassed
by few men I have ever seen." The same passage defends Nat almost
indignantly from the charge that he was "ignorant and cowardly,"
that his object was to steal "money to make his escape." Besides an
incident showing "the decision of his character," Gray was led to
relate that "it is notorious, that he was never known to have a dollar
in his life; to swear on oath, or drink a drop of spirits."[30]

The portrait, then, betrays a kind of chilling admiration for the rebel Negro, a blend of horror and furtive esteem that raises the narrative well above that of any other contemporary account. Gray's parting glimpse of the prisoner ascends, indeed, to an exalted poignancy as we read of the "calm composure with which he spoke of his late deeds and intentions, the expression of his fiend-like face when excited by enthusiasm, still bearing the stains of helpless innocense about him; clothed in rags and covered with chains; yet daring to raise his manacled hands to heaven, with a spirit soaring above the attributes of man; I looked on him and my blood curdled in my veins."[31]

Eight hundred miles to the north, William Lloyd Garrison read those words and called sardonically for "Grand Juries in the several slave states to indict Mr. Gray and the printers of the pamphlet forthwith," even as they had lately indicted the fiery abolitionist editor and his journal, the *Liberator*. "Let Southern legislatures," he counseled, "offer a large reward for their apprehension," for the *Confessions* must "only serve to rouse up other leaders and cause other insurrections, by creating among the blacks admiration for the character of Nat, and a deep, undying sympathy for his cause."[32]

Garrison had seen what few other whites had allowed themselves to see in the pamphlet, the quality of sublime dignity in the impenitent rebel leader. The source, moreover, of the pathos and grandeur of the portrait of Nat seemed unmistakable: on the face of the defiant black prophet, Thomas Ruffin Gray had read the mirror image of his own ravaged soul. Born in the same county and in the same year as Nat Turner, Gray must have understood only too well the sources of the turbulent emotions in the breast of the enigmatic black man. The same blind destiny that cast Nat into a life of slavery had robbed Gray of his patrimony, his wife, the affection of his father, his standing in the community. As with the narrator, so with the recorder, might the pattern of regulatory beliefs and devices of white dominion have appeared more as an enemy than an ally. Unwilling to acknowledge his affinity with the rebel, yet unable to escape it, the young attorney seems to have found in the recesses of his own heart a chord that responded vibrantly and in unison with the savage confessions of the slave.

Diaspora

The panic that seized hold of the white community in Southampton and surrounding counties in the fall of 1831 found its chief expression in a wave of repression against the black population, especially against the free Negroes. A young free black woman of Halifax County, North Carolina, would recall in later years that "the white people who owned no slaves" would have killed many Negroes had not masters put their slaves in jail to protect them. No such security however, was available to the free blacks. "They came to my mothers," she related, "and threatened us—they searched for guns and ammunition. . . . One of them put his pistol to my breast, and said, 'if you open your head, I'll kill you in a minute!' I had told my mother to hush, as she was inquiring what their conduct meant." [33]

A Quaker in Perquimans County complained to the head of the American Colonization Society in early September that blacks in his neighborhood were "so severely punished they had rather go any where than to stay here where they are persecuted for innocency." A Pasquotank County observer in the same month noted that "there is no safety for free people of Colour." One had lately been killed in his own house there by two drunken white men, and "the mere imprisonment" of the killers had generated much resentment "among our non slave holding population." John W. McPhail, Colonization Society agent in Norfolk, learned that the free Negroes of Southampton were "suffering severely . . . altho confessed by all to be inoscent inofending people . . . they have been obliged to leave their houses and take refuge in the houses [of] benevolent white men" such as Joseph C. Lewis and Dr. Carr Bowers. [34]

Apprised by Henry Lenow, a fifty-seven-year-old German shoemaker of Southampton, that the whites hoped "every one" of the free blacks might "leave this part, as they can be well spared, and great advantage to themselves," [35] the Colonization Society sought to turn the situation to the advantage of itself as well as the oppressed Negroes. Free blacks from Southampton and elsewhere had already started arriving in Norfolk in early September when the society began making preparations to send a ship to Liberia. Fifty applied to Henry Lenow for assistance in arranging transportation to Africa, and Thomas Pretlow emancipated three slaves for the same purpose. Joseph C. Lewis, arriving in Norfolk on September 23, announced to McPhail that 200 were ready to leave Southampton "immediately," all of them "honest industrious people." By October 20 the list had grown to 245, or nearly one-sixth of the free black population of the county.[36]

These and other Negroes from other places were taken aboard the schooner *James Perkins* at Norfolk at the end of November, and the vessel embarked on December 5 for Africa.[37] They comprised probably the ablest and most talented of Southampton's free Negroes, including James and Peggy Ben, "a celebrated Black Doctor and Doctress,"[38] brickmakers Charles Hamblin and George Artis, blacksmiths Willy Brown and Willy Jordan, cooper Henry Bowlin, house carpenter James Cotton, and shoemakers Joshua Gardner, Isaac and Simeon Overton, Willis Scott, Andrew Turner, and Hamilton Tann.[39] Mostly in families of from three to eight people,[40] they included many named Brown, Butler, Duncan, Jones, Ricks, Scott, Turner, Vines, and Williams. They ranged in age from some two dozen infants in arms to seventy-five-year old George Liberty, whose memory spanned the ages since before George III had become king of England. No doubt few had been landowners in Southampton, but James Cotton and Hamilton Tann were among those who had to sell their property at whatever price they could get in order to make the voyage to Africa.[41]

The *James Perkins* reached Liberia in thirty-five days from Norfolk, all of its passengers bearing certificates, according to agent McPhail, "of good Character from gentlemen known to me to be of the first character themselves." After visiting for a few days in the town of Cauldwell, they indicated to the captain of the *James Perkins* their satisfaction with "the general appearance of the Country & Town, their prospects of gaining a livelihood &c. . . ., and thought they could with industry get a good living there, and be their own master to boot."[42]

Others from Southampton County followed as rapidly as transportation could be arranged. Fourteen Whiteheads (one was named Colegate) and sixteen Whitefields departed on the *Jupiter* from Norfolk in May 1832, eleven more on the *American* in July of that year, and twenty others on the *Jupiter* in the following November. The

five Artises who embarked on the *Roanoke* in December 1832 apparently represented the end of the flight occasioned by the insurrection
panic.[43] Still others, of course, had fled west or north in search, if not
of true freedom, then at least of relief from the life of insecurity and
harassment that Southampton County meant for them. For slavery
and race relations in the South had now entered upon a critical and
dangerous new phase, one that would culminate in tearing the
nation apart.

For those free Negroes who chose to remain in Southampton, the
holocaust of the uprising continued to haunt them through the
winter of 1831–32 while the fate of the four free black suspects
remained undecided. Ben Blunt, last of the slave suspects, was
hanged on December 20, 1831, but the cases of Thomas Haithcock,
Berry Newsom, Exum Artis, and Isham Turner were not decided
until the following spring.[44] Haithcock, miraculously surviving
adverse testimony given in the fall by his wife and stepdaughter,
was released and was registered on the county's roll of free Negroes
on June 13, 1832, as a forty-year-old freeborn man.[45] The case
against Exum Artis, apparently consisting of testimony by a slave
named Burwell Vick that Artis had flourished a pistol on August 23
and boasted of the whites he might kill, ended with the defendant's
release.[46] Isham Turner was also released, but Berry Newsom,
accused of having expressed to some fellow blacks his intention of
joining the rebels (evidently not carried out), was convicted and, on
May 11, hanged.[47] This brought the number of people convicted
to thirty, nineteen of whom were hanged and the rest transported.[48]

Scar Tissue

Shock waves from the slave rebellion continued to reverberate
through Southampton for many years after the event. The forms
taken by these tremors included a legacy of recriminations among
some of the principals in the affair, perhaps an inevitable consequence of personalities maimed and distorted in the crucible of
panic and retribution. Among the first to feel such an aftereffect of
the rebellion was Jerusalem's innkeeper, Henry B. Vaughan, whose
unhappy fate it was to be castigated publicly about the quality of
his services to the Richmond troops during the insurrection.

Vaughan, whose sister-in-law Rebecca was among the victims of the uprising, was described by the Richmond *Whig* in early September as one whose "base and sordid love of pelf" led him to furnish the troops "with the commonest of stinking fare" and then submit to the state an outrageous bill of over $800.[49] At an entertainment given in Petersburg for the Richmond Dragoons shortly afterward, editor Pleasants of the *Whig* went so far as to propose a toast to "Henry B. Vaughan—the publican, who speculated upon the bones of his kindred, which the dragoons went to bury and avenge."[50]

A more serious injury was that incurred by Harriet Whitehead, who had survived though her sister was killed in the room in which Harriet was hiding. Years afterward she would have occasion to tell a Southampton court that "the fright and alarm" she experienced during the uprising had left on her a "powerful and overwhelming effect." As a result, she often "became depressed in spirits weak in body and mind, hysterical and easily excited and in such a state of mind has resorted to stimulating medicines and the like."[51]

The reason for these disclosures was a lawsuit brought by Miss Whitehead in 1848 against Nathaniel Francis. The suit alleged that Francis, "seeing that she was hopeful of a considerable estate, and that in consequence of her unfortunate state of mind, was a fit subject for him to defraud . . ., accordingly set about to obtain it from her."[52]

It appears that in 1843 Francis, characterized by Harriet as "notorious for his love of money" had come into possession of several small notes of debt owed by Harriet to other persons. With these, it was alleged, Francis set out to force her to deed all of her property to him. Failing to wear her down by frequent visits and by pressure applied through female intermediaries, it was charged, Francis resorted to having warrants issued against her. He also threatened to expose her to the congregation at Clarksbury Methodist Church, where both had for many years been members.[53] Harriet, unable to hold out against such tactics, agreed in November 1843 to sign over her property to Francis, the consideration to be a payment of $800 (never made) and a promise to take care of her for the rest of her life (never honored). Harriet was able to get the court to void the deed; when she died in 1852 she left her property to two of her brothers. Nathaniel Francis died of pneumonia in 1849, bequeathing his own respectable estate to his wife and children.[54]

There were others for whom the psychological stress of the rebellion was severe, though probably less permanent than in the case of Harriet Whitehead. Levi Waller's temporary derangement has been noted previously. At Littletown, O. M. Smith had written on August 29, 1831, of "[o]ne young Lady and two men to my knowledge," who were "frightened out of their senses, so that they have been perfectly deranged for four days!" "I must tell you," Smith added, "that one of the three is no other than Mr. William Harrison, my patron." Harrison was "very dangerously sick, perfectly crazy, and growing worse very fast, unless he is better very soon, my next to you will announce his death!" Benjamin Harrison, brother of William, was ill before the rebellion began, "and it cured him immediately."[55]

Southampton slaveholders who petitioned the General Assembly at the close of 1831 for compensation for slaves killed in the uprising were all disappointed in their hopes. Applications by Richard Porter, the Elizabeth Turner and Fitzhugh heirs, Peter Edwards, and Levi Waller, though citing legislative precedents going back to 1691, were all rejected. Nor did the legislators see fit to recompense the innkeepers whose fare, for good and ill, had nourished the men and horses engaged in suppressing the revolt.[56]

A less enduring injury was the one sustained by those who looked for an early revival of religion in Southampton. Baptist Elder Robert T. Daniel wrote glumly to a church newspaper in early September of the effect of the revolt on churchgoing: "The confusion produced by the outrage of the blacks in this county, has given a vital stab to our blessed cause in this section, as well as to the tranquillities of every family. When all things are to become still and harmony prevail, I know not. We had some hopeful appearances in a few of the churches here before the insurrection took place." Because some Southampton residents had been attending a camp meeting in neighboring Gates County, North Carolina, on the day of the revolt, a local historian in 1900 professed to find that "camp-meetings were not so frequent in this section after this."[57]

Within a short time, however, the scene had brightened enough for James Delk, whose ministry included a portion of Southampton, to write that he was now "much encouraged" for the future. During the period of panic, he conceded, "it would be impossible for me to describe . . . the effects which it produced." He had "tried to preach a few times" but without effect until September 9, when he baptized nine people at one service.[58] There appeared to be some hope that the aftereffects of the rebellion might even include a greater earnestness about religion than before.

But the insurrection, of course, had not affected adversely every individual touched by it, even in the period of greatest terror. Benjamin Phipps had reaped his small fortune from the arrest of the fugitive leader. Another whose prospects were greatly improved was Simon Frazer Blunt, fifteen-year-old son of Dr. Blunt and a hero of the defense of his father's farm against Nat Turner's final assault. Commodore Eliot of Norfolk, reporting directly to President Andrew Jackson on September 8 in regard to the navy's role in the affair, gave him "a minute account" of the revolt and the conduct of young Blunt. The president thereupon authorized Blunt's appointment to the Naval Academy, opening for the youthful appointee a career of more than twenty years as a naval officer. He was a member of the Wilkes exploring expedition of 1838–42 which circumnavigated the globe.[59] He was married to Ellen Key, a daughter of Francis Scott Key.

Gray's Elegy

Thomas R. Gray knew no better fortune in the wake of the slave rebellion than he had before. Although the *Confessions* pamphlet is said to have sold well enough to require a second printing in 1832,[60] proceeds from it did not measurably alleviate the author's financial distress. He appears to have acquired no real estate during the rest of his life, though he was able to purchase a gig in 1834, which, with his horse, constituted the whole of his taxable property during his remaining years in Southampton County. His daughter Ellen Douglas became the ward of Gray's fellow attorney William C. Parker in July 1832.[61]

Gray's meager role in public affairs reflected his worldly poverty. He had served briefly as a justice of the peace before his resignation at the end of 1830, but he was not to hold so consequential an office again. He occupied for a time the positions of overseer of the poor and commissioner of Indian lands in Southampton,[62] but both were offices to which he was appointed before his financial collapse in 1830 and 1831.

In the fall of 1839 Gray moved to Portsmouth,[63] and there, in the summer of 1845, he fell mortally ill with bilious (or congestive) fever. He was heralded to the grave by an anonymous eulogist who acknowledged "the impetuosity of his temper" and conceded that the deceased had been "a scoffer at religion." The obituary, strikingly out of character with the panegyrics customary on such occasions, drew a harsh sketch of its subject. "Whatever were his faults," the writer began, "there was in the character of the deceased much to admire and much that was worthy of esteem." After directing attention to Gray's lack of malice or "vindictive passion," the writer made a gallant effort to praise the "independence and fearlessness of [his] mind, which disdained alike concealment and restraint— what he tho't on any subject, as of any individual, that he said, whether in or out of his presence." The latter trait, unhappily, was sometimes "misdirected," and it was a "reflection deeply painful to his friends, that he invaded with unhallowed lips the sanctuary of religion."[64]

His last day on earth was Saturday, August 23, 1845—fourteen years and a day since Nat Turner had swung the hatchet that gave the institution of slavery its mightiest jolt. Like the black prophet whose confessions he had broadcast to the world, Thomas R. Gray had been a rebel. But confrontation with death had drawn a sharp distinction between the rebel against an earthly master and the rebel against the divine. Nat Turner, boldly owning the full scope of his leadership in the revolt, spurning an opportunity to offer words of contrition at the gallows, had "in a firm voice" "hurried his executioner in the performance of his duty" and entered eternity "with the utmost composure"—"not a limb nor a muscle was observed to move."[65]

But Gray, summoning in his final hours Rev. Mr. Eskridge of the Episcopal church, had chosen to offer what his eulogist deemed a "contrition . . . as sincere as its evidences were impressive": "I have been (said he to the Rev. Pastor) the vilest of sinners and nothing could have awakened me to a knowledge of my lost condition, but a blow like that which struck Saul of Tarsus to the earth. O, that I could be permitted to go abroad but for an hour. I would cover myself with dust and ashes and cry aloud to sinners to repent and flee the wrath to come!"[66]

The souls of saint and sinner flew forth to face the judgment of a righteous God, who alone in all creation was certain which was which. But there had been a period of a few days in the autumn of 1831 when Nat Turner and Thomas R. Gray conspired to create the most compelling document in the history of black resistance to slavery. Despite the stilted prose in which Nat's confession was clothed by the young attorney, it was the vein of compassion and identity he felt that gave the account its enduring power and haunting validity. Nat's literary legacy to unborn generations was made possible by the chance that brought to his prison cell perhaps the only educated man in Southampton County who was prepared to appreciate the prophet's calm assurance that what he had done was what had to be. If the *Confessions* may be said to have sounded the death knell of American slavery, it was Nat who swung the gong and Gray whose resonant metal rent the air.

8

Trojan Horsepower

The P. & R.

The new steam train was emphatically the marvel of the age. Ten years before, the very suggestion of steam railroads would have relegated the advocate to the class of those who talked of perpetual motion and squaring the circle. Now, in the spring of 1835, you could ride on one of these things from Portsmouth to the Nottoway River and back again, making the whole excursion in a single day. The possibilities for commerce and industry were astounding, but there was a world of entertainment in simply being transported in this way between distant points. No one who could afford the dollar fare would think of missing it.

The cosmopolitan Norfolk resident, up to now serenely confident that he had seen just about everything there was to see on the planet, caught his breath at the wheezing five-ton iron machine. He could take the early morning ferry over to Portsmouth, be conveyed rapidly by carriage to the railroad depot, step aboard the cars, and in eighty minutes' time be deposited in front of Elliott Whitehead's tavern in Suffolk, a full seventeen miles away. The really adventurous excurionist could elect to continue the trip on past McClenny's and Carrsville to the latticed bridge over the Blackwater above South Quay, passing on an elevated trestle some twelve to fifteen feet above the Blackwater low grounds and coming out again on terra firma for the final leg of the journey to the east bank of the Nottoway.

The scenery along the route was admittedly somewhat bleak and uninviting, a swampy wilderness sufficiently devoid of interest to make the village of Suffolk seem the traveler "worthy of a poet's lay." The occasional farm clea   ooked as though "they blushed at being exposed to the public gaze by the intrusion of the rail upon their privacy."[1] But dull was the ima   tion that would ever forget "the chimney of the locomotiv   as a passenger described it, "with its stream of sparks lighting up the gloom of the Great Dismal Swamp."[2] Any who took the trip could be assured of "such a ride," extolled a Norfolk commentator, "as he cannot but be delighted with, over a road which has no superior."[3]

Thomas G. Broughton, oracle of the Norfolk *Herald,* was, as usual, precisely on target with his assessment following his first visit to the western reaches of the line. The railroad bridge at Blackwater, he wrote, "will be the principal intermediate depot for the produce of the line . . ., and we should not be surprised if, in a few years, the Bridge . . . were to exhibit at either end a thriving village, where now there is nothing to be seen but swampy wilderness."[4]

Already there was a clearing at the Nottoway where the engineers were constructing a massive bridge of heart pine resting on tall beams well above the river's flood crest and pointing the Portsmouth and Roanoke toward its ultimate southwestern terminus. The clearing, containing nothing much more than a storage warehouse for the work crew, had been somewhat hopefully dubbed Crocketsville (for Davy Crockett), and landowners in the vicinity were dreaming of broad avenues and flourishing market houses. When Jesse Lankford of Southampton County in early August 1834 shipped 10,000 pounds of bacon and lard and ten barrels of vinegar on the produce cars to Portsmouth, "all of which was disposed of next day, at liberal prices," the cornucopia began to pour forth its riches.[5]

The special treat out on the far end of the line was to dine at Murfee's, a mile and a half east of Nottoway, where the traveller could enjoy Virginia ham, roast pig, fresh fish, poultry, potatoes, beets, peas, snap beans, pickles, and a variety of other delicacies in any combination or all together. There were also excellent pies and beverages, the product of Murfee's own apple orchard. Leaving Murfee and his groaning board at 2 P.M. the wayfarer was back in Suffolk at 4:30 and in Portsmouth by 6 o'clock, having covered eighty-four miles in only about five hours of actual travel time. Passengers from Halifax, North Carolina, could come by the new stage line via Jackson forty-five miles to the Nottoway near Murfee's, depart from there at 5 A.M. on the cars, and be in Norfolk in plenty of time to catch the Baltimore and Washington steamboats up the Chesapeake. "Not an accident occurred to mar the enjoyment of the occasion," wrote an exultant Norfolk excursionist, "save the death of an unfortunate cow, who very indiscreetly . . . took post on the line of the road; and although solemnly warned by the powerful voice of steam, and the thundering of the approaching train, that her position was untenable, . . . refused to retreat." The editor of the Norfolk *Beacon* was "happy to see that the ride to Nottoway is becoming one of the most fashionable recreations of the day."[6]

It was, of course, much more than that. For instead of the bone-wrenching carriage ride over the swampy road to Edenton and the long wait there for an unpredicatble ferry over Albemarle Sound, the southern tourist now headed west to Blackwater and connections with the Edenton steamboat. A New Yorker took the new route on his way to Cuba in early 1836 and enjoyed himself immensely: "We left the cars in the midst of a cypress swamp and took stage, eight miles, to Blackwater River. . . . On arriving . . ., we were not a little gratified to find, moored to the trees, the little snug convenient steamboat Fox, which used formerly to run from New York to Flushing, and was a favorite of [essayist] Grant Thorburn's, who presented it with a print of 'A Fox on the Lookout.' A trio of us had the whole boat to ourselves, there being no other passengers."[7]

The *John Barnett*, first locomotive on the Portsmouth and Roanoke, was supplemented in March 1836 by a new one from Robert Stephenson's works at Newcastle-upon-Tyne, but the papers complained that there was "not yet a sufficient number of Engines for the business of the Road. Travelling continues to increase and produce is collected at the several depots, even faster than it can be transported." By December the line had been completed to Weldon, on the Roanoke River, one day's ride from Portsmouth and at a fare of $5.[8]

In spite of the fine prospects for commerce along the line, however, the P. & R. was beginning its history with a heavy burden of debt and competition from another railroad whose managers seemed to devote every waking hour and the greater part of their dreams to the earliest possible destruction of the road. The Petersburg Railroad, already in operation from the Roanoke since 1833, not only offered a more direct route between Washington and the South but connected at Petersburg with oceangoing vessels that could handle any merchandise that the wharves of Norfolk and Portsmouth could. There was a great deal of new business to be garnered in the river valleys of Tidewater Virginia and the Roanoke, but probably not enough to sustain both railroads at the same time. In what shaped up as a fight to the death, the Petersburg line had a good headstart and no scruples about striking straight for the jugular vein.

Whatever the outcome of the railroad competition, the farmers, millers, and lumbermen of Southampton County could scarcely avoid benefiting from it. The Petersburg route, skirting the western fringes of Southampton, gave to a great many residents of the county an equal choice of trading either on the Petersburg or Norfolk markets. It would be an unimaginative businessman who could not wring a profit from this situation so long as it lasted, and Dame Fortune seemed to have taken out Southampton citizenship and settled down permanently. The legendary bitchiness of this lady was forgotten for the time being, and the Blackwater-Meherrin region prepared for the cloudbursts of money that must surely rain down soon upon it.

Too Much Too Soon

The railroad revolution descended upon Southampton almost before people were aware there was such a thing. George Stephenson's *Rocket* had executed its first passenger run less than a decade before the *John Barnett* was huffing back and forth across the county frightening the stock and starting brushfires along the railbed. Many Southampton residents had gone over the Meherrin in 1833 to gawk at the first trains of the Petersburg Railroad grunting and belching past Belfield, and not much more than a year had passed after that before the trestles of the P. & R. were being pushed across the Blackwater. Some of the implications were immediately obvious: word of a Negro rebellion in Southampton, which had taken more than twenty-four hours to reach Norfolk in 1831, could have been delivered in less than three hours in 1835. The security of slave owners seemed much greater than ever before.

The economic life of the county was swiftly reoriented toward the depots along the rail lines and away from the old post routes that had marked the pathways of commerce in former times. Dusty crossroads and sidings such as Branchville, Boykin's, Newsom's, and Murfee's Depot now became the hubs of business enterprise, and

older communities suffered in dismal silence as old familiar stores
and taverns shut down or were removed to more promising sites.
Jerusalem, the focus of so much of the county's business since long
before it was incorporated as a town, was one of the places hardest
hit by the new scheme of things.

In 1835 Martin's *Gazetteer* described Jerusalem as a town that had
"neither retrograded nor advanced" in twenty years. But the place
had four mercantile stores, a saddler, a carriage maker, two hotels,
two taverns, a Masonic hall, and about twenty-five dwellings, besides the public buildings.[9] It had been the county's metropolis for
almost half a century, but in 1837 Elliott L. Story would decline
employment in Theodore Trezevant's store there, because "the
trade of that place was much curtailed" in consequence of the shift
of business south toward the railroad.[10]

Fortune favored the agile and flexible entrepreneur who could
cast aside the years spent building a reputation and a trade in one
vicinity and shift readily and smoothly to another. J. W. Murfee
was among the earliest to seize the initiative in the new business of
catering to the railroad trade, and his Half Way House was quickly
a landmark to the rail clientele. Situated midway between Blackwater and Nottoway and halfway between Portsmouth and Weldon,
Murfee's establishment was one of the places where the locomotives stopped for wood and water, during which interval hungry and
thirsty passengers thronged to his bar and tables. Murfee could seat
a hundred guests for a meal and arrange stage accommodations for
those who wished to embark in other directions from his house.[11]

The railroad was not a ribbon of gold but of iron: it could bring
misfortune on wheels that turned as fast as those of profit. The financial epitaph of William Murfee, kinsman of J. W. Murfee, was pronounced in 1858 after the failure of his business at Franklin Depot:
"He started with but very little money," wrote Elliott L.. Story;
"when he first grew up and for many years his friends thought that
he was making quite a good little income every year, but he was in
a hurry to be rich, bought a large stock of old goods in order to get
into the mercantile business . . ., and after doing business in this line
about two years he had failed and I suppose will loose more than he
has ever made." It was reported some years later that Murfee "took
an unexpected, and somewhat hasty departure; and *never returned*"
to Southampton.[12]

A similar lament might have been made on behalf of others in the county who had gambled on the glamorous promises of the railroad men. Much of the trouble that plagued the P. & R. was of its own making, including the shoddy equipment it installed. Its locomotives and loaded freight cars were supposed to glide smoothly over rails made of heart pine overlaid with two-inch-thick strips of iron. Such rails, however, were frequently crushed by the burdens to which they were subjected, causing many accidents.

On December 10, 1837, a P. & R. engine pulling three passenger cars and nine lumber cars loaded with cotton struck the loose end of a projecting iron strip about two miles west of Nottoway River. The engine, headed east after leaving Rochelle Depot, pitched off the track, and the freight cars came slamming against the passenger cars ahead of them, smashing the latter into "one common mass of ruins!" Some riders were thrown clear, but others were mangled in the wreckage. Those killed were Misses Blow and Rochelle of Southampton, and the injured included Capt. James D. Bryant, whose legs were broken, Col. Nathaniel Rochelle, a Mr. Blow, and Misses King and Simmons, also of Southampton. Prominent among those who escaped injury was Senator William C. Preston of South Carolina. [13]

The P. & R. probably did not need any extra shoves into oblivion on the part of its Petersburg competitors, but it got them anyway. The Petersburg managers, their line now considerably extended and incorporated into the Richmond, Petersburg and Fredericksburg Railroad, tried and failed to cut off the P. & R. from access to the Roanoke River. [14] They sought to dissuade Halifax stage drivers from carrying P. & R. passengers, linked their own rails to those of the new Raleigh and Gaston to monopolize north-south traffic, sharply reduced fares, and spread the rumor that they would "run *for nothing* and give a bottle of wine, should the Portsmouth Company reduce correspondingly." [15]

Portsmouth managers fought back by installing better track, replacing heavy engines with lighter ones, and linking up with the Weldon and Wilmington, completed in 1840. But the burden of debt incurred by these and other alterations drove the P. & R. into bankruptcy in 1843, and its assets were bid off at auction to James Magett and James S. French of Southampton. When their bid was assigned to a representative of the R. P. & F., the Portsmouth and

Roanoke was closed down and would not be permanently reopened until it was newly incorporated as the Seaboard and Roanoke in 1846. Even then it was another three years before the North Carolina portion of the tracks was back in operation, but now the whole system was rebuilt. During the 1850s the line would finally begin to enjoy some of the prosperity envisioned by its founders twenty years before. [16] The two decades of floundering had been a frustrating period for the people of Southampton County.

Southampton was beginning to take on the appearance of the crossroads of the Mid-Atlantic region in 1858 with the completion of the Petersburg and Norfolk Railroad. Five years in construction, this line included a remarkable stretch of fifty-one miles, passing through Ivor and the northeastern part of the county, without a single turn. The engineering for the railroad was performed under the direction of young William Mahone, a graduate of the Virginia Military Institute (Class of 1847) and native of Southampton. Mahone conceived the idea of negotiating the Dismal Swamp section of the Petersburg and Norfolk by forming a platform of logs and dirt over the surface of the swamp and creating a foundation that effectively supported the heaviest equipment of the railroad. The depot at Ivor, like several other way stations along the P. & N., was given its name by Otelia Mahone, wife of the engineer, who chose the names from Sir Walter Scott's *Waverley* novels. [17]

Blackwater Station

The growth that Thomas G. Broughton predicted for the site adjacent to the Blackwater railroad bridge took place in spite of the disasters that befell the P. & R. The steamboat connection with Edenton and intermediate points survived the hard times of the railroad and provided an important trading route for Southampton's commerce. The steamboat *Fox* was troubled by no competition on this route for almost fifteen years. Her captain, Joseph Middleton, became a legendary figure for competence and courtesy who was so thoroughly familiar with these waters that he "used to swear, that if the *Fox* was turned loose, with her machinery in motion, she would make her way to Franklin depot without captain or helmsman, vowing that he had frequently seen her *bend* in turning some of the curves of the Blackwater River."[18] The *Fox,* which could cover forty miles in four hours on a cord of wood,[19] was replaced in 1851 by the *Stag,* also operated by Captain Middleton. Rated at 166 tons, the *Stag* was more than twice as large as her predecessor, but she would have to share the Blackwater business with the *A. R. Schultz,* which was put on the route in early 1851 by a group in Portsmouth.[20]

The Blackwater depot, described in 1836 as "a swampy wilderness," was already a trading center known as Franklin when Elliott Story went there on business in the autumn of 1838 and recorded the name in his diary.[21] Richard Barrett, who boarded construction crews at his farm there while the railroad was being rebuilt in 1842, opened a regular boardinghouse which soon blossomed into a hotel. The railroad depot, until it was moved to Franklin in 1857, stood on the east, or Isle of Wight, side of the river, but it was on the Southampton side that business developed most rapidly. One of the first stores was that of John F. Pinner at the point where Jerusalem road crossed the railroad tracks. Robert Edwards soon put up a store on what is now South Street, but Pinner sold out in 1847 to Alexander W. Norfleet, who became antebellum Franklin's leading merchant. A Dr. Cox from New York, settling there in the 1850s, was the community's first physician.[22]

At the Southampton end of the bridge stood a small house occupied by that dark and eccentric survivor of the Southampton rebellion, John Ruffin "Choctaw" Williams. He had lost his wife and child in the uprising, but after remarrying in 1832, he had sired a large family of children and was agent and stationmaster for the railroad as well as postmaster for the village. Nearby stood John Frisbee's sawmill, progenitor of what would later become Franklin's dominant industry. Self-appointed to the position of Franklin's first police officer was a colorful Corsican named Napoleon Bonaparte Raziere, or "Captain Razor," as he was locally known. Raziere had come into the region as an employee of the railroad company, married an Isle of Wight girl, and adopted Franklin as his home until his death on the eve of the Civil War.[23]

A brief moment of glory for antebellum Franklin was the arrival there on Saturday, August 11, 1851, of Gen. Winfield Scott, Petersburg native and the most celebrated military officer of the American army. General Scott, Whig candidate for president in the following year, was en route to Nag's Head for a gala reception and was scheduled to take the *Schultz* down the Blackwater and Chowan to his destination. [24]

Unfortunately, Scott stepped off the cars at Franklin Depot to learn that orders had arrived there ahead of him summoning him immediately back to Washington, D.C. His trip to North Carolina was summarily canceled. A local diarist set the episode to somewhat ungainly verse in the lines:

> The boat was full and the wharves with people crowded,
> So "hail to the chief," guns fired and all shouted;
> A despatch from Washington which the General regretted,
> Stopped his journey at Franklin and the people fretted. [25]

The sequel was remembered as long as the event itself. As the *Schultz* proceeded down the Blackwater with a throng of passengers who had come to escort "Old Fuss and Feathers" to Nag's Head, it occurred to some of the wags on board that they might have some fun at the expense of waiting crowds along the route. John B. Odom of Northampton County was on board, and his tall, 240-pound proportions almost rivaled those of the general in stately corpulence. A uniform, complete with epaulets and cockade hat with feathers, was borrowed from Lt. Lawrence S. Baker, freshly graduated from West Point, and Odom was stationed majestically on the upper deck of the *Schultz,* beside the pilothouse. As the boat neared Edenton Wharf, the crowd on shore took Odom for the hero of Lundy's Lane and gave forth a lusty cheer, accompanied by a considerable booming of the old Boritz cannon. After the steamer reached the wharf, Dr. Edward Warren delivered a fifteen-minute address of welcome. A hush fell over the crowd as the distinguished visitor prepared to respond, and Odom, a stutterer, announced that "if-if I was General Scott I-I would make-make you a speech, but-but as I-I am only John-John B. Odom, I shan't do it." Astonished cries of "Kill him" and "Throw him overboard" were, with some little difficulty, quieted and the hotheads at length conceded that it was a pretty good joke, whereupon all accompanied their ersatz hero to the hotel for champagne. [26]

Paddlewheels and Planks

Southamptonians living closer to the Nottoway and Meherrin looked with longing upon the rapid progress of steamboating on the Blackwater but could not lure such craft into their own shallow and winding waters. In 1853, however, the aggressive mercantile interests in the town of Petersburg completed a plank road down to Jerusalem, offering a sleek and convenient new route for produce from the border counties. So smooth was the wooden surface of the road that horses were said to have died from being driven along it too rapidly. Built at a cost of only about $1,900 a mile, a tenth of the cost of railroads, the plank road provided convenient, all-weather transportation and seemed to be an enormous improvement over the rutted quagmires into which ordinary roads were often turned by wet weather.[27] People in Murfreesboro began to talk of a plank road to connect their town with the one at Jerusalem,[28] and it appeared that a great new movement had begun.

A couple of years' experience demonstrated the wretched miscalculations of the sponsors of the plank-road scheme. Rotting boards gave way continually under heavy wagons, causing accidents and delays all up and down the line. Tolls failed dismally to make up the initial costs of construction, and maintenance became a fiscal nightmare. In 1858 a Petersburg newspaper editor complained bitterly that "of all the abominable burlesques upon internal improvements . . . these plank roads are the most unmitigated. There is nothing under heaven to admire in them or be made out of them, and their . . . impassable character render them the object of universal complaint." If the routes could not be paved or graveled over, the paper concluded, they would soon be abandoned altogether.[29]

The failure of the plank road proved to be less critical than it appeared at the time. Residents of the village of Jerusalem were surprised on the afternoon of January 11, 1859, by boys running through the streets shouting, at the top of their voices, "A Steamboat's coming—a steamboat's coming!" Skeptical adults ran down to the water's edge to discover that there was, indeed, a steamer on the Nottoway, the first such vessel ever to enter the river. "I was utterly astonished on arriving at the water," wrote Jerusalem mer-

Plank-road certificate. James D. Bryant of Southampton bought four shares in
the ill-fated plank road in 1855. (Southampton County Historical Society;
photograph by Colbert Howell)

chant Seth W. Cobb, "to see so many. The village was deserted by
both black and white, young and old—all were standing on the
banks, watching with an eager eye the approaching steamer."[30]

The visiting craft was the little steamboat *Hope,* a Norfolk vessel
bound to Freeman's Bridge in Sussex County for a load of lumber.
Declining an invitation to free lodging and entertainment at John
Barham's Union Hotel, Captain Blount hurried on upriver but was
back in four days pulling two large barges of white oak timber.
Further inquiries revealed that the *Hope* had come south through
the Dismal Swamp Canal and that she was owned by Dr. George
W. Peete of Portsmouth, who had a charter permitting him to
operate as much as ninety miles up the Nottoway.[31] The event was
enough to shake Jerusalem from the torpor that had descended upon
it since the opening of the P. & R. and to cause its residents to dream
once more of growth and prosperity for their town.

Other allied events appeared to confirm the anticipations of the
people of the upper Nottoway. In 1856 the steamer *Curlew* was intro-

U.S.S. *Crusader*. Built in Murfreesboro in 1857 as the cargo steamer *Southern Star* by Jesse A. Jackson, later a resident of Franklin, the ship was purchased in 1858 by the U.S. government and converted to a cruiser which was used against the South in the Civil War. Jackson was grandfather of Edgar B. Jackson, well-known Southampton writer and historian. (Naval Photographic Center)

duced on the Chowan and Blackwater by Dr. Thomas Warren of Edenton,[32] its cargo holds and ample decks providing space for the accumulated produce of the feeder lines from the Nottoway and Meherrin. A tiny stern-wheel boat called the *Leonora* was placed on the Meherrin as far up as Murfreesboro, and merchants in that town laid the keel of a behemoth steamship ultimately to be known as the *Southern Star*. This vessel, 460 tons in displacement and more than 135 feet long, was to be sailed when completed to Wilmington, Delaware, and there provided with engines for a regular connection between New York City and the Meherrin.[33] The firm of Riddick and Burbage, headquartered at Riddicksville, a Chowan River station almost adjacent the Southampton border, began running several small steamers on the feeder routes of the upper Chowan and its tributaries.[34] When the *Seabird* was placed on the Chowan by Messrs. Delk and Lindsey of Portsmouth in 1860, the owners boasted of staterooms, sleeping apartments, two saloons, and a freight room with space for 250 bales of cotton, besides facilities for livestock, slaughtered beef and pork, and "all other kinds of produce fit to ship in steamboats."[35]

Greater things were yet to come. In 1860 a conglomerate of businessmen in Tidewater Virginia and northeastern North Carolina chartered the Albemarle Steam Packet Company and ordered from the firm of Harlan and Hollingsworth in Wilmington, Delaware, a huge new steamer. The vessel was to be known as the *Virginia Dare*, and it would be a 357-ton side-wheeler, more than 160 feet in length and capable of operating at thirteen knots. The venture, known in later years as the Albemarle Steam Navigation Company, was to provide the upper Chowan and Blackwater with reliable service for a period of almost three-quarters of a century.[36]

In the scant quarter century since the spring of 1835, the immense strides in transportation had catapulted the region in some respects from the Stone Age to the industrial era. A brother of Clara Barton, busily engaged in erecting a new mill town on the upper Chowan (known as Bartonsville), wrote excitedly home to Massachusetts that he had "never seen as good a time to make money as at present."[37] Many others echoed the same sentiment, never dreaming of the fatal hour, not many months hence, when the *Curlew* and the *Virginia Dare*, flagships of opposing navies, were to engage in a fierce gun battle to test which government would control the Albemarle Sound and its tributary waters.[38]

"Porte Crayon"

The Blackwater connection was already well known to travelers long before *Harper's Magazine* made it universally famous in 1857. In the previous April, writer-artist David H. Strother, gathering material for a series of articles to be entitled "North Carolina Illustrated,"

Captain Thomas I. Burbage and steamboat crew. Burbage (with X over his head) was for many years a well-known master of vessels of the Albemarle Steam Navigation Company. (Mrs. R. G. Whitley)

took the cars at Portsmouth and made the trip over to Franklin Depot where he embarked downriver on the Blackwater steamer. His account, published under his nom de plume "Porte Crayon," lent to the water passage an air of romance and adventure that most of those familiar with the route had perhaps never paused to contemplate.

On a pleasant morning, we find our adventurous traveler . . . standing on the promenade deck of the steamer *Stag*, which is just backing out from the Blackwater station, on the Sea-board and Roanoke Railroad.

On approaching this station, about twenty miles distant from the town of Suffolk, one looks in vain for the promised steamboat that is to convey him to Edenton. His search for the navigable river whose waters are to float the boat is equally fruitless; and not without many misgivings does he see the train go off, leaving him standing agape beside his baggage, in the midst of an apparently interminable cypress swamp.

Anon, a blowing and fizzing draws his attention to the swamp on the left. He starts, supposing it to be the noise of an enormous alligator, but is relieved on perceiving a white column of steam rising from the midst of the forest, and a black smoke-pipe peering above the dense undergrowth. At the same moment, a negro approaches and shoulders his baggage.

"Gwine aboard, Massa?"

The traveler cheerfully follows him down a narrow path, and presently is surprised to find himself aboard of a very promising steamboat. Then, for the first time, looking over her stern, he sees the Blackwater River, a narrow, black ditch, embanked with tangled bushes and cypress-knees, and over-arched completely with trees clothed in vines and hanging moss. The stream being barely wide enough to float the boat, she is obliged to *crab* her way along for a considerable distance, her alternate sides butting the cypress knees, and her wheel-houses raked by the overhanging boughs.

At length the river begins to grow wider, and, taking advantage of a sudden bend, the boat turns round and pursues her course headforemost. One of the passengers openly expressed his satisfaction at this change, for he said it always made him sick to ride backward. . . .

The tortuous stream lay motionless, like a dead serpent, under the dismal shadow of the never-ending forest. When the prow of the advancing boat disturbed its glassy surface, the waves heaved up as if they might have been uncouth, lazy reptiles, hastening to get out of her way, and flinging themselves over the skeleton-like cypress roots, disappeared, tumbling and wallowing among the reeds.[39]

What Porte Crayon accomplished for the Blackwater was not

Deck of the *Stag. Harper's Magazine* artist "Porte Crayon" sketched this deck scene when he took the *Stag* from Franklin down the Blackwater River in 1856. (*Harper's New Monthly Magazine* 14 [April 1857]: 434)

unlike what Harriet Beecher Stowe, in her novel *Dred: A Tale of the Dismal Swamp* (1856), or, earlier, poet Thomas Moore had done for the Great Dismal. A report from a railroad passenger in July 1857 described how, when his fellow travelers reached Blackwater Station, they made "quite a rush from the cars" for a glimpse of the celebrated river. [40]

It was a curious contrast—the dark, narrow, primeval stream and the great, gleaming steam vessel, its enormous wheels churning the water into foaming whirlpools. As Porte Crayon made his way down toward the sounds and across North Carolina, his facile pen enlarged upon the anomaly of archaic charm and rustic simplicity surviving into an age of steam and iron. Edenton Bay, for example, was "all the prettier for not being . . . interrupted by those forests of shipping which usually mar the appearance of seaport towns." [41] North Carolinians were quick to take offense at the slightly patronizing tone, the frequent hints of economic and cultural deprivation sprinkled throughout the *Harper's* series.

But Porte Crayon was being kinder than they knew. He might have stressed the point that these strange and wonderful steam machines were all of alien origin: the *John Barnett* and its rails from Liverpool, the *Fox* and the *Schultz* from New York, the *Seabird* from New Jersey, the *Curlew* from Delaware, the *Stag* itself from Baltimore.[42] So far, intersectional bickering gave little hint of a day when the *Stag* would lie scuttled athwart the Blackwater channel and Porte Crayon would be a colonel in the Union army. But it was, in part, the failure to take due account of the steam machines and the technology they symbolized that was to turn Southampton soon again, as in 1781, into a fearful battleground.

9

The Restless Calm

The Rockbridge Conspiracy

The story as partially unraveled by scholar James A. Shackford has all the intrigue of a modern spy-thriller. Four or five men, whose purpose it is to destroy Andrew Jackson and the Democratic stranglehold on the White House, gather in secret at Natural Bridge, Virginia, sometime around 1830. Together they choose Davy Crockett of Tennessee as a man with the characteristics they seek in a future Whig presidential candidate. But Crockett is still only a regional figure, not well known to the rest of the public. He must have a national audience and for that he must be provided with an image, a mystique, sufficiently colorful and captivating to challenge the "log-cabin" charisma exuded by the flamboyant Jackson.

The scheme devised by the Natural Bridge junto is that of writing a series of plays and popular books, both fiction and fact, as vehicles for publicizing Crockett's exploits, real and imaginary. Crockett's consent for the effort is obtained, but the ulterior motive of the literary productions must be kept in strictest secrecy. So Mathew St. Clair Clarke, anti-Jacksonian clerk of the House of Representatives, writes a biography of Crockett that becomes one of the most popular books of the decade. Entitled *Sketches and Eccentricities of Col. David Crockett of West Tennessee,* the book portrays Crockett as a rough-hewn and unlettered but unflinchingly honest and able frontiersman, a modern Daniel Boone with just a touch of George Washington in his iron integrity. It is a magnificent portrait, and following the book's publication in 1833, Colonel Crockett becomes almost overnight a new legend of the West, a great man of the people who turns to look sternly eastward at the graft and corruption in Jackson's Washington.

The interest of Edgar Allan Poe and other curious bookmen reveals that the copyright for the anonymous biography has been issued in the name of an obscure country lawyer, a certain James S. French of Jerusalem, Virginia. No one suspects the real author,

Rochelle-Prince house. This early nineteenth-century Courtland house was home of Southampton clerk of court James Rochelle. His son James Henry, Confederate naval hero, and daughter Martha, who married the son of President John Tyler, were born here. (Photograph by Colbert Howell)

and as more books and plays by the Whig junto come off the presses, Crockett's star rises and Jackson forces take alarm at the danger he represents to their hegemony in national affairs. It begins to appear that the Rockbridge County Conspiracy is about to achieve its design and that Andrew Jackson's reign as "King Andrew I" is soon to come to an end.[1]

It is a fascinating story as traced by Shackford and in all likelihood largely true if not entirely so. What is known for certain is that Clarke, the author of the Crockett biography, and French, the copyrighter, as well as the other Jackson enemies who helped to build the Crockett legend, all had ties of one kind or another with Natural Bridge and could well have gathered there at the time Shackford surmises they did. French, for instance, was a relative of the Strange family who lived at Natural Bridge, and his education had been pursued under the direction of Judge Robert Strange, an uncle in Fayetteville, North Carolina.[2] As a young attorney in 1833, French's identification with the Crockett biography would not raise questions about ulterior political motives, and such an identification might well help to promote his own literary aspirations.

So James Strange French's name was handed down in history as that of the author of Crockett's biography and is still listed as such by the Library of Congress and other leading repositories, despite strong evidence that French did not write a line of it. An important argument in the denial of French's authorship of this work is that obtained through examination of a book he did write, a novel entitled *Elkswatawa; or, the Prophet of the West,* which appeared in 1836. The difference in style and merit between the two indicates that the author of the bumbling novel could not have been the writer of the polished and popular biography.[3]

But French's novel, like the biography, had as one of its purposes the popularization of Davy Crockett, for a leading character in it, named Earthquake, is clearly modeled after the Tennessee frontiersman.[4] It also contains an admiring portrait of Gen. William Henry Harrison, already being touted by the Whigs as their anti-Jackson candidate, Crockett having lost his seat in Congress in 1835. Whether the Rockbridge junto was involved in this enterprise too is not known, but French was clearly still at work to further the interests of the new party.

Elkswatawa, however, had other apparent purposes for French than that of assisting Whig leaders. The title character, actually Tecumseh's brother, Tenkswatawa, was the Shawnee leader of a great Indian uprising against the whites in 1811. As Elkswatawa in the novel, he is portrayed as holding "daily converse with the Great Spirit," as one who "never mingled with the common herd," who taught the Indians that they were "invulnerable to the bullets of the whites," one who "was reserved and mysterious in his manner, and when not preaching, would wander about and commune with his own thoughts."[5] The portrayal of the Indian "prophet," in other words, appeared also to reflect what French knew of Nat Turner as well.

The story dealt with the adventures of a young man who, like the author, was a lawyer from Petersburg. Like the author, too, the hero, Richard Rolfe, was a graduate of William and Mary whose education had been supervised by an uncle.[6] The writer modestly described Rolfe as "[g]enerous to a fault, ardent in temperament, and glowing with youth, . . . a being of high order." The love interest is that of Rolfe for a young lady of fifteen named Gay Foreman, a maiden with auburn hair, "rich and glossy, . . . curling and clustering beautifully down her shoulders, forming a rich drapery for the loveliest face my eyes ever beheld."[7]

Driven by financial setbacks to abandon his profession and seek his fortune in the West, Rolfe hints to Gay that he wishes her to go with him as his wife. This the girl's family rejects, probably because of Rolfe's want of an estate as well as the fact that he had lately "courted dissipation, and neglected his studies" in consequence of his finances.[8] There follow adventures on the northwestern frontier involving Rolfe, his homespun companion Earthquake, and the Shawnee Prophet who is seeking to bring together the Plains Indians for a great war on the whites. Some time elapses before Rolfe discovers that Gay Foreman has become a captive of the Shawnees, her family having also fallen upon hard times and migrated west. The happy ending, following the defeat of the Indians at Tippecanoe, is the marriage of Gay to her rescuer, Richard Rolfe, and her husband's rapid rise to political prominence in Washington.[9]

If Richard Rolfe was the image of his creator, who was the pattern for the lovely heroine who became his wife? The solution to the romantic mystery is probably to be found in a letter written home to Southampton on May 10, 1838, by Cadet George Henry Thomas at West Point. To his brother John, Thomas wrote: "From what I can learn you are about to have grand times in Southampton this summer. Bob Parker told me the other day that his mother wrote him Mattie Rochelle was engaged to Judge Tyler's son, the Galant she brought home with her from the Williamsburg ball or some great doings; this seems to be rather a sudden affair, so much so that I fear it will be the death of the Squire. And then farewell to any more such novels as E---- unless I shall be able to supply his place."[10]

Martha "Mattie" Rochelle and John Tyler, Jr., son of the future Whig president, were married at Jerusalem on December 6, 1838,[11]

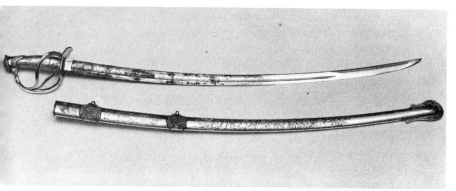

George H. Thomas sword. This sword was presented to Major Thomas (later general) by Southampton citizens in appreciation for his service in the Mexican War. (Reproduced through courtesy of Virginia Historical Society)

but Thomas's letter indicates that she had been courted, through the instrumentality of the novel and otherwise, by James Strange French. There was irony in the fact that Judge Tyler would reach the presidency in 1841 partially through the earlier efforts of French and the Whig junto in behalf not only of Davy Crockett but of "Tippecanoe and Tyler Too."

James S. French was eventually to enjoy some success of his own as president of the Alexandria, London and Hampshire Railroad.[12] But he may have departed Jerusalem under a cloud not less dark than that of his former colleague, Thomas R. Gray. In another letter to his Southampton kin in 1840, George Henry Thomas made reference to some "scrape" into which French had "got himself" and pronounced the novelist "a hard headed fool." The writer suggested that French had had "sufficient warning" and should long since have "ceased visiting a house where he had met with such strange and inconsistent treatment, and above all when he found that his visiting the house might create some of those slanders incident to the relation in which he stood to the family."[13] Had the marriage of his heroine not cooled French's ardor? The question was but another enigma in the mysterious career of James Strange French.

The Social Fabric

As the antebellum era drew to a close, Southampton seemed to be trying to appraise itself critically, to develop some measure of that detachment that enables us to see ourselves as others do. The self-examination was rooted partially in the publicity surrounding the slave revolt, but it was also created by the triweekly and even daily visitations of strangers along the routes of the railroads and steamboats. The wayfarers not infrequently brought with them curious customs shaped and nurtured by environments strikingly different from those of the Blackwater-Meherrin country. Opportunities to visit far-off places such as Richmond and Norfolk reinforced the impression that Southampton's folkways were in some respects peculiar. As the era waned, the county was not only the home of a novelist but the locale of several novels, including Harriet Beecher Stowe's *Dred* (1856) and G. P. R. James's *The Old Dominion* (1858). These and other circumstances helped to bring on an introspective mood, a prelude, perhaps, to a shaking-off of the provincialism of the past.

A manifestation of the new mood was the question that arose in 1860 over the propriety of snuff dipping and tobacco chewing. An anonymous Southamptonian aired in a Suffolk newspaper his impression that "ladies lips do not look well after dipping snuff."[14] There were, to his knowledge, gentlemen who could not bring themselves to kiss a snuff-dipping lady, though "most ladies of refinement, who use snuff" had the delicacy to withdraw to the parlor or otherwise out of male company when they did so.

Unfortunately, as Southampton's Philip Lemont observed in a rejoinder, the men themselves often revealed but slight sensitivity when it came to the custom of tobacco chewing but persisted in standing "right before you, with their chins dripping, their bosoms besmeared, squirting in every direction, and seem[ing] to think all is right. They will spit in the parlor, over the neatly painted hearth or polished stone. I have seen such persons sitting in the company of ladies, draw from their pockets the three cent twist and cram their mouths full and then begin to sputter and spit as though they had a bird caged in their mouths and feared its escape." It ill-behooved the inveterate chewer, thought Lemont, "his mouth besmeared with tobacco-juice, and his whiskers as thickly set as a double-sowed wheat-patch, all struck together as though they had been dipped in a glue pot, with the filthy juice still trickling down the well traced furrows of the chin," to withhold his cherished embraces from the snuff-dipping lady.[15]

Sobriety's zealots began to experience some little success in Southampton, spurred in part by the example of the Abstinence Society at Tucker Swamp Baptist Church, which enrolled sixty-five members in 1833 despite what one member cited as "the circumstances of the surrounding country.[16] Abstinence was, however, too great a burden to attempt seriously to impose on Southampton, and better results probably attended Rev. Putnam Moore's temperance group at Black Creek, a cause which, thought one who heard Moore discourse on the subject, seemed "to be gaining ground in this community."[17] A small but significant concession to such efforts was the political innovation adopted by Robert Ridley of Rock Spring plantation in the 1840s. Candidates for office were expected to partake generously of the local brandies and buy a round at taverns in the vicinity of political meetings. Ridley, who served three terms in the state legislature, "employed a man to ride with him and drink in his stead,"[18] rather than risk being bested on the forum by an opponent with a greater capacity.

Perhaps more persuasive than either abstinence or temperance groups was the fate of some such luckless inebriate as Bray Saunders, tried at Jerusalem in 1858 for murdering his wife. Evidence showed that Saunders was drunk on whiskey at the time of the murder, but the court found no reason to mitigate the penalty and he was sentenced to hang. When the appointed day came, a throng of prospective onlookers filled the jail yard and clambered atop the enclosure surrounding the gallows, "where they sat for hours, with the rain descending in torrents, and themselves drenched to the skin." The knot slipped on the first try, but Saunders was led back up the steps and, on the second try, satisfactorily dispatched. "Such," wrote farmer-teacher Elliott Story, "are the dire effects of whiskey drinking and improper training while young."[19]

If personal habits and beliefs came more and more under scrutiny, social diversions remained what they had been in colonial times. Elliott Story and other farmers, still by far the leading occupation in Southampton, passed their leisure hours fox hunting, fishing, reading, and conversing. Christmas, not invariably an especially festive season, could sometimes be the high point of the year, as in 1848 when Story enjoyed a round of parties where games, molasses pulling, and general merriment among "the jovial sort" went on intermittently for a week or more. A political or military gathering at Jerusalem could be a time of fine entertainment, such as the militia muster in May 1847 when Story spent his time

sauntering the streets and talking about the news of the times with an acquaintance . . . til parade time. . . .

After muster was over there was a sort of concert-Negro-dance perform-ance in the court house, twenty-five cents admittance. I went in and [was] very much amused, with the negro-like songs and odd manoevers.

After the performance was over I left town, and left it echoing with the songs and speeches and hubbub of those who had practiced too much at the bar.[20]

Any time was a good one to talk with old neighbor Moore, who had been "a poor boy, living in Philadelphia, at the time the smoke and thunder of the revolutionary contest . . . was boiling up" and who could "tell about the doings of those days with the accuracy of a historian." An evening in late summer, like the one in 1839, could provide opportunity for an all-night outing to James Wells's stur-geon hedge on the Nottoway. Story and his friend James Williams caught none of the big fish on this particular evening but, near morning, they "went out on the river bank where there were several Negroes and a white man who also had been fishing for sturgeon, and quit and built them a fire; we contrived to . . . get a clear space . . . where we threw down some brush and a blanket, and in a few moments we were entirely senseless to the surrounding scene."[21]

A rare trip to Portsmouth or Norfolk to buy ready-made clothes and other supplies, or the annual Christmas trip to Petersburg to sell lard, chickens, and other farm produce, might prove to be a fine adventure. The wagon ride to Petersburg market in 1842 was made by Story in company with Sam Williford in cold, rainy weather that dampened bodies aplenty but spirits not at all. "We travelled on and fun flowed copiously," Story wrote in his diary, until about 8 o'clock in the evening when we called a halt, hove to, struck a light, unhitched our steed and fed him, built us a fire and cut wood enough to keep it up all night. By this time the drops of rain had turned to flakes of snow, which the roaring winds drifted upon us most cheerlessly. Notwithstanding these dismal prospects . . . we spread a piece of covering . . . partially to screen us from the storm, and under this we dispelled the . . . scene about us . . . with merry jokes and cheerful tales and oft our . . . voices were heard to break forth, above the howling of the storm . . ., in merry peals of laughter. [22]

A favorite recreation for Story was the debating society he and other young men of the neighborhood formed in the spring of 1847. The group, including Joseph Pretlow, Orris Moore, Ichabod C. Edwards, Joseph E. and James A. Gillette, William Murfee, and George W. Griffin, met twice monthly at Story's school and usually with a good audience. The topics of debate included such questions as whether "pride or deceit is the more pernicious," whether "a Savage enjoys more happiness than a civilized man," whether, "if a person is condemned unjustly . . . he commit[s] a crime by escaping from prison," whether it is "in Solitude or in Society" that one may live the more virtuous life, and so on. Good attendance and often spirited discussion confirmed Story in the view that participants tended to become "very familiar and free and easy" with one another and that his was, indeed, "a fine neighborhood for good company." [23]

Nothing, however, in the rural environment quite rivaled a wedding party for sheer enjoyment. The wedding of a Miss Joyner in August 1846 found Story free from both school and farm responsibility for the time being and able to give his full attention to the affair. Arriving at Joyner's about sunset on the wedding day, he was soon engaged with others in pairing off attendants for the ceremony:

It was arranged that Mr. Boykin Pastor was to wait with Miss Maria Morrison , Mr. George T. Nelms with Miss Elizabeth Boykin, Mr. W. W. Joyner with Miss M. H. Pretlow, Mr. J. Pretlow with Miss E. S. Joyner, Mr. Elijah Joyner with Miss Emily Dick, and Miss Jane Joyner with myself.

About 8 o'clock it was announced that the ladies were ready and we soon entered the chamber where they were assembled. We . . . selected our partners and . . . formed in procession for the parlour, two candle waiters in advance and two behind the other waiters, and the bride and bridegroom behind the whole. Each one occupied his and her post . . . and the parson (The Rev. Saml. Holmes) pronounced the ceremony in a low, but impressive voice, and soon the union was confirmed which only death should part. The usual salutations were given, and . . . supper was announced, when the company went to eating and the waiters to waiting. I suppose there were at least a hundred persons, and it was eleven o'clock before supper was finished.

After supper, some plays were proposed in which a part of the company joined, and went through with one or two, but the ladies were very backward in playing and at length it was given up and the remainder of the evening passed in the usual talk for such occasions and about 1 o'clock the company began to leave.[24]

Not every such union was attended with as much gaiety as this one. When Bennet Griffin took Susan Joyner to wed in 1840, the groom and his thirteen-year-old bride-to-be dashed past Story "with all speed to N. Carolina" and "with Allen Edwards her guardian" in hot but futile pursuit.[25] Such liaisons often made up in savory gossip what they denied the community in festivity.

The Nurturing Toil

The life of Southampton revolved slowly around the rigors and routines of farming, and the business of agriculture was a demanding one that gave little rest to those who depended on it for a livelihood. New Year's Day 1848 began on Saturday and was, for Elliott Story, a workday like any other. His journal for that day contained the kind of intersectional contrast that one heard more and more frequently nowadays: "With our folks in the northern states, I suppose this is a day of high living merry-making and holy-day; with us it is considered a time of laying aside all such, and for commencing the year's work, and he who does a good day's work to-day will keep it up and make a good year's work of it.[26]

Those who gained less inspiration from the promptings of folk wisdom had only to observe their hogs grinding away voraciously throughout New Year's Day at last season's corn crop and hour-by-hour depleting the precious bushels representing the thin margin of subsistence for the family itself. If hog-killing had not already begun, it was high time it should. The Storys, benefiting from last year's experience when much of their pork was spoiled by a spell of warm weather, were taking added precautions this year, salting it heavily, packing it in close bulk, and leaving it so until after the weather turned really cold. They had made an early start at slaughtering this year and should come through winter with plenty of corn and pork, including some for sale.[27]

But pork raising was never anything more than a mad throw of the dice. In a year of low pork prices, such as 1848, feed cost more than the hogs brought on the market and it was unwise to raise more than necessary for the family's bacon. The Storys, solely because it was the customary thing to do, raised some for market anyhow, the idea being, as Story told his journal, that "although we should make more money from some other source, mother would be extremely uneasy, and almost ready to say that it was so much clear loss. . . . We never sell any corn. It matters not how much we make, it is all fed away to the hogs that can be spared for them and often in the course of this time the corn they have eaten would much more than pay for them."[28]

A good year in Southampton was likely to be a good year also in counties to the west, so that, as in 1846, Story would complain that "western hogs are swarming into this section of the country. . . . The price commenced this season at six dollars, but it is now down to five and I understand some have sold for four [dollars] and fifty cents" per hundred pounds. Those with bacon to sell saw the price drop from eight and a half cents down to seven, and still the drovers came with their grunting caravans.[29]

Smart farmers waited until their corn had a good start in June and then planted some peas among the stalks. The result was perhaps to reduce the corn crop a bit, but peas were excellent feed and saved much more corn in that way than was lost through the mode of planting. The only question was just how soon ought the peas to be planted after the corn in order to maximize production. On this, as on nearly every other practical question, each farmer had his own views, and more than a hundred years of experience in Southampton had not led to much in the way of consensus. Anyway, hogs could always be turned loose to forage for acorns in the woods, and sometimes they thrived on them.[30]

The same differences of opinion held in the matter of ploughing. Most of Elliott Story's neighbors were breaking their land as soon as they could get started after Christmas. But Story felt that a wet period between the end of ploughing and the start of planting could leave the ground almost as stiff and hard as before. Such land, he had found, "continues cloddy and in bad order the whole year. . . . The generality of our land I think would produce as well if it was broken up only the week before it was planted."[31] On the other hand, to start planting late was to run the risk of a rainy spell just when the planting needed to begin, thus causing delays that it might not be possible to make up in the spring.

Whether there was anything to sell, whether there was even enough to eat, depended upon a thousand things besides the weather. The chickens and crows sometimes got into the newly planted corn, the caterpillars—"as numerous," wrote Story in 1858, "as I suppose the locusts in Egypt are"—into the orchard, the chinch bugs into the wheat. There was a constant fight against wire grass in the corn and peas and always the danger of illness to the farmer at some critical moment of sowing or harvesting. Those like Elliott Story who owned no slaves and depended on hired help might find, as in 1857, that adult hands were not available at less than a hundred dollars a year and were, therefore, out of reach.[32]

The land itself often seemed to betray the care lavished upon it, as though, used up and farmed out, it was simply too old to go on producing. "How hard it is to dig a scanty support out of our barren soil in this poor region of country," wrote Story in a moment of despair. "When I converse with persons who have seen the rich lands of the southern and western states or read descriptions of them, and then look and compare the products of our industrious farmers with what others from the same labour gather in those countries, the contrast is disheartening, and it is surprising that the emigration is not greater than it is."[33]

But there were other times when Elliott Story counted his blessings and took not only pride but genuine pleasure from the toil of his farm. The business of agriculture, he declared in his journal in 1846, depended on

a great many circumstances for its success, and in this part of the world it requires hard digging and close economy to keep out of debt and live comfortably on farming alone. But of all the employments I like it best and the longer I live the more I like it. . . . It is the occupation for which man seems to have been chiefly designed by his creator, . . . the employment in which it seems to me the mind is left most unprejudiced to enjoy quietude and tranquillity and therefore is best qualified to judge of things as they really are, unbiased by the many things that are thrown in the way of a bustling life of business. It is the business in which the domestick ties grow most strong and are cherished with the most tenderness, . . . in which our health and constitutions are most likely to be preserved sound and vigorous, . . . in which we are most likely to preserve peace and friendship with our neighbors, . . . in which although we are not likely to grow rich, yet we are apt to enjoy more pleasure than wealth can buy.[34]

Southampton's free Negroes were mostly farmers too, but the majority of these were tenants or else they existed as bleakly on a patch of clay that exacted brutal labor for slight results. Despite the exodus following the insurrection, the county continued to have a high proportion of free blacks; and a few, such as Colgate Whitehead, triumphed over a maze of civil afflictions to become successful at their trades and owners of productive farms. Whitehead, indeed, "ranked in a class with many white farmers of Southampton" and well ahead of any other free black in this part of Virginia.[35]

The Making of a Soldier

By the 1840s those planters who could afford to do so were sending at least one son on for further training at one or another institution of higher learning, frequently a military one. James Henry Rochelle graduated from the Naval Academy in time to see service in the Mexican War, and several Southamptonians were graduated from the Virginia Military Institute, including William Mahone (Class of 1847), William Hill Urquhart (1850), James T. Murfee (1853), and James Rochelle Tyler (1861).[36]

A military education could provide a sound background for careers in other fields, though some, such as Mahone, would make superb soldiers as well. Cadet Murfee embarked on a teaching career after finishing at VMI and in 1854 became professor of natural sciences at Madison College in Pennsylvania. When the Civil War began he was serving as professor of mathematics at the University of Alabama, and after service as a Confederate artillery officer he became, in 1871, president of Howard College in Marion,

Alabama. After sixteen years at the college, in 1887 he founded
Marion Military Institute, which he headed until his retirement in
1906.[37]

The most outstanding product of an antebellum military education was George Henry Thomas of Newsom's Depot, where he was
born in 1816. Following his early training at James Parker's school
near Jerusalem and at Southampton Academy,[38] Thomas began
the study of law with his uncle, James Rochelle of Jerusalem. He
was briefly deputy clerk of the county court following Rochelle's
death in late 1835, but he resigned in 1836 to accept appointment
to West Point.

As a cadet, Thomas showed early the qualities of judgment and
bearing that were to carry him to the rank of major general later
on. It was his rule at the academy "never to speak to an officer but
on business," and the effect, as shown in later contacts with the same
men, was to heighten their respect for him. At graduation in 1840,
Thomas stood twelfth in a class of forty-two, and although he
accumulated 109 demerits, they compared favorably to the 380
awarded to his irrepressible roommate, William T. Sherman.[39]

Assigned to the third Artillery Regiment, Thomas joined it at
Fort Columbus, New York, in September 1840 and was soon en
route with it to Florida for service in the war against the Seminole
Indians. Several month's service at Fort Lauderdale was a pleasant
experience, and Thomas wrote home to his brother that he "would
not be at all surprised if this became a very populous country." The
soil was well adapted to cotton, and an inland waterway might, with
little expense, be cut all the way to Saint Augustine. It was not until
November 1841 that he saw any action, but his performance won the
praise of his commander and he was breveted first lieutenant.[40]

During the Mexican War, Thomas earned fame for gallantry on
battlefields at Monterey, Buena Vista, and elsewhere. Word of his
exploits soon reached Jerusalem where, in July 1847, James Maget
chaired a citizens' meeting which adopted William C. Parker's
proposal that Thomas be presented with a testimonial sword. The
instument was ordered from Horstman and Sons of Philadelphia
and had a steel blade inside a solid silver scabbard engraved with
the names of Thomas's chief battles and a vignette of the Battle of
Monterey.[41]

The effect of the action on Thomas was both interesting and prophetic: he hated the whole idea. In a letter from Brazos Island, Texas, in which he complained of being "so much a stranger in Virginia," Thomas called the proposed public presentation "a great source of annoyance to me and will take away a great deal of pleasure I anticipated . . . in visiting the county again . . . at first I was determined not to go to the county for one or two years, but upon reflection I have concluded to go as soon as I . . . get a leave and have the thing off my Mind. . . . I hope they will not enact the absurd ceremony of presenting me with the sword. . . . If I could get off with a dinner only I should have great cause to congratulate myself."[42]

Perhaps inevitably, the long absences from Virginia were taking their toll on Thomas's associations not only with the state but with his family as well. Judy and Lucy, his maiden sisters in Southampton, seemed to him "to lead a lonely life" with "no associations which are more than barely tolerable," and he thought they might be happier in Norfolk. He was married now to a New York girl, Frances Kellogg, and every passing year seemed to take him emotionally farther away from his boyhood ties. Poor crop years on the Thomas farm contributed to domestic unpleasantness there, leading the soldier-brother to hope that "time will gradually deaden all feeling of irritation, and our home will once again become as happy as it had previously been.[43] But the strains on the Thomas family paralleled those of the nation, and it would be a great while indeed before the United States could be "as happy as it had previously been."[43]

Thunder's Roll

A religious revival in Southampton in the fall of 1858 betokened the currents of emotional electricity that were discharging themselves among the masses of the people. Elliott Story's diary spoke of the revival as evoking "more feeling" than ordinarily among both blacks and whites and "considerable excitement" attended the October protracted meeting at Nottoway Chapel. "I have lived," Story wrote, "to see one more happy time at old Nottoway."[44]

The excitement was fanned by the arrival in early 1859 of Rev. Benjamin Franklin Woodward, a forceful pulpit orator who ignited a New Hope Church congregation in September into yielding up forty-five professions of faith at a single meeting. This was on Christianity's North Carolina side of the line, where the challenge was perhaps less severe, but Woodward followed up his New Hope triumph by turning out the largest meeting ever held at Applewhite's. More great days followed at Whitehead's, where so many ladies appeared that "not a single gentleman was able to sit beneath the roof of the sanctuary, but a dense mass occupied all the available standing room in every direction." There were even ladies listening to Woodward from inside carriages parked at the front door.[45]

Southampton's Methodists universally regretted Woodward's reassignment to Brunswick at the year's end, and many "were moved to tears" by his farewell sermon in December. But religious enthusiasm was already beginning to be diverted into another channel: the same newspaper article that reported Woodward's departure observed that citizens of Southampton "have determined to check the wanderings of northern pedagogues, chiropodists, pedlars, etc. who have so long infected our county. A rigid lookout is maintained for all suspicious characters."[46] Not Jesus Christ but John Brown had become the urgent concern of the people.

General William B. Shands addressed the citizens of Southampton at Jerusalem in late November about forming a military company and, though professing to be "no alarmist," suggested that it was requisite "for Southern men to be armed and prepared for any emergency." A Southamptonian warned a Petersburg newspaper in December that slave property was "in *imminent danger*" from the "cloud which is now rising in the North. . . . *We already hear the mutterings of the distant thunder, and it is now time for us to close the shutter, and prepare for the approaching storm.*"[47]

Seth W. Cobb, addressing the Petersburg *Daily Express* over his usual nom de plume "Black Eagle," reported that "daily crowds have thronged around the Post Office" at Jerusalem since the Harper's Ferry incident, "eager to procure the latest intelligence." Captain Joseph E. Gillette had summoned his cavalry company to Jerusalem for drill, and many had come "prepared for an immediate journey" to Harper's Ferry. Formation of chapters of the

Knights of the Golden Circle in the summer of 1860 at Boykin's and Franklin insured the continuance of high political emotion. Elliott Story visited Franklin in early August and found the KGC plan for creating new slave states in Cuba and Central America to be "the chief topic" of conversation, though one, in his words, which would "I fear divide the Union."[48]

A Bell and Everett (Unionist) Republican in the presidential canvass, Story was alarmed to find that Southamptonians were almost unanimously Breckinridge Democrats and in favor of a rigid posture of state's rights militancy. In late October, just before the national election, he heard about "a company of men" who had "gone to the house of a man of the name of Headly, from N. York, who has been residing for some time in our county, and ordering him to leave the community, I suppose upon suspicion of his being hostile to the institution." But a sizable part of the community resented such extremism and the deed was "very much condemned by many of our citizens." There remained ample evidence "that the days of peace and union in our nation are drawing to a close."[49]

John C. Breckinridge carried the county in November, but Abraham Lincoln won the election and, within a few days, Story was hearing "a great deal of talk about the secession movement in the southern states." A month later South Carolina seceded, and inexorably, those who wanted initially to preserve the Union at all costs were drawn into the rising tide of sentiment for Virginia to follow South Carolina's lead. "It seems to me," wrote Story in the spring of 1861, "that Virginia has done all that she could do consistent with honor and justice to settle it peaceably in the Union and there [is] nothing left for her but to withdraw from the Union and cast her fortunes with the South. This she had done and I am with her."[50]

Later generations would debate the question whether the national conflict had its origin in Southampton County in the summer of 1831. Some would contend that Nat Turner's Revolt so hardened proslavery and abolitionist sentiment South and North that there remained no real hope of compromise and no means of resolution short of war and the dissolution of the Union. But most Southamptonians probably shared Elliott Story's hope this spring that military preparations and a show of armed resistance might demonstrate to the North the determination of the South, so that "peace and brotherly love may speedily be restored."[51]

Major George Henry Thomas wrestled with his conscience that spring, vainly hoping that he would not have to choose between his country and his native state. The struggle ended, however, with a decision to retain his position in the United States Army. His decision was to have important consequences on the course of the war, for he would prove to be one of the ablest commanding officers on either side. But perhaps he recalled again the sage advice given to him in 1836 as he was about to leave Southampton for the Military Academy: "Having done what you conscientiously believe to be right," John Thomas had said, "you may regret, but should never be annoyed, by a want of approbation on the part of others."[52]

10

The Civil War

The company banner was the handiwork of the Misses Thomas and it had the new Stars and Bars on one side and the state flag on the other.[1] It was inscribed with the words "Justice and Truth, Liberty or Death,"[2] and somehow on this June morning the defense of chattel slavery and the disruption of the American Union seemed as grand and noble as the fight for independence eighty years before. "Though each volunteer was impressed with the solemnity of the occasion," intoned a Jerusalem Confederate, "there glowed from his eye a beam of content, and from the heart there seemed to leap an honest conviction that he was engaged in an honest, noble, holy and patriotic cause. Though they have odds to contend with, they are satisfied that God is with them and that with Him they are invincible."[3]

No one had ever yet come up with a thoroughly tactful and appropriate way of asking people to go off somewhere and die. The accepted procedure was to play a great deal of stirring music and fire off some ceremonial cannon and do other things that caused dogs to bark and street urchins to run about excitedly and girls to wave their handkerchiefs. So Richard Clements and his Rough and Ready Guards had been presented by General Shands with a handsome address and a lovely flag on behalf of the ladies of the county. The boys all sang "Dixie" and hurrahed and then were marched twice up and down the street, stopping at each house to serenade the occupants. At Barham's Hotel they got bouquets and flowers, and all of them "seemed to go off in fine spirits."[4]

A long time afterward it might seem that music and flowers and fine words by elderly patriots was not nearly enough, but the boys of 1861 went off to war thrilled by the honor that was conferred upon them. Awkward farmhands grinning self-consciously in gray uniforms were cheered on from hamlet to hamlet as they marched, and James Fenton Bryant wrote home from the Southampton Cavalry's training camp at Smithfield that he could not imagine a place that contained more generous, kindhearted & hospitable people. . . . They (the ladies) offer to do our soeing, washing, mending &c for nothing, and are anxious and proud to do it. The citizens send down to our quarters every day such vegetables as they have, such as Irish Potatoes, beets, cabbage, onions &c.

The greatest thing of all about the place is the abundance of the intelligent & pretty young ladies. . . . It is a fact, I never saw so many . . ., for the size of the place, any where else in my life. They compliment us highly, and every evening they pass our Barracks and throw us bouquets &c. I went to church last Sunday & fell dead in love with one of them.[5]

The summer passed in a hard labor of drills and marches and work details, but the war itself was far away somewhere, and the news that came from the front told of glorious Rebel victories over numerically superior odds. Joe Johnston and P. G. T. Beauregard ran Gen. Irvin McDowell out of northern Virginia in July, and the vaunted Lincoln blockade of the Southern coast turned out to be nothing much more than paper shuffling at Washington. Southern editors were optimistic that the Yankees would soon see that the effort to force the South to return to the Union was not worth the price and the war would end.

The occupation of Hatteras Island by a Union force at the end of August was chiefly a blow at Confederate pride, but the capture of Roanoke Island at the beginning of 1862 appeared to be a matter of some strategic concern. Theoretically at least, Union gunboats might now venture into the Chowan River and its tributaries or land troops along its banks for assaults against Norfolk or the vital rail junction at Weldon. There was even talk of a possible strike up the Blackwater at Franklin railroad bridge, but Gen. Benjamin Huger sent some troops down to the mouth of the river to barricade it and put up a masked battery to cover the obstruction. Franklin seemed secure, especially after February 21 when a Federal flotilla attacked and burned Winton on the Chowan but turned back upon learning of the Blackwater defenses.[6]

The Southampton boys now began to get their first experience of war, and the business seemed not so terrible by half as it was sometimes represented. Captain Joseph E. Gillette's cavalry was one of the companies that ignominiously fled from Winton in February, but the unit redeemed itself somewhat at South Mills, at the southern entrance to the Dismal Swamp Canal, in mid-April, when

Union forces tried and failed to destroy the canal locks there.[7] "Now the battle commenced in earnest," wrote Private Bryant to his cousin Mollie Bryant at Jerusalem, "and as soon as it did Col. Wright ordered Capt. Gillette to detach 20 men to act as scouts on the line to prevent the enemy from flanking our forces. I was in, the detachment, and we had to pass through the range of musket balls. The Yankees shot too high, fortunately for us, for the balls passed over our heads on horses. They certainly know but little about the use of the firearms. If they had shot right they would have killed several of us." "A large nine inch shell passed near my horse," wrote Lt. Irvin Wills of the same company, "so near that I thought he was wounded, as he sprang into the air with all his might, but was not touched." Never mind: "I have reinlisted," wrote Wills, "for the war, also most of the company."[8]

It might take a number of such thrashings as the one at South Mills before the North was convinced of its errors in judgment, but the Private Bryants and Lieutenant Willses of the Confederate army were still confident the thing could be done. A little more sacrifice, a bit more exertion of Rebel strength, and everybody could go back home, and life would go on just as it had before.

Thoroughfare

The Burnside expedition entrenched itself on the North Carolina coast in early 1862, but the Union menace in that region was not great and interior areas did not fear that enemy armies might suddenly break through in that quarter and ravage the upcountry. George B. McClellan's offensive on the Yorktown Peninsula in the spring appeared to endanger Richmond, but General Lee took the matter in hand and, in a few weeks, sent McClellan packing back to Washington. But even as the one menace dissipated, another arose.

The Rebel evacuation of Norfolk in May threw the Tidewater into pandemonium. Federal troops, pushing on through Suffolk, established a wide perimeter of tentative control stretching southward to the Chowan and west almost to the Blackwater. Panicky Confederates destroyed not only the railroad bridge at Franklin but the one across Nottoway as well. The *Stag* and two small schooners were scuttled below the ruined Blackwater bridge, and Franklin seems for a time to have been virtually abandoned on the mistaken premise that the Yankees would soon be in Southampton itself.[9]

As demoralizing to the Southamptonians as the fall of Norfolk was the failure of the Confederate river defenses. Rebel authorities in the summer of 1861 had purchased almost every steam vessel in the Tidewater-Albemarle region and, from a dozen or so passenger vessels, tugboats, and canal steamers, slapped together a makeshift "navy" for defense of the Albemarle Sound area and the canal to Norfolk. The *Curlew* and *Seabird* were converted to warships by the marvelously simple device of mounting a couple of guns on each, but nobody was particularly surprised when the former was sunk and the latter chased off (and soon captured) at the Battle of Roanoke Island in the opening days of 1862. By a cosmic irony, the Federal flagship on that occasion, possibly the same ship that sent a cannonball hurtling through the hull of the *Curlew* and sank it, was the U.S.S. *Delaware,* formerly the *Virginia Dare.* It was this ship that had been ordered for the Albemarle Steam Packet Company in 1860 but, falling into Union hands at the start of the war while still on the stocks in Delaware, was converted into a fine gunboat. The *Delaware* was also flagship of the flotilla that burned Winton a month later.[10]

Inspired by the example of the ironclad *Merrimack* in Hampton Roads, Confederate authorities began casting about in the spring of 1862 for a suitable place to build a ram for the defense of the Blackwater and its important railroad bridge. Norfolk resident J. Marsden Smith in March proposed to a Confederate congressman that such a craft might be built at Franklin or some other place on the Blackwater, provided that the river could be guaranteed against Union gunboats. Another suggested that a battery might be built at or near Franklin as there was plenty of timber and a sawmill at hand. North Carolinians expressed interest in raising a subscription for building the vessel and were known to be receptive to the idea of a joint-stock company for the purpose.[11]

Even though the stream's tributary to Albemarle Sound lay open to Union naval encroachment after the fall of Roanoke Island, neither side sent large forces into the region and the Confederates

Major Joseph E. Gillette. Gillette recruited and led Southampton cavalry unit in some of the major engagements of the Civil War. (Daniel T. Balfour)

were able to continue to use the Chowan-Blackwater route to collect supplies from the rich agricultural region of northeastern North Carolina. Flatboats and small sailing vessels gathered provisions on the Chowan and took them up to Fort Dillard at the mouth of the Blackwater where they were conveyed to the Steamer *Stag* for shipment to the cars at Franklin. A Union gunboat commander who visited the site in May reported to his superiors that the route had become "one of the great thoroughfares to the army of General [Robert E.] Lee, as regards provisions."[12]

The extent of the commerce here indicated that the Army of Northern Virginia would suffer by its interruption, and on May 24 the gunboat *Hunchback* was sent up to the mouth of Blackwater for that purpose. Finding the battery deserted, the gunboat crew made a thorough and unhurried work of ripping out the 400 fathoms of chain they found strung across the head of the Chowan and clearing a path through the three schooners sunk in the Blackwater, two

miles upstream. Some logs and timbers were pulled from the channels of both the Chowan and Blackwater, whereupon the *Hunchback*
preceeded unmolested to Franklin itself. Since the Rebels had already destroyed the bridge and ships there, the gunboat returned
downstream without effecting anything warlike.[13] Mysteriously, the
whole region seemed to have been written off by the Confederacy
and Lee's most vital supply line lay completely unprotected.

It might appear later that there was method in the Confederate
madness here, but the Federal forces made no effort during the
summer to exploit the open route to Franklin. The place was visited
again on August 5 by the U.S.S. *Henry Brinker,* whose captain was
reduced to making war on the sunken hulk of the *Stag* by burning
a part still above water, but there remained nothing here to lure
aggressors and the ship left after a few hours. The situation, indeed,
might have remained so for much of the war had not reports started
coming into Suffolk in late September that up to 12,000 Rebel
troops were now concentrated at and near Franklin and that a floating bridge (swung from the west bank so it could be taken up when
not in use) had been thrown across the river there to bring artillery
and railroad cars to the east bank.[14] Clearly, so many troops were
intended for something more than the defense of the Seaboard and
Roanoke Railroad, and Union commanders, fearing an assault on
Suffolk, hurriedly arranged an effort to disperse the Confederates
and destroy the floating bridge. The attack was to be performed
by 1,900 troops from Suffolk acting in conjunction with gunboats
which would come up the Blackwater.

The Union force left Suffolk on the evening of October 1 in order
to be in position to strike at Franklin by dawn. Meanwhile, three
gunboats had come as far as South Quay, where they spent the night
of October 1 and then got under way next morning at 5:45 for
Franklin, four miles away.

The Action at Crumpler's Bluff

The Union flotilla was composed of the *Commodore Perry, Hunchback,*
and *Whitehead,* all of them formerly ferryboats whose shallow draft
made them ideal for river operations. Inching toward Franklin in

the early dawn of October 2, all three soon came under fire from Rebel sharpshooters on both banks of the river, but the pilothouses had been protected with piles of sandbags and the crews of the deck guns responded steadily with grape and canister to keep the riflemen at a respectful distance.[15]

It was about 7 A.M. when the *Perry,* flagship and leading vessel, started around a tight bend under Crumpler's Bluff, a west bank promontory three-quarters of a mile below Franklin. Here the Confederates had posted a sizable force of infantry in ambush, and the Yankee sailors were dismayed to see a curtain of musketry descend suddenly between the *Perry* and her objective, now almost in sight upstream. There was still no sign or word of the Federal infantry that was supposed to be attacking Franklin by this time, and the prospects for a successful expedition seemed to have vanished.

What gave this engagement its special interest was the personnel on the Union side. The flotilla commander was Charles W. Flusser, known to his fellow officers as "Lion-Hearted" Flusser in compliment for his courageous conduct in several earlier actions. Aware that he was incurably ill with heart disease, Flusser was recklessly bold and would willingly run any risk required by a mission.[16] His executive officer on the *Perry,* unquestionably one of the most daring and resourceful men ever to wear the uniform of the United States Navy, was a nineteen-year-old lieutenant named William B. Cushing. It was Cushing who, when Flusser was killed trying to sink the ram *Albemarle* two years later, planned and executed the spine-tingling expedition that blew the famous ironclad out of the water. Suicidally audacious under fire, Cushing was to be a legend among military men on both sides long before the war was over.[17]

As Flusser headed the *Perry* around the bend at Crumpler's Bluff, he ordered his crew below deck and began the tortuously slow process of sliding the big steamer around in the twisting channel. A great hailstorm of lead pellets poured down on the *Perry,* and the bow of the vessel, swinging too close in toward the left bank, ran hard up on the mud and stuck fast to the river's margin. Confederrates on the bluff, realizing the stricken condition of the boat, let out a Rebel yell and dashed forward down the slope to board the *Perry* and perform with bayonets what could not be done with bullets. As the Rebel mass surged forward, Cushing called from a gang-way for volunteers and rushed onto the exposed and riddled rear deck where stood a field howitzer resting in a gun carriage.

Aided by six other men, Cushing tore the weapon loose and swung it around in the direction of the charging Rebels, but as he began to aim, he found that he was alone in the work, all the others having been cut down in the withering fire. With unruffled deliberation, the young officer aimed and fired directly into the gray-suited attackers, now within thirty yards of his boat. The canister charge exploded with devastating effect, killing or injuring some, dis-orienting others, and shattering the Rebel charge. To Cushing's astonishment, however, the Rebel leader, "a splendid looking fellow with long curly hair," came racing on ahead, waving his sword and preparing to board the craft alone. Cushing, who had lost his pistol in the scramble to aim the howitzer, stood transfixed as the attacker, now within ten feet of the *Perry*, suddenly pitched forward face down into the mud. A wounded sailor, leaning against the ship's railing, had sent a musket ball into the charging man and saved Cushing for more exploits in campaigns yet to come.[18]

The danger remained acute for all that. It took several more minutes of frantic effort to back the *Perry* into the channel once more, but Flusser, undaunted by the near-fatal mishap, drew off far enough to bombard the bluff clear of riflemen and then move up past the point in order to cover the boats behind him. The *Hunch-back* and *Whitehead* also cleared the bluff, but now, a quarter-mile farther, they all were brought up short by a barrier of trees which had been cut down across the channel. Since the boats now lay between thick swamps, Flusser concluded that he might wait there in relative safety to see if the land force from Suffolk would arrive and make the mission a success in spite of everything. By 10:15 A.M., with no evidence that the troops were near, Flusser decided to make his retreat. Again the gauntlet was successfully run, and the gunboats, pushing at full steam through tree barricades thrown down in the river behind them, got clear of the Blackwater in early afternoon and headed for the wharves at New Bern.[19] The Suffolk troops, apparently stalled by a handful of Rebel pickets, reached the Blackwater during the afternoon, but withdrew that evening without achieving anything. Franklin and the floating bridge were saved, but the boldness of the Yankee sailors left the defenders with an uneasy feeling that these ungainly ferryboats were invulnerable to the weapons that were supposed to stop them. A disconcerting discovery on the Union side had been the observation that Negro riflemen had played a conspicuous part in the ambuscade of the gunboats.[20]

The Longstreet Raid

From the autumn of 1862 until the beginning of the following spring, the fifty-mile Blackwater defense line was under the command of Gen. Roger A. Pryor of Petersburg. Unwilling to tolerate further threats from gunboats, Pryor proceeded to block the river effectively with fallen timbers and to erect long lines of rifle pits and earthworks down the west bank to discourage enemy crossings.[21] The Federals, content merely to hold their Norfolk-Suffolk perimeter, organized no large offensives and devoted the next six months to tentative probing at the Blackwater line and talking halfheartedly of cutting the railroads that supplied Lee's army.

West of Blackwater, Pryor was soon confident that he could hold the line, though he was too far outnumbered to the east to carry on offensive operations. With his river barricade and rapid rail communications to Petersburg and Weldon, he could summon quick assistance at any crisis. There was intermittent skirmishing from Ivor all the way down to South Quay and beyond, and occasionally small parties crossing and recrossing the river, but the line would remain intact throughout the fall and winter.[22]

Early December brought a flurry of Federal assaults along the Blackwater intended to create a diversion to draw Rebel units away from Weldon and Goldsboro, North Carolina, where more important attacks were in preparation. These, in turn, were supposed to help Burnside in his campaign against Fredericksburg,[23] but Lee, though outnumbered by two to one, abused his latest opponent even more roughly than previous ones and the effort of the Army of the Potomac again went for nothing. The Suffolk command had hopes of seizing Franklin, but news of reinforcements for Pryor and of a bombproof railroad-iron gun battery at Franklin dampened their enthusiasm, and the flurry amounted to nothing more serious than a harassing cannonade of a Rebel camp at South Quay and a brief dash across the river at Ivor.[24]

Despite the security of the river defense line, Southampton was slowly bleeding to death that winter. Slaves ran off in whole families to freedom within Union lines and farms decayed for want of either black or white laborers. Captain Louis H. Webb, a longtime resident of Franklin after the war, led an artillery battalion from Petersburg to Ivor in November 1862 and commented that Southampton, "once the center of civilization, refinement & wealth," was now "poor and desolate and hardly (pecuniarily considered) worth a battle for." Webb's gun crews, "half-fed, nearly naked & shoeless" at the start of the worst winter in sixty years, were still more pathetic, especially on the morning of December 7 when Webb awoke in his tent at Black Creek Church with "hair & beard . . . heavy with ice, from my congealed breath, and when washing my face, the water froze on my hair."[25]

Notwithstanding the gloom, there was still fight in the Rebel soldier. With a few days' adequate rations and comfortable lodgings at last near South Quay, Webb on December 12 chronicled in his diary a fine little action along the riverbank: "Heard firing up the river in direction of Lawrence's Ford. Found our 3rd sec. engaged with the enemy who appeared on the opposite side of the river. The boys behaved well, fired seven rounds with remarkable accuracy & the enemy soon turned & fled leaving one horse, saddle and bridle, caps, knapsacks, & other equipment. Nobody was hurt on our side, though shot and shell flew closely and thickly around us."[26]

For the soldier in the line, these little encounters were always measured in terms of victory and defeat, and it would be a long time before they could be seen as tertiary diversions and demonstrations in behalf of armies hundreds of miles away whose existence was but half-perceived from the pine barrens and pocosins of southeastern Virginia. Winning the war still seemed to depend in some measure on turning back the next cavalry charge at Lawrence's Ford or digging a deeper rifle pit at Zuni. And maybe it was not so much in the outcome of great battles as in the day-to-day attrition of scratches and bruises that the fate of the American nation was being decided.

For about two months, beginning in February 1863, the Federal high command at Norfolk heard from escaped slaves, deserters, and others a stream of reports that a heavy buildup of Rebels was taking place on the western bank of the Blackwater. Pryor, it was learned, was being braced by cavalry and artillery, and the still of any night betrayed the ominous rumble of Confederate railroad engines coming and going on the Weldon and Petersburg roads. By the time the reinforcements reached 20,000 and the Blackwater command had been taken over directly by General James Longstreet, Suffolk's defenders were making feverish preparations to hold on against an expected attack. From his headquarters at Petersburg, Longstreet made weekly and even twice-weekly visits to Franklin and other points nearby, and the Tidewater was alive with rumors of his intentions.[27] The band of tension and suspense stretched needle-thin in the first days of April and then snapped abruptly on April 11 when Longstreet put down his pontoon bridges and sent 35,000 men pouring across the Blackwater toward Suffolk. Union reserves rushed forward to try to save the town, and for three weeks the Tidewater experienced the bloodiest fighting it was to see in the four years of the war.

Longstreet would gladly have taken Suffolk if he could have, but that was not his primary objective. Under orders from Lee, he had come into the region east of Blackwater and Chowan on an immense foraging expedition to gather provisions for the Confederate army. Organizing great caravans of vehicles known as "ox-sulkies,"[28] the only sort of conveyance left in the ravaged region, the Rebels confiscated tons of bacon, grain, cotton, and other supplies, leaving the population of Gates, Chowan, Nansemond, and other counties almost starved until the lean harvest of the following fall.[29] The seige of Suffolk was pressed until the opening days of May when, the last wagons having crossed the Blackwater into Confederate territory, Longstreet sped north with the rations that would carry the Army of Northern Virginia to Gettysburg. In his fiery wake lay a vast countryside of denuded farms and devastated fields and a population no longer much concerned about who won the war as long as it ended soon.

During the Longstreet raid, the Baptist Church in Jerusalem had been turned into a hospital for injured Confederates and for victims of an epidemic of measles that swept Hood's Texas Brigade. The

disease cost the lives of some of the soldiers, as did the wounds of
war, and the dead were buried behind the church.[30] Another cemetery at Franklin contained some of the Rebel dead as well as a few
Union men who died as prisoners, including, it is said, a Negro
hanged there as a Federal spy.[31] With the departure of Longstreet,
the defense of the Blackwater line was left to scattered Rebel units
and to such Home Guard detachments as could still be mustered
in the area. Again the region lay open to Union assault.

The Smoking Earth

By 1863 the war bore down on Southampton with crushing weight.
"Sugar and coffee became almost unknown," wrote Dr. W. B. Barham of Drewryville,

and flour was indulged in only once a week. Sunday morning was hailed
as "Biscuit Morning" and even then we were not given a very lavish
allowance. For coffee we struck upon the device of a drink made from
toasted corn, rye and sweet potatoes, and this, sweetened with sorghum
molasses, made a fairly palatable drink. All the farm products except those
that were actually necessary for the sustenance of life were sent to . . . the
front. The women . . . formed societies, where lint was picked from old
worn-out fabrics to dress the wounds of the boys at the front. Old trunks,
chests and closets were ransacked, their out-of-date gowns were brought
forth, cut and remodelled to suit the times, hats and bonnets were made
of platted wheat and rye straw. The looms were called into requisition
and home-spun garments became the order of the day.[32]

Farms nearer the Blackwater, such as George Camp's place outside Franklin, suffered still more severely. Long after the war, Virginia Camp Norfleet remembered that these days on her father's
farm were "full of sorrow and anxiety . . . and through the night
the heavy roaring of cannon like thunder, and the whole earth full
of smoke, and everything in an unsettled condition." It was impossible to raise a crop in this vicinity, and the depredations of the
enemy were hardly worse than those of the Rebels themselves.
"Longstreet's Brigade was camped on my father's farm," wrote
Mrs. Norfleet,

and the lame, sick, halt and maimed, and all those who did not want to go
to the front were there and they were not very desirable neighbors, no

hungry people are. Pig after pig disappeared until there were none left and the same with the chickens, turkeys, calves and lambs and the last of all the bee hives. Peas and sweet potatoes were our main support. . . . After this army was removed, we were left without any protection and we lived in awful terror of the Federals. They went all through the country and took their pick of what was left, so my father kept his horses back in the forest and other valuables concealed in the most unheard of places.[33]

The Negroes—those who remained—knew still greater privations than the whites. A Yankee schoolteacher at Norfolk in November 1864 interviewed Mary Pope, an escaped Southampton slave, and passed along to the newspapers Mary's account of her experiences. She recounted how her husband had been sold away to Richmond early in the war by her master, Amos Pope, and that the large slave gang on the farm had dwindled to ten as the war progressed. And then, "some six weeks ago," Mary related,

one ob dem ran away. Missus told me we had better all go to the mean Yankees; if she did not get rid of us, they would come and kill them all. Missus was very kind to us till after the war [began] when Massa went away. Den 'pears like she could not work us hard enough. . . . She used to make us spin all day, and far into the night. She was a mighty weaver herself, and 'pears like she wanted to done get all de cloth she could. Every little while Missus tell me I better go to de Yankees; dey'd work me harder than she eber did, and I'd starve at that. I'se allus used to minding Missus, so ob course I did dis yer time.

Early on a November morning Mary Pope "put up a few tings in a bundel," awakened her four children, and with six other Negroes, requisitioned some meat, chickens, and cornmeal from the storehouse and set out for Nottoway River. The group was put across the river that night by a Negro man and next day walked thirty miles, crossing the Blackwater, and finally entering Union lines near Suffolk. One of her children died on the way, but two others were soon in school in Norfolk. "She says when her feet get well," wrote the interviewer, "if she can find any thing to do, she can take care of herself. Her oldest ones can spin and knit."[34]

Somehow, even in the depths of war, there were moments of relief. An episode that brought smiles for a long time afterward was the launching of Jack Poythress's submarine in the Blackwater in April 1863. The inventor was a three-and-a-half-foot midget who could drink a glass of whiskey without the use of his hands—while

standing on his head. Jack's seventy pounds were all but camou-
flaged behind a ten-inch growth of black whiskers, and nobody took
his submarine project seriously until he actually brought the thing
down to the river a little below the railroad bridge and announced
that it was about to make its first cruise. Onlookers found that
Jack had fashioned for the defeat of the Union navy an "infernal
machine" from a smokestack stoppered at both ends with pine
blocks and outfitted with a canvas hose for underwater breathing.
The *Mushrat,* as Poythress christened his vessel, was to be driven
by means of a hand crank that turned a stern propeller. Unhappily
for naval science, the *Mushrat* capsized upon launching and almost
drowned its inventor. The craft lay for some time thereafter half
submerged and was finally carried off by a freshet to its final resting place at George's Bend, five miles downstream. Jack's own end
was sadder still: he was convicted for second-degree murder in 1875
and spent his final years in prison.[35]

Soldiers in the war zone sensed the despair at home and sometimes wrote determinedly cheerful letters about the success and good
treatment they were enjoying. "We are getting the greatest quantity
of Bread and Bacon," wrote James F. Bryant in the spring of 1864.
"Everything is going on gloriously for us," he insisted, "and I think
this campaign will virtually close the war."[36] The soldiers' families
tightened their belts and resolved to brave out yet another winter
season which, for better or worse, must be the last.

Two Soldiers

By the close of the second year of the war, both of the great armies
had been able to identify those men in their ranks whose achieve-
ments demonstrated superior qualities of leadership and ability. An
arresting result of this process of selection was that two Southampton men, William Mahone and George Henry Thomas, had become
leading general officers, the former in the Confederate, and the
latter in the Union army. The two never met in battle, but both
were to emerge from the war with outstanding records—that of
Thomas, indeed, ranking him with the foremost military figures of
the century.

William Mahone. A native of Monroe, Mahone was distinguished in the Civil War as "Hero of the Crater," the climactic action near Petersburg. He was later a railroad engineer, businessman, and U.S. senator. (Reproduced through courtesy of the Virginia Historical Society)

George H. Thomas. Newsom's native became a major general in the U.S. Army during the Civil War. A brilliant tactician, he was renowned as the "Rock of Chickamauga." (Reprinted, by permission, from Richard O'Connor, *Thomas: Rock of Chickamauga*, ©1948 by Prentice-Hall, Inc.)

The two Southamptonians differed as much in personality and temperament as they did over the issues that brought on the war. Mahone, a brilliant engineer and business leader before the war, was a tough, wiry, profane little man whose passions were poker and tobacco.[37] Thomas, his tall physique bronzed by his career as a soldier, was a reserved and sensitive lover of domestic life and children who was never to have either. The Rebel, for all his military talents, was the born politician and manipulator; the Unionist, in spite of his record of valor, might have found life as a naturalist closer to his heart's desire.[38] They had been reared within a few miles and years of one another, but "Billy" Mahone had learned of life in his father's tavern while George Thomas was coming of age on a nearby farm.[39] Both knew much of fortune and acclaim, but Mahone seemed always to be wrenching loose by main strength the jewels that the gods cast repeatedly at Thomas's feet.

The fame of "Pap" Thomas, as he was known to his men, was won in the western theater of the war. It was he who gave the Union one of its earliest victories—at Mill Springs, Kentucky, in January 1862—opening the way into East Tennessee if the government had had initiative enough to seize the opportunity.[40] Thomas saw major action in the West during the next eighteen months, but it was at the end of the summer of 1863 that he began to distinguish himself as one of the towering leaders of the war. The action that earned him his immortality, the first in a series of major successes, occurred in northern Georgia in September 1863.

The Army of the Cumberland, after driving the Confederates out of Tennessee in the summer of 1863, pressed on southward across Lookout Mountain on the Georgia-Tennessee border to deal a knockout blow to Braxton Bragg. In separating his forces for the trek across the mountain, Gen. William S. Rosecrans marched straight into a death trap set for him on the Georgia side by Braxton Bragg, one that might spell catastrophe for the Union war effort. On September 18, with the main Union army in position before him near Chicamauga Creek, Bragg, joined by James Longstreet, delivered a heavy assault against the left side of the Union line under Thomas's command. Thomas coolly held his position against a furious assault, but Longstreet now dealt his coup de grace, a bludgeon blow by the other half of his army at the right side of the Federal line. The latter strike succeeded in driving a huge wedge into the Federal lines, sending Rosecrans in flight back toward the mountain. Thomas held firm, but now Longstreet wheeled quickly about to come in behind Thomas and serve the left side as he had just served the right. "Federal control of everything west of the Alleghenies suddenly teetered and rocked," in Bruce Catton's words, "ready to come down in a Humpty-Dumpty crash that could never be repaired."[41]

What Thomas accomplished in the next few hours was the tenacious defense of his position against the entire Confederate army.

Wave after wave of Rebel troops were beaten back, and when ammunition ran low, Thomas sent men out into the front of the lines between assaults to gather bullets. He held on somehow until Rosecrans, collecting his wits, sent in some reserve forces to bolster Thomas and permit an orderly withdrawal instead of a rout. Thomas, in the interim, had become "the Rock of Chicamauga," the great defensive general of the era. But it was not merely in defense that he was a master tactician, for the attacks he led later at Chattanooga and Nashville were equally skillful. In the whole course of the war, as Catton observes, there were only two instances when a major Confederate army was forced to abandon "a prepared position in complete rout—at Chattanooga and at Nashville. Each time the blow that routed it was launched by Thomas."[42]

William Mahone, appointed a lieutenant colonel at the outset of the war, was brigadier general before the end of November. Fort Sumter had barely surrendered before he was bluffing the Yankees into evacuating Gosport Navy Yard by running a railroad engine all night up and down a stretch of his Norfolk and Petersburg so as to give the impression of major reinforcements arriving.[43] He saw action in almost every major engagement in the East during the war—at Seven Pines and Malvern Hill and Second Manassas in 1862, as a major general at Chancellorsville and Gettysburg in 1863, at the Wilderness in 1864. But it was a brief moment during the long seige of Petersburg that was to earn him his renown and the sobriquet he would proudly bear down through the years. The day was July 30, 1864.

Sultry dawn had just broken over the Petersburg defense line when drowsy Confederate sentinels suddenly saw a great bank of earth and debris dislodge itself from the Rebel barricades and explode in an awesome eruption of clay clods and iron cannon and quivering flesh. In the next seconds, an enormous expanse of trenches and embrasures and parapets, the perfected result of months of brutal labor, crumpled into a huge refuse pit 25 feet deep and 150 feet long. A wide door into the sealed vault of Petersburg had suddenly flown open, and the next few minutes could see a Union assault that would make it impossible for Lee to last through August. A war that seemed a moment ago likely to go on for years now appeared to be within weeks of its end.

It would take days before the Rebels could ascertain that Pennsylvania troops had tunneled under the Confederate defenses and mined them with tons of powder, but there was no time now for speculations over the cause of the great, smoking gap in the line. If Lee's thin reserves could not close it instantly, then the war was lost. While hundreds of Union troops poured into the Crater, Wright's Georgians and Mahone's Virginians rushed forward to try to reestablish the line. Aided by a fatal miscarriage of Federal orders, the Rebel troops caught their enemies milling aimlessly about in the gaping void and stormed into the Crater with terrible effect. Before the main body of the Union assault could reach the scene, the defenders had killed or captured enough of the vanguard to reassert Confederate control. Petersburg was saved and Mahone would come down to posterity as the "Hero of the Crater."[44] It would require over eight more months to defeat the Southern armies.

Nottoway Lifeline

From early May 1863 until the war's end, Southampton County and the region of North Carolina adjacent to it were so haphazardly defended by the Confederacy that Federal units roamed almost at will throughout the area. Fortunately for the civilian population, the Union itself maintained only small units there, and weeks on end could pass without the appearance of forces from either side in the Chowan-Blackwater country. Both armies concentrated their strength at more critical points and sought some opening that might hasten a successful conclusion to the war.

The new situation along the Blackwater and Chowan was no sooner apparent than the old supply line for Lee's army, perhaps never entirely interrupted, stole stealthily back into flourishing existence. A Unionist mayor of Edenton testified after the war that the Albemarle section of North Carolina furnished along this route up to ten million pounds of bacon and pork a year along with 40,000 bushels of corn. Confederate commissary agents, he stated, were stationed throughout the area with large supplies of cotton and tobacco to trade for food, clothing, shoes, boots, corn, meat, sugar, coffee, and so on. The result was a form of blockade-running that saw up to a hundred small boats a night pass Edenton headed for the railroads in Southampton County.[45] The point of the testimony was that the war could have ended much earlier if a determined effort had been made to interdict this supply line.

By 1864 the clandestine commerce had developed an important additional feature. Union merchants in the Norfolk area circulated throughout the Chowan-Blackwater country offering to trade many sorts of contraband goods for cotton and tobacco. The Norfolk military command, aware that much of the material so exchanged went forward to the Army of Northern Virginia, averted its eyes and made only a pretense of regulation. When criticism mounted, the Twentieth New York Cavalry was sent on a cosmetic raid across the Blackwater at South Quay and to Murfee's Depot near the Nottoway. Here the Federals destroyed a post office and telegraph office, several warehouses, and stores of cotton, bacon, salt, apple brandy, yarn, cloth, small arms, and so on.[46] But the traffic went on unabated and criticism grew.

Eager Rebel traders raised from the bottom of the Blackwater the little canal steamer *Arrow*, captured from the Yankees and sunk at Franklin earlier in the war, and sent it down the Chowan with cargoes of produce in exchange for bacon, salt, "northern packed pork," and other supplies. What might have become a lucrative new adjunct to the contraband trade was halted, however, in July 1864 when the *Arrow*, on her second trip, was captured at Gatesville by a Federal gunboat.[47]

An investigation in early 1865 resulted in the replacement of the Norfolk military commander and a crackdown on contraband traffic. But a group of enterprising Baltimore merchants was among those who found means to continue the trade. In June 1864 they contrived to get from President Lincoln a permit to trade in Union-claimed northeastern North Carolina, exchanging such items as plows and twine for cotton and tobacco. The steam-tug *Philadelphia* was sent to Norfolk, where Gen. Benjamin F. Butler endorsed the permit, and the boat proceeded through Currituck Canal with its cargo. But the *Philadelphia* not only carried unauthorized goods; it also spent the following months making trips as far as Murfee's Depot and Franklin in search of cargoes. The tug would usually stop at Winton, pick up Confederate pickets to insure safe passage, and then steam off to Murfee's, where Jacob Lenow[48] or some other hospitable middleman would arrange exchanges of illegal goods.

Responsible Richmond authorities quietly encouraged the trade. A Confederate officer at Murfee's wrote home in exasperation to his wife in January 1865 that "we have now lying within two miles of us a steamer loading with cotton for northern markets. I was on board of her one day. Her commander has his papers all right from his government, and the parties loading him has theirs too." The officer complained that how "such a trade can be conducted is incomprehensible," and felt that "such a thing two years ago would at the bare mention of it have shocked our government, the President and the whole cabinet. . . . To save my life I cannot understand to what end we are rushing."[49]

Official suspicions resulted in detention of the *Philadelphia* briefly in the opening days of 1865 by Federal authorities, but her captain, George W. Lane, talked his way to freedom and was soon up to his tricks again. The vessel was later impounded and Lane jailed,[50] but still the illegal trade continued.

The irritated Norfolk command, convinced that the Albemarle-Tidewater route was all that kept Lee in the field after the fall of Wilmington and Charleston, dispatched the Third New York Cavalry to Murfee's in early March. Refugees had reported that the Confederacy was using nine mule teams to move huge amounts of cotton and other stores there and that nearly all of Lee's sugar and coffee was brought through Murfee's and Weldon on its way to Richmond and beyond. Others from Edenton insisted that "a regular line of vessels" was coming into that place at night from the Chowan, "each carrying one hundred bales of cotton." The Federals this time found fifty bales of cotton and some corn at the depot, which, along with warehouses and other buildings, was burned. The trade was now so nearly cut off that the Norfolk officer who ordered the raid was pleased to learn a few days later that Richmond "must soon be evacuated; provisions were becoming very scarce and bacon could not be purchased at any price."[51] On the night of April 2, his supply lines ruptured beyond recovery, Lee retreated from Richmond and Petersburg. He surrendered a week later at Appomattox Courthouse.

Epilogue

The scene at George Camp's farm was reenacted hundreds of times throughout the county in the weeks following Lee's surrender. As Virginia Camp Norfleet recalled it half a century later, nothing had been heard from her brother in the army for many months. "We were not expecting him for we did not know where he was, but some of the family saw a ragged, poor, pitiful, weak human being coming down the avenue, and as he came nearer we saw that it was our own dear brother that we had not seen for four long years; we all wept for the very joy."[52]

The sound of martial airs and hurrahs had died for Private Camp a long time ago, along with the fragrance of bouquets and the image of colorful parades and gay banners. But he might have heard the echo, borne on April's breeze, of the company of phantom horsemen that galloped along the Barrow road and cheered for the victory that was theirs. For the time had come when the first should be last and the last should be first.

11

The Convalescence

Blackwater Metropolis

At the end of three years as an outpost on the battle line, Franklin was a forlorn ghost-hamlet of sixteen people, its railroad and bridges gone, its wharves and warehouses in decay.[1] But the relaying of the tracks and reestablishment, in 1866, of the Albemarle Steam Navigation Company quickly brought to the place a hum of commerce louder than that of the prewar era. The ASN Company acquired title to the side-wheeler *Ella*, a sleek Rebel blockade-runner, and placed it on the Edenton route. Spurred on by demands from cotton-starved northern textile mills and a good market for lumber, hams, bacon, and agricultural products, the company added two Baltimore-built boats in 1868. The *Ella* was sent to Wilmington, Delaware, in 1874, rebuilt, and renamed *Chowan,* giving the ASN "altogether the largest, staunchest, and the best adapted [boat] to the needs of the route" of any "that ever plied the inland waters of eastern North Carolina and Virginia."[2] On a single day in April 1875, Franklin's wharves were visited by the *Chowan, Lota, Helen Smith* (of the Clyde Line), *Silver Wave,* and *Harbinger,* and the tug *Lane.* A Norfolk paper gushed that "no place on earth could have undergone more change in two years than Franklin. Our surprise was unbounded as we looked in vain for old and familiar residences and business stands, only to find them improved beyond recognition, or entirely removed, and their places supplied by others neat and pretty."[3]

An ornament of the place was Mrs. Barrett's hotel, which, at least in the memory of Judge Francis D. Winston of North Carolina, "ranked as high as the reputation of the hotels of Norfolk, Richmond and Baltimore." This was a big two-story frame structure with double verandas that stretched along Main Street on the northwest corner of its intersection with the railroad. There was no church until the Baptists completed theirs in 1872, but services were conducted by several denominations at the Masonic Hall.[4]

Municipal government in Franklin began with Governor Gilbert C. Walker's authorization in 1869 for the election of a mayor and council, and Dr. James Fenton Bryant became the town's first mayor in that year.[5] During 1873 two newspapers were established there, J. Abner Harrell's *Monitor* selling out in 1877 to Theodore N. Ramsey's *Tribune,* after which both appear to have been combined into the new *Seaboard and Roanoke Times.*[6] Perhaps the most notable event in these early postwar years was the tournament of 1870. Tournaments were very much in vogue at the time, and Franklin's was highlighted by mounted "knights" who sought to pluck off with the points of their lances, while riding at full gallop, two-inch suspended rings. Each knight chose a fanciful name and gay costume and competed for the right to crown the queen at the evening's ball in the hotel dining room.[7]

Fannie Lawrence Webb, daughter of Capt. Louis H. Webb (CSA) was a girl of eight when her family settled in Franklin in 1876 and she began collecting the impressions for the memoirs she would write some eighty years later. The town at that time was still not much more than a "crossroads hamlet of perhaps a dozen or so wooden buildings," including a few stores and residences and the railroad station. Nearly all the stores of this period were two-story frame buildings with grocery counters down one side and dry and fancy goods counters down the other and a big kerosene tank in a far corner. A drugstore, awe-inspiring in its array of plasters, patent medicines, quinine, chill tonics, Epsom salts, and other mysterious potions, dispensed from its soda fountain iceless lemon and vanilla soda at a nickel a serving. There was a single small school in the basement of the Norfleet home conducted by Burilla P. Carnes, but the social center of the community was the railroad depot. "The ladies waiting room," Miss Webb recalled,

was furnished with some degree of elegance, carpeted and fitted out with rocking chairs, center table, footstools and other accessories. In addition, a colored maid met every passenger train, to assist feminine travelers and care for children. . . . The windows on the east side looked out on a tasteful little flower garden on one side, laid out with walk and flower bed. . . . Two elderly women wearing dark calico dresses and sunbonnets made daily trips from a small farm on the outskirts of the town with split baskets on their arms. They paraded up and down the length of the train and, with

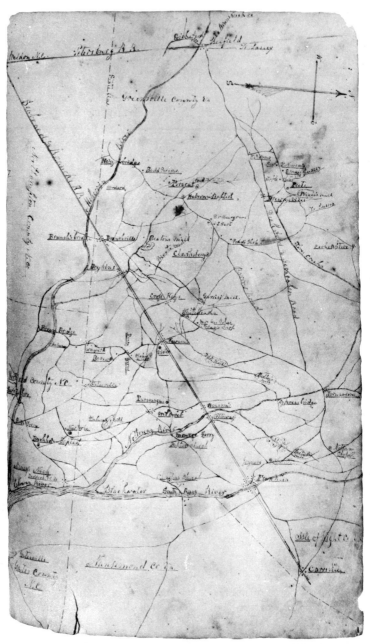

The Leigh map. Reverend Joshua Leigh drew this map of Southampton and adjacent areas as a convenience in serving his Meherrin circuit during the 1870s. (Southampton County, Historical Society; photograph by Colbert Howell)

baskets raised to shoulder height, presented a variety of homemade delicacies to tempt hungry passengers—fried chicken, ham, big soda biscuits, baked sweet potatoes, homemade cookies, a few apples or pears . . ., or wild black grapes . . ., also chinquapins.[8]

With regular steam connections to Norfolk, Edenton, Murfreesboro, and many intermediate points, Franklin by 1881 had become the center for a wide and flourishing business. The chartering of the Farmers and Merchants Steam Transportation Company in 1877 brought a reliable new firm into competition with the ASN Company, insuring better opportunities for commerce.[9] The federal government, impressed by the quantities of corn, cotton, wheat, tobacco, lumber, and fish carried along the Chowan-Blackwater route, in 1879 began clearing stumps and other obstructions between Edenton and Franklin.[10] The town earned incorporation in 1876 and promptly began putting on city airs by forbidding hogs to run in the streets and requiring licenses of anyone exhibiting a stallion or jackass "for the purpose of letting to mares." There was even an effort by the council to prohibit barrooms from keeping their back doors open on Sunday and selling or giving away liquor. That such injunctions ran clearly in opposition to long-standing custom may have motivated a petition to the legislature in 1877 calling for repeal of Franklin's charter.[11] In any case, it failed to carry.

On the night of Saturday, February 26, 1881, the mournful wail of the steamboat *Chowan*'s siren aroused the town to a fire near the railroad office on Main Street. The blaze was soon out of control, working its way down and across the street and finally consuming every business in town but one—containing an undertaker's stock of coffins. A telegram went out to Portsmouth appealing for emergency equipment, but it arrived only around 8 A.M. on Sunday, the fire by this time having spent itself in the destruction of forty-three buildings, including Barrett's Hotel and the post office.[12]

The stricken community, seizing upon the advantage offered by the disaster, enjoined businessmen from replacing burned-out structures with any other than brick and stone buildings. Despite a temporary setback, the result was a modernized and much improved business center.[13] Neither the disasters of war nor those of peace could detract from Franklin's favorable location as a rail and river market, and the town within two years was once again growing and bustling as before. Important industrial and agricultural innovations of the post-war years played a major role in the irrepressible prosperity of the Blackwater depot.

Pine and Vine

The economic gains enjoyed in Franklin and elsewhere in the county during the quarter century following the Civil War were made largely on the strength of the demand for two products which Southampton produced in vast abundance—lumber and peanuts. The lumber industry had flourished there since colonial times, but it was the introduction of the steam sawmill in the last decade or so before the Civil War that brought the business to maturity. One of the earliest such mills was that established at Delaware Station on the east bank of the Nottoway at the railroad crossing. Edward Hedley, a Pennsylvanian, built his mill there in 1853 and, though burned out by Federal troops in the closing days of the Civil War, was back in business soon afterward.[14] Among the numerous suppliers of logs to the mills were three brothers from Franklin— Paul D., John S., and William N. Camp—who were to dominate the lumber industry in this region within a few years.[15]

Another firm supplied by the Camps on the eve of the Civil War and afterward was that of R.J. and William Neely, also Pennsylvanians, whose Blackwater mill opposite Franklin was built in 1856. Both Hedley and the Neelys employed steam tugs to bring logs from lower down the Nottoway and Blackwater to the mills, from which huge amounts of wood products were sent out by rail to the Norfolk market and elsewhere. In 1876 Paul Camp bought out the old Hedley mill at Delaware Station and turned out lumber at a rate of 6,000 feet a day until moving his operations to the Maney's Neck section of Hertford County in the following year. Here, with his younger brother James, Paul organized P. D. Camp and Company. When the firm in 1886 purchased the Neely mill, the foundation of a great industry had been laid for Franklin and its environs.[16]

In 1887 Paul D. Camp and three of his brothers—James L., Robert J., and William N.—created the Camp Manufacturing

Company, which within four years was producing lumber at a rate more than twelve times that of the original mill at Delaware Station. The Camps also added a planing mill to turn out flooring, weatherboarding, and smooth lumber and soon began expanding beyond the Franklin area.[17] At the turn of the century the company was well on its way toward becoming the largest such organization in the southeastern United States and the greatest spur to Franklin's progress.

Completion of the Atlantic and Danville Railroad through Franklin and Courtland in 1888 reflected the rapid rise of the lumber business, but it also betokened the dramatic advance of the peanut to acceptance and popularity with the American public. Before the Civil War, the lowly "ground pea" had been cultivated only in small quantities and then mainly because it was enjoyed by Negroes and white children and was useful for fattening hogs.[18] Like bright-leaf tobacco for smokes, peanuts became popular as a nutritious food among soldiers of the Civil War, a fact which helped to create a northern market for the crop in postwar years.

A Nansemond farmer is said to have marketed peanuts at Jerusalem during court week as early as 1844, but it was at the end of the war that cultivation became extensive in the Upper Tidewater. By 1868 peanuts had become the leading money crop of Southampton and adjoining counties, bringing Virginia farmers a revenue of a million dollars a year.[19] Even so, the potential market remained much constricted owing to the slow methods of harvesting the nuts by hand and, in Virginia, the poor color given to them by the clay soil of the Tidewater area. An Assamoosick farmer, speaking on behalf of America's greatest peanut-growing county, felt confident in 1872 about instructing readers of the Petersburg *Rural Messenger* in the most approved method of harvesting. It required, he wrote, the use of the two-horse plow invented by Dr. Charles W. Nicholson of Southampton to cut the taproot and loosen the soil around the vines. The next step was to lift the vines from the soil, shaking them gently to remove clinging dirt, and then leaving them on the ground until dry. The vines should then be shocked on six-and-a-half-foot stakes, from fifty to eighty stakes to the acre. After three to four weeks, the nuts were ready for threshing with Crocker's threshing machine and sale "to the candy and peanut oil makers."[20]

The Crocker machine, invented in 1869 by a Norfolk preacher, at length proved unsatisfactory, and other enterprising artisans turned their talents to the problems of peanut production. The result was an ingenious array of machines, culminating in a successful mechanical harvester in the opening years of the twentieth century.

Among the inventors upon whose ingenuity the future of the peanut depended, few made greater contributions than Caleb R. "Chick" Everett, a farmer near Newsoms. During the 1880s Everett patented and marketed a "planter for field peas," besides his guano sower, lime drill, peanut cleaner, and other inventions. In cooperation with Fenton Ferguson, a gifted machinist at Murfreesboro, he designed and built a peanut planter "that would be little improved on in half a century."[21] Further notable contributions toward the development of the harvester were made by a Negro blacksmith in Vicksville named Benjamin F. Hicks, who is also said to have patented a peanut planter and manure spreader.[22]

Marketing techniques kept pace with mechanical innovations. John Pretlow, Jr., of Franklin was one of the first to envision the commercial future for Virginia peanuts and to develop the market for them. Pretlow and Company evolved from a country store into one of the principal suppliers of peanuts for the expanding Norfolk market during the late nineteenth century. With partial control of the Albemarle Steam Navigation Company, the Pretlow family was able to tap the production of the rich agricultural region below Franklin and bring the crop to Southampton and Isle of Wight mills for processing. Out of this combination of facilities arose the Pretlow Peanut Company, chartered in 1900, which was expanded in 1906 into the Virginia-Pretlow Company.[23] By this time the peanut had been adapted to a thousand commercial uses and was a common item of consumption from coast to coast.

Country Crossroads

Lengthening miles of rail lines, along with burgeoning commerce and industry, gathered an ever larger proportion of Southamptonians from farms into small towns and loose settlements which took shape around lumber mills and crossings. Scores of places

Ferguson clan. Composite photo shows inventor Fenton Ferguson (*upper left*), his brother-in-law Benjamin R. Griffin (*upper right*), his father Caswell Ferguson (*lower left*), and his uncle Elbert Ferguson (*lower right*). Fenton helped develop first successful peanut picker and other farm equipment. (Gary M. Williams)

known only to history through brief entries in the records of the Post Office Department came momentarily into existence only to fade within a few years—places with names like Airfield (a post office in 1876), Jockey Club (1883), Koskoo and Pinopolis (1885), Uggal (1891), Baffle (1895), and Pumpkin (1902).[24] Other places, especially those that grew up along the railroads, fared better. The Atlantic and Danville spawned new settlements and reinvigorated old ones in the central part of the county as the S. & R. had done earlier in the southern and the N. & P. in the northern part. The long-depressed county seat, renamed and incorporated as Courtland in 1888 on the initiative of the postmistress, Fannie Barrett, was granted by the A. & D. a new lease on life.[25] Farther west along the A. & D. was Capron, known at first (1889) as Cairo, and, farther still, Drewryville, a post office since 1838. Pope (1889) and Adam's Grove (1881) were still smaller sites along the railroad.[26]

Jerusalem's notable days came on court week and at tournament time. A visitor in 1878 had this to say of the November Court:

Every man, woman, and child in the county seems to consider it his duty as well as privilege to visit Jerusalem on court day, and on that important occasion, there is to be seen every character and description of mankind. Among the teams there exists the same variety. The finest blooded horses, as well as the plucky sumac bull, have their representatives. Oyster carts, horse-traders, and venders of various wares abound, and add to the general confusion. The farmers are cheerful and express themselves as being satisfied with their crops. This has been a most excellent year for peanuts, and the yield will be very large.[27]

The tournament of December 1869 began at 10 in the morning when "the joyous throngs began to gather, and conspicuous in the swaying multitude were many groups of bright-eyed, smiling lassies, . . . assembled to honor the festive hour with their presence and greet the contestants in the coming struggle with their sweetest smiles of approval." Then came the train of knights "bedecked with sash and plume and bearing the trusty lance" to compete "in skillful feats of horsemanship" and win the honor of crowning the "Queen of Love and Beauty." R. A. Drewry was outfitted as the Knight of the White Lance, J. E. Rowe as the Knight of the Golden Fleece, J. Williamson as the Knight of Indifference, Willie Wilson as the Knight of Do-Nothing, and so on. After hearing a charge at the judges' stand by Thomas Cross, the contestants vied for three hours before J. N. Sebrell, the distinguished Knight of Minnehaha, bore off the title and the right to crown the queen that evening at Howard's Hotel. A dinner and dance concluded the festive occasion.[28]

As viewed, at least, from the railroad, Boykins in the 1870s was a collection of only three stores and six residences. A visitor commented on the "neat appearance of its white stores and beautiful shade trees," but the place came in for some unfavorable publicity engendered by a Murfreesboro correspondent of the *Norfolk Journal*. Annoyed at a want of wheeled accommodation that forced him to walk fourteen miles through the night to Murfreesboro from the depot at Boykins, reporter Charles H. Foster had the temerity to refer to the latter as a "half-horse town."[29] Upbraided by several pro-Boykins critics, Foster responded that his experience there had actually led him to suppose that "Boykins was a no-horse locality." The village was "all right, what there is of it; but the trouble is there isn't a great deal of it." A humorless antagonist reminded readers of the paper that Foster was a carpetbagger who might prefer the frigid wilds of his native Maine to the pastoral pleasures of Boykins Depot.[30]

Held back in part by the *Anopheles* mosquito, which had established its leading metropolitan center on Tarrara Creek, Boykins struggled against an incidence of malaria approaching 50 percent and was finally incorporated in 1884.[31] Business increased at Boykins with the completion of the Roanoke and Tar River Railroad, a subsidiary of the Seaboard and Roanoke, in 1888. This thirty-two, mile link with Lewiston, North Carolina, also had a six-mile branch between Pendleton and Murfreesboro. The latter route was scheduled for discontinuation in 1897; the town of Murfreesboro attached the property to prevent it, but Seaboard management sent in a nocturnal track gang that removed all rails and equipment, so that the people of Murfreesboro awoke on the morning of May 8 to find that their railroad had disappeared.[32]

Post–Civil War Ivor, its railroad facility spanning the northern edge of the cotton belt, was seen by a visitor in 1879 as "a thriving village of several hundred inhabitants" with four stores, two churches, and "several work-shops and other evidences of enterprise." Corinth Church was founded by the Quakers in 1882 as an offshoot of Black Creek Meeting, and the Quaker community provided a lively industry and culture though still quaintly distinguished by their "plain modest bonnets and broadbrims" from their neighbors.[33]

Berlin, six miles south of Ivor, had been a crossroads community long before the Prussian immigrant Henry Lenow gave the place its name around 1830.[34] It was typical in most respects of a score of such places, including Zuni, Newsoms, Branchville, and Manry, which might boast a general store, a blacksmith shop, or some other rural facility that served a scattered community of a few hundred people, nearly all of them farmers and lumbermen. Each year now witnessed a further shift toward integrated community life and further steps away from the deeply rooted provincialism so characteristic of the antebellum years.

Freedom's Snare

County politics in the years immediately following the Civil War quickly resolved itself into a struggle for control between black voters and white. A great many politically active whites were temporarily disfranchised for participation in the Rebellion, but the overwhelming black majority was uncertain in its new circumstances, unsure about how to organize and pursue its interests. Easily subverted by those with long experience in the machinery of government and politics, blacks enjoyed a brief hour of influence in local and state administrations and were then forced into a new submission from which they had not fully emerged a century afterward.

The new political order of the postwar era pitted Conservatives (as the Democrats were styled for the time being) against Radicals (Republicans) and was structured in such precisely racial terms that a Southampton Conservative could claim in 1868 that "we have no radical whites among us." Leading spokesman for the blacks was a Baptist minister, Rev. Joseph Gregory, and the embittered atmosphere in which he labored was illustrated by an incident at Courtland in July 1868. Conservative John Goode and Radical Lucius H. Chandler, both of them Norfolk whites campaigning for Congress, were scheduled to appear at the county seat for political rallies. Goode had already begun to address the whites when Chandler arrived in a buggy, according to the Norfolk *Virginian*'s Conservative informant, "with a notorious mulatto scamp . . . named Gregory." As Chandler dismounted, "a prominent citizen . . . stepped up to [him] and cursed him and told him he wished to fight; like a whipped cur, he sneaked off to the negro stand and made his speech, which I am told no white man heard through." Chandler appeared a little later at the Howard Hotel bar to order a drink only to be confronted by

a mercurial gentleman [who] rushed to the door shouting "run here boys, I have a white negro to show—only five cents a head." The crowd thronged the bar, and the poor fellow—amid groans, hisses and curses—hastily swallowed his grog, and went on the porch; while standing there, a gentleman went up to him and said, "Come sir, this is no place for you, go over there where you belong among the negroes"—and he went.

He came back to get his horse, followed by a crowd of negroes, whether for his defense or not nobody knew or cared, and the whites opened on him again with redoubled powers: "Do you want a negro wife? see, he has just offered a darkey two dollars for his sister, &c." and he left hastily, followed by hoots and hisses. . . . We are at a white heat on politics.[35]

Chandler, a native of Maine, was to be the victim in 1876 of what the Norfolk authorities referred to as suicide.[36]

An explosion of racial violence in Southampton seemed inevitable and almost came in June 1869 when two Franklin men, one black and one white, engaged in a dispute that resulted in the latter, Charles Holland, shooting his antagonist in the thigh. When a crowd of Negroes failed to apprehend Holland, they took out their anger on Neely's sawmill in a $20,000 fire that brought out a detachment of Norfolk troops. A Norfolk paper reported on June 25 that "great excitement existed" at Franklin, "and as the whites also were armed a serious disturbance was imminent."[37] Miraculously, it failed to take place.

Reverend Mr. Gregory, a Franklin teacher as well as spiritual leader, had won election to the state Senate in 1867, but it was a clear sign of white resurgence in the spring of 1870 when he lost his race for justice of the peace in Franklin. He was defeated for reelection in 1869 by Dr. Richard U. Burges and in 1871 by George E. Beaton; he was afterward reported to have incurred the anger of many Southampton Negroes by urging his friends to vote conservative.[38] Other Negro leaders, including Orville Artis and Allan Murfee, were gradually subdued, and Joseph B. Pope, elected to the House of Delegates in 1879, was the last Southampton black to hold state office up to the present writing. In June 1875 a newspaper correspondent writing from Berlin felt confident to say that radicalism in Southampton "is dead and, I trust, buried forever."[39]

Political leadership after 1870 returned largely into the hands of those who had exercised it before the war. General William Briggs Shands of Courtland, a state senator in the 1850s, was a notable craftsman of the political reorganization of postwar Southampton, along with Capt. George E. Beaton of Branchville, for four years (1871–75) the county's representative in the House of Delegates, and Kenneth R. Griffin, state senator from 1877 to 1879. Influential at both the local and state levels of Conservative politics were Dr. James F. Bryant and John H. Bogart, the latter as mayor of Franklin, member of the House of Delegates, and in other capacities.[40]

An index of the doleful suppression of black hopes in Southampton and across the old Confederacy was the research conducted by William Sidney Drewry of Drewryville in the 1890s and the volume, *The Southampton Insurrection,* which he published in 1900. The author's doctoral dissertation at Johns Hopkins, the book reproduced from Southampton "folklore" the litany of stories about loyal slaves who protected their masters and mistresses against brandy-soaked rebels. But Drewry was also able to extrapolate from his material the conclusion that the slave had been "a more obedient and law abiding citizen than the modern free negro," that education rendered the Negro "a useless and discontented citizen," that the Southampton rebellion had been "instrumental" both "in bringing about" abolition and in tending to "delay rather than quicken emancipation."[41] The book's clumsy special pleading and jarring methodological deficiencies did not, however, prevent it from becoming the definitive work on its subject for most of the century that followed.

Heroes and Exiles

The only Southamptonian of the postwar era to make his mark on national politics was William Mahone. The "Hero of the Crater" set out at the end of the war to regain control of the Norfolk and Petersburg Railroad, did so, and then, by a series of mergers, created the Atlantic, Mississippi and Ohio Railroad (later renamed Norfolk and Western) to give Norfolk a 408-mile link to the rail systems of Tennessee and Kentucky. This line made Norfolk the Atlantic outlet for the exports of a vast region stretching out toward the Ohio and Mississippi rivers and lined the Norfolk waterfront with lumber, wheat, and tobacco from southern Virginia and cotton from the Deep South. It also put Mahone well on the way toward becoming one of Virginia's earliest millionaires. [42]

Mahone's efforts on behalf of his great railroad system led him into politics, where he headed the moderate wing of the Conservative party and though losing a bid to become governor in 1873, he threw his support to Gen. James L. Kemper, whose victory launched Mahone's career as a kingmaker in Virginia politics. In the long ensuing struggle between "Funders" and "Readjusters" over payment of the state debt, Mahone sided with the latter and emerged from the stuggle with greater support from the state's Republicans than among his old political allies. Readjuster success made him the outstanding political figure in Virginia, and in 1879 he was elected by the legislature to the United States Senate, where his talents were employed in behalf of Republican policies. Denounced as a traitor by the Democrats, he served effectively as a senator but was defeated in 1889 in another bid for the governor's office. He was socially ostracized in his native state for his cultivation of Negro support, which, with his autocratic manner and growing financial problems, left him an isolated and much maligned figure. Confident that history would vindicate his role and proud of the services he had rendered to Virginia and the nation, he disdained his critics until his death from a paralytic stroke in 1895. His political testament reflected his character as a man:

I have stood upon Cemetery Hill and looked down on the scene of the great crater fight, and wondered in my heart if God could have any forgiveness for those men who led the South into that awful war, and are answerable for the blood, the misery, the ruin that followed. Yet under their teaching I was one of the most bitter and irreconcilable of all who flew to arms in the cause of the . . . Confederacy, and I never learned my wretched error, the awful blunder of the South, the curse of her institution of slavery and her traditions until I sat in the United States Senate, and day by day had borne in upon me the amazing significance of our form of government, what it meant, on what basis it was founded, how great and grand it was above any previous human effort, what it meant for humanity, and how much greater the nation was than any State. [43]

Mahone cartoons. Mahone's enemies portrayed him as greedy capitalist and political conniver. (Reproduced through courtesy of the Virginia Historical Society)

Southamptonians looked on Mahone with the same mixture of feelings they held for George Henry Thomas. A county resident, stung by Mahone's cultivation of a constituency among society's underdogs of both races, was quoted in the press in 1879 as announcing that Southampton had "produced two noted characters—Nat Turner, the insurrectionist; and Billy Mahone, the communist; and the latter might profit by the example of the former."[44]

The astigmatic perception that could transmute Mahone's populism into communism betrayed the open and festering emotional wounds left by the war. George Henry Thomas, dying in 1869, had not seen his Southampton home again after a brief convalescence there from a railroad accident in the winter of 1860–61. His Confederate sisters had utterly disowned him and refused any further contact with him after he cast his lot with the Union.[45] But the Rebel hero fared little better than his Federal counterpart, having forsaken—or been forsaken by—his old friends and neighbors in Southampton. It was not perhaps altogether coincidental that the three notable figures given by Southampton to the nation—Nat Turner, George Thomas, William Mahone—were all for so long rejected and despised in their native county, or at least by the white opinion makers there. It may not have been so much in spite of the fact that they served a larger interest as because of it that none of them found favor with Southampton's white community in these years. A provincialism intensified by defeat could see only betrayal in actions that set social justice ahead of service to the white bourgeoisie.

And yet, Southampton could love as ardently as it could hate and not every son and daughter who went forth to service in a wider world or a greater cause was scorned for having done so. If Thomas and Mahone evoked the darker side of Southampton's nature, James Henry Rochelle was one to call forth the better side and to reveal the nobler impulses of the society that nurtured him. When Captain Rochelle passed away at Courtland on March 31, 1889, Southampton mourned the loss of an honored and venerated son. A neighbor composed a eulogy that sought to portray the feelings of those who had known him and followed his career from its auspicious beginning through its illustrious close half a century later: "Euripides, I think it was [Solon, rather], said no man should be called fortunate or happy until he had been placed with his good

James H. Rochelle. Captain Rochelle was
a Confederate naval hero, member of
hydrographic surveying expedition on upper Amazon, and biographer of Admiral
Tucker. (Naval Photographic Center)

name by death beyond the reach of accident or change. Then,
indeed, is this noble soldier happy, for he lived without reproach
and died without fear. Another noble son of Virginia has gone down
below the horizon of time, but his name will be held in sweet re-
membrance by his old comrades and his memory cherished and
honored by his kinsmen."[46]

The subject was not less admirable than the sentiment. Appointed acting midshipman as a boy of fifteen, Rochelle had seen
service under Commodore Matthew C. Perry in the Mexican War,
won appointment to the Naval Academy, cruised the Mediter-
ranean, accompanied Perry on the celebrated expedition to Japan
on the U.S.S. *Southampton,* and participated in the Paraguay Expedition in 1859. On the latter cruise he was an officer on the *Crusader,*
built at Murfreesboro for commerce in 1857 but acquired by the
navy when its own vessels proved too few for this assignment.[47]

Resigning from the navy at the outbreak of the Civil War, Rochelle was on the ironclad *Virginia* when, in 1862, it engaged the *Monitor* in the fight that introduced a new epoch in war at sea. He commanded the C.S.S. *Nansemond, Patrick Henry,* and other ships of the James River Squadron and elsewhere before his appointment to head the Confederate Naval Academy in Richmond late in the war. The end of the conflict seemed to augur the end of his naval career and Captain Rochelle returned to Courtland, but soon he embarked on further maritime adventures.

In 1873 Rochelle was invited by his former comrade-in-arms, John Randolph Tucker, to join a hydrographic survey of the upper Amazon River under the auspices of the government of Peru. He accepted the invitation and remained in South America for three years, during which time he and Tucker ranged far into the unexplored hinterlands. It was in the course of this survey that Rochelle visited a village of the Amazon where a fort was projected by the government, to which place he gave the name Letitia in honor of his niece in Courtland, Letitia Tyler, granddaughter of President Tyler.[48] Rochelle's *Life of Rear Admiral John Tucker* (1888) gave a graphic account of the explorations in Peru as well as an affectionate portrait of his friend. As a writer, military man, explorer, and distinguished citizen, Rochelle represented the best qualities of the Southerner of his age.

The New Generation

Franklin celebrated its recovery from the fire of 1881 with the Franklin Agricultural and Mechanical Society Fair in November 1884, when thousands gathered for what the *Franklin Gazette* hailed as "A Carnival of Bucolic Joys." A traveling dramatic troupe put on *Kathleen Mavourneen,* and other favorites, the Democrats held one of their "grand jollifications," and a phalanx of pickpockets, gamblers, and shakedown artists worked their way though the crowds at the skating rink, in the exhibition tents, and among "the votaries of Terpsichore" at Pretlow's Hall.[49]

C. C. Vaughan, Jr., an energetic young graduate of Randolph-Macon College, introduced banking to Southampton in 1886 when he organized Vaughan and Company at Franklin, the only such institution between Norfolk and Weldon. Vaughan also brought organized athletics to Southampton with the formation of the Kildees baseball team, a regional powerhouse that would send Pitcher Bob Lawson on to the major leagues. The Methodist Church on First Avenue installed a naphtha streetlight around 1890, quickly followed in this by the Baptists on Main and then by some lights paid for by the municipal corporation. A pumper fire-fighting apparatus, a telephone system, and other innovations of the advancing technological age placed Franklin in a position to enter the new century as a thoroughly modern town.[50]

Temperance advocates prevailed upon the local judiciary in 1891 to deny licenses to liquor dealers, and the town experienced an awkward and uncomfortable year as a "dry" community. As with previous experiments of the kind, this one enjoyed little genuine support. A newspaper correspondent in 1872 had described at some length how "the rural tipplers, who love to spend a social day," would arrive in Franklin with "a host of whiskey flasks, punch bottles, and brandy jugs wending their way to the bar-room." The object of each such visitor, according to the writer, was that of "getting gloriously drunk," and a brief interval was always sufficient to bring forth "the ringing laugh of hilarity and the high-sounding voice of bacchanalian revelry" to the business district. It was scarcely surprising then that buckboard rumrunners desecrated the 1891 prohibition year to the extent that any thirsty citizen had only to "go to some vacant lot and 'shake a bush,' and a coffee pot or tin bucket would be found containing his favorite brand." The wets carried a liquor referendum later in the year that returned Franklin to law-abiding good cheer once again.[51]

The century closed with Southampton formally recognizing its return to the Union by sending a sizable complement of men to the ranks of the United States Army for the Spanish-American War. C. C. Vaughan's Company I, Fourth Virginia Regiment, saw service in Cuba and returned home in April 1899 to a gala reception at Armory Hall in Franklin. A company of Confederate veterans, headed by Capt. I. C. Wills, joined the boys of Company I in a banquet of Southampton ham and turkey and spent some pleasant hours exchanging tales of Malvern Hill and Gettysburg for those of San Juan Hill and Santiago.[52] The occasion was symbolic of the passing of the torch of county leadership from the old generation to the new, with its implied promise that the resentments of the past might soon give way to a more positive mood of unity among the states and races. The old century passed unmourned, and the new one bade fair to be a better time.

12

The Age of Wheels

The *Olive*

The unexpectedly rough waters of the lower Chowan had caused Captain Withy to bring the *Olive* around and head back toward Holley's Wharf, a mile and a half upstream, but it was already too late. Apprehensive passengers, startled by the deafening roar that burst suddenly from the starless night sky, peered through the port windows to see a giant white column snaking rapidly toward the straining steamboat. An instant later the *Olive* was thrown crashing onto her beam-ends, the deckhouse smacking heavily against the river's surface and a massive wave bringing tons of water breaking through windows and compartment doors. The *Olive*, jerked upright again by the water pouring through every opening into the hold, hung soddenly motionless for a moment and then dropped like a rock to the river bottom, carrying down with her all of the thirty-one passengers and crew.

Those who bobbed to the surface in the next seconds fought for a hold on the protuding smokestack or the half-sunken lifeboat jammed against it. And now, over the shrill whistling of the wind, they could hear the horrifying sounds that arose from the flooding staterooms below—the shrieking prayer of Rev. George White, the doomed black minister, the voice of the Bennett girl shouting to her grandmother that they were about to die, a last few muffled screams, and then silence, except for the mournful howling of the wind. Half a minute had been enough to take the lives of seventeen people in the worst disaster in the history of the sprawling river country.[1]

The chilling drama of the survivors from the *Olive* unfolded slowly in the days ahead from the half-hysterical accounts that were carried in the newspapers, how Captain Withy and several others chose to stay with the sunken hulk while the rest spent more than an hour bailing out the remaining lifeboat and scrambling into it out of the freezing river. All were rescued in the early hours of the next morning, February 27, 1903. By some miracle of salvation, no further lives were lost after the sinking, even among those who spent the long and stormy winter's night in the icy water. But the stories of trapped and screaming passengers in the flooding coffin of the steamboat were enough to cause the most experienced of travelers to take sober stock of the means of transportation available to them with an eye for safety on their next trips.

The sinking of the *Olive* on its regular Franklin-to-Edenton run that February night is believed to have been the only fatal accident in the long history of the Albemarle Steam Navigation Company. But the misfortune cost the lives of several from Southampton as well as elsewhere, and it represented one more burden the steamboats would have to shoulder in a time when their future seemed insecure. The ASN still had some useful years ahead, but the disaster to the *Olive* signaled the approaching end of the riverboat, a nineteenth-century conveyance that could not survive the age of the wheel.

The Autoists

Southampton had gone quite mad over wheels four years before Claude J. Edwards came home from Norfolk with the county's first automobile. When the Parker Buggy Company opened business at Franklin in the fall of 1903 its line of light, inexpensive, factory-built vehicles were snapped up as fast as they rolled out the Second Avenue doors. O. W. Gray and Brother at Boykins carried the whole line of Parker rigs, hearse included, but fretted much over "freight charges" from Franklin and lobbied openly for a buggy and wagon works for Boykins itself. By and by they got it, too. A mayor's committee composed of Gray and others worked out an agreement with the Hines Buggy Company of Murfreesboro, raised $15,000 in seed money from interested citizens, and provided Hines with a free lot adjacent to the railroad. The four-story brick factory was started in early 1911, and Boykins had its first home-produced buggies before the year's end. Before long Hines was turning out buggies at a rate of 150 a month.[2]

In the meantime the business at Franklin had become the new century's first undiluted boom. In 1909 C. C. Vaughan, Jr., was

Camp Hugo loggers. A 1909 photo shows R. T. Lassiter, Sr. (in overalls), Tom Bunch (at his left), and other loggers at a camp south of Boykins on the Seaboard Railroad. (R. T. Lassiter, Jr.)

Peanut wagons. This early twentieth-century photo shows a familiar scene at Boykins as wagons await railroad pickup of peanuts for expanding market. (Gertrude Mannes)

already rattling about town in his Stanley Steamer, and R. A. Pretlow owned a fire-engine-red Rambler touring car, but Parker Buggy
Company was so overwhelmed with orders that it kept its entire
force of sixty working overtime for seven weeks in the fall in the hope
of catching up by Christmas. John D. Abbitt opened his Virginia
Buggy Company down the street in early 1910, and the Franklin
Buggy Company a few weeks later acquired a lot on Middle Street
from the Pretlow estate for its own factory. But Parker Buggy behaved as though the other two were only pausing in town for a visit
and the automobiles were the toys of the idle rich. Having already
doubled the size of their plant in 1906, they announced plans in late
1910 for a new factory more than twice as large as their two older
buildings combined. The new place would have 2¼ acres of floor
space, the largest in the South, and would double Parker's output to
6,000 vehicles a year.[3]

Demonstrably, the new century was to be the age of the wheel,
and the fate of the *Olive* only underscored the fact. The era was not
yet six months old when Franklin's town council in June 1901 found
it necessary to ban the riding of bicycles on Main Street sidewalks
between Second Avenue and the railroad and to require that riders
stop and dismount before passing pedestrians on any other sidewalk.
An ordinance of 1906 forbade roller skating on sidewalks, and
another of June 1910 limited automobiles to eight miles per hour
within city limits. (This speed was found to be unreasonably low
and shortly afterward the limit was raised to twelve.)[4] "Night soil"
(sewage) at Franklin was carted off daily in the town's "honey
wagons," and Sampson Johnson of Sedley in 1909 began using a
motorcycle on his rural mail route. Courtland in 1912 acquired a
Ford dealership, giving wheel-happy Southamptonians an alter-
native to the Metz that was carried by the Franklin Automobile
Company.[5]

The craze for wheels generated demands for streets and roads
freed from the tyranny of mud, a cause spearheaded by the Southampton Good Roads Association. Motorists growing accustomed to
cruising along dry surfaces at twenty miles or more an hour fumed
over ferries that might dawdle for half an hour on a round trip across
a river or creek. C. C. Vaughan, with his father and civil engineer
Paul F. Darden, in the fall of 1907 drove the Stanley from Norfolk

to Richmond to survey and map a proposed highway that would connect those cities through Southampton County. The wooden Blackwater bridge at Franklin was replaced in 1910 by a $5,000 steel structure, and many of the county's other wooden bridges were similarly displaced in the next three years. Sol Rawls in 1913 became the Franklin outlet for Hupmobiles, Cases, and Reos, and the *Tidewater News* reported that Maxwells and Overlands were selling well in Southampton though the Ford was still the most popular car in the county.[6]

A different sort of wheel, the projectionist's reel, was also altering the living patterns of many in Southampton. Herky-jerky "movies" had been shown at carnivals and tent shows around the county since the beginning of the century, but it was not until 1907 that they were regularly shown in Franklin's Armory Hall. Townspeople turned out in large numbers to sit on wooden benches in the old, unheated building to watch such silent dramas as *The Trapper's Prize, The Ten of Spades, Dooley Referees a Fight,* and *A Strike at the Ranch.* This venture was short-lived, but movies came to stay with the establishment soon afterward of the Skydome Theatre in a store on Main Street, where, for ten cents—reduced in 1912 to five—the viewer could watch three different films every night, provided the machinery did not break down.[7]

But the wheel that put its stamp on the new century was the one that freed Southamptonians from dependence on the public facilities of railroad and steamboat and offered to Everyman a means of going where he pleased and when. Passenger service on the railroads was not as yet threatened by the advance of private conveyance, but the steamboat lines, dependent upon winding along those courses established by nature herself before the advent of man, were soon in peril.

The Great War

Company I of the Fourth Virginia, no doubt somewhat rusty after almost twenty years of inactivity, was off to service again at Newport News on April 1, 1917, a day ahead of President Woodrow Wilson's message to Congress calling for America's entry into World War I.

Franklin, with the South's largest lumber mill, expected also to lend significant material support to the war effort,[8] and Southamptonians seemed relieved at the nation's commitment after so many long months of suspense. Blacks held a mid-April rally at Cool Springs Baptist Church to show their united loyalty to the cause, and further rallies were held during the month by members of both races in Courtland, Capron, Drewryville, Newsoms, Ivor, and elsewhere. General C. C. Vaughan was commander of the Virginia state troops and set an admirable example of energetic patriotism until army physicians at the beginning of 1918 found him still overweight and out of shape and sent him home in retirement. Draft registrants in Southampton by the beginning of June totaled 838 white and 1,336 black, or about the same proportion as whites were to blacks among the county's 26,000 inhabitants. The Franklin Protective League organized a Home Guard to keep the Germans on the east side of Blackwater, and everybody turned out to cheer the trains that carried the Fourth Virginia south to Camp McClellan, Alabama, in early September.[9]

The war for most residents of Southampton was experienced in terms of Liberty Loan drives, fuel shortages, and news from the local boys, who by the end of 1917 had begun to arrive at the war zone in France in considerable numbers. Country folk who had not yet quite adapted themselves to the idea of the permanence of automobiles or the practical utility of airplanes received a jolt in late June 1918 when a fleet of thirty-two government trucks roared through Ivor, Berlin, and Franklin en route to some Hampton Roads destination, alarming the horses and throwing a blanket of dust over everything along its route. Ten days later, at the Fourth of July celebration in Franklin, a Curtis biplane dazzled the crowd by swooping along Main Street just above the treetops at ninety miles an hour.[10]

And Southampton had its war heroes, whose exploits helped P. D. Camp reach the quotas set for his War Savings Bond drives. Prominent among the county's volunteers was young Colgate W. Darden, Jr., who had gone on his own to France in 1916 and become an ambulance driver with the French army. Debilitated by rough campaigning in the Argonne and elsewhere, Darden was returned to the United States in 1917 for several months of hospitalization but reenrolled as a Marine Corps fighter pilot and returned to the

Colgate W. Darden, Jr. Later governor of Virginia
and president of University of Virginia, Darden was
early enlistee and aviator of the French front in World
War I. He is shown here at Verdun in 1916. (Colgate
W. Darden)

front in 1918. In October 1918 a plane in which he was riding
crashed in northern France, throwing Darden clear of the wreck
but killing the pilot. Though severely injured and hospitalized for
a year, he was able to complete his studies at the University of Virginia in 1922. His war service was among those qualifications that
were soon to recommend the young man to a career in politics.[11]

Again, as in 1899, the return of the troops was a time of gladsome celebration in Southampton when 4,000 people turned out to welcome home the white boys on June 27, 1919. A triumphal arch and reviewing stand were erected on Main Street in Franklin, and three automobiles, draped with Confederate flags, carried a last contingent of old Confederate soldiers along ahead of the marching doughboys. The largest contingent of "colored soldiers and sailors" reached Franklin three weeks later and was led by Capt. Jesse Joyner on a Main Street parade through soaking rain.[12] The newspaper on this occasion made no mention of Confederate flags.

The war had cost the lives of only a small number of Southampton's men and had, indeed, made important economic contributions to the citizens of the county. Brief participation and painless victory in Teddy Roosevelt's "splendid little war" against Spain and Wilson's war "to make the world safe for democracy" helped immeasurably to reunite the shattered sections of the nation and to obliterate the awful lessons of war taught by the "irrepressible conflict" of the 1860s. A new generation of Southamptonians had been launched into life with unrealistic expectations of what the post-war epoch held in store for them. As a result, the "Roaring Twenties" were to be a prelude to crushing disillusionment.

Thrust and Bust

A beginning toward the uniform education of children of both races and sexes had been made as far back as the year 1870 when Dr. James F. Bryant became Southampton's first school superintendent. For some years afterward, however, the outstanding schools in the county continued to be private institutions such as the fine Male Academy and the Female Seminary in Franklin, the former of which opened in 1890 and the latter in 1894. These were among the earliest schools in the county to offer a high-school curriculum and were among the few schools in Southampton whose teachers were generally college educated. The Franklin Male Academy was converted in 1903 into a military academy, but the new institution lasted only five years. The Female Academy continued to operate until 1912, when it was converted into a public high school. By this time, the thirty-one schools of 1870 had grown to more than 120, though most were one- or two-room affairs conducted by a single teacher, usually white.[46] There were nine accredited high schools in the county by 1913, all of which, of course, were racially separated, the black teachers receiving salaries averaging slightly more than half those of white.[13]

Of special importance to the black community was the Franklin Normal and Industrial Institute, founded by Mrs. Della Hayden. Mrs. Hayden was a well-educated and energetic black leader who was able to persuade northern philanthropists to provide funds for a dormitory and other facilities for her school. She conducted the school for several years before her death in December 1924, as the victim in Franklin's first fatal automobile accident.[14]

Another asset to the Southampton community was the Hungarian colony founded by Count Bela Kalman Basho. A native of Hungary, Basho came to America in 1890 at the age of eighteen. He studied at Oberlin College in Ohio and took a degree in divinity there in 1910. In the same year, Basho moved to Southampton, acquiring a farm near Courtland. Here he set about organizing a community of immigrant Hungarians. His Basho Cement Works at Courtland was only one of a number of enterprises launched by the industrious colonists. Basho died at Richmond in 1931, but the Hungarians continued to prosper as an integral part of the life of Southampton County.[15]

A more literate public opened the way for the growth of newspaper circulation, and several adventurous publishers hastened to cultivate and supply the need. Southampton's earliest newspaper had been the *Herald,* published briefly at Jerusalem in 1860. Franklin's weeklies, the *Tribune* and *Monitor,* merged in 1878 into the *Seaboard and Roanoke Times,* gave way in 1880 to K. R. Griffin's *Franklin Gazette,* which also had a brief history. The *Southampton Democrat, Blackwater Courier, Messenger,* and *Graphic* were other Franklin sheets of the last years of the nineteenth century, but it was 1905 before Paul Scarborough's *Tidewater News* finally established the profession of journalism firmly on Southampton soil.[16] The Boykins *Times,* edited by Rev. Thomas E. Johnson, was founded in 1916 but lasted only a few months before the editor moved to Richmond.[17] For the most part, the early newspapers were four-page weeklies with per-

Della Hayden. Founder of Franklin Normal and Industrial School, a pioneering black educational institution, Mrs. Hayden died in an auto accident in 1924. (Mrs. S. P. Morton)

haps a column or two of county news, mostly in the form of editorial nuggets or letters from regular correspondents. They were poor fare in comparison with the banquet of news served up by the big dailies in Norfolk and Richmond.

There were, however, more impressive signs of enlarging cultural horizons in and about Southampton County. Literary clubs enjoyed a popularity in the larger communities. The early twentieth-century Chatauqua movement brought high-level music and oratory on occasion, and the town of Boykins, so history records, in 1924 organized its own Civic Symphony Orchestra.[18] But the motion picture and the introduction of radio were the features of the postwar cultural explosion which reached the greatest number of people and had the most immediate impact on the level of public awareness of the world beyond the Meherrin and Blackwater.

Cultural pursuits were retarded by the coming of the Great Depression when many Southamptonians lost their jobs or were forced to abandon all pursuits except the narrowly economic. Economizing town commissioners cut Franklin's water rates and the salaries of all town employees in October 1931, when the pay offered by the town for common labor was 12½ cents an hour. But the Roosevelt New Deal brought immediate relief for many of the county's poor, forty-six of whom were sent off in May 1933 for labor with the government's new Civilian Conservation Corps. Farmers in July began plowing up more than 2,400 acres of cotton, for which relief to the cotton glut the government paid them $29,000. Make-work projects in the county included the draining of Tarrara Creek, the painting of school buildings and grading of school grounds, and the extension of sewer and water systems. By painfully slow degrees, Southampton emerged from the time of troubles, the end of which was signaled by the organization at the end of 1936 of the Chesapeake-Camp Corporation, which would bring the county a huge paper mill and would offer employment to some seven hundred people when completed.[19]

The Talents

The progress in education and the gradual enrichment of the cultural opportunities of Southampton offered to a larger number of its young people careers that would benefit not only the region but the nation. The *Tidewater News* in 1926 took notice of the career of Dr. John J. Kindred, a native of the county, who had lately been reelected to Congress from New York. Dr. Kindred had been educated at Randolph-Macon College and in medicine at the University of Virginia, after which he continued his studies at the University of Edinburgh in the field of mental diseases. He later served with the staffs of several large hospitals for the insane in England and Scotland.

In 1896 Dr. Kindred established River Crest Sanitorium at Astoria, New York, and later a Farm Colony and Sanitorium at Belle Mead, New Jersey. Having subsequently studied law and obtained a law degree, he entered politics and was elected in 1910 to the first of his five terms in Congress. His most notable activities as a legislator were in the field of mental health, where he sponsored a number of bills, but he was also an early advocate of a Federal Narcotics Bureau. He died in New York in 1937.[20]

A career in some respects parallel to that of Kindred was that of Dr. William Francis Drewry, who was born at Westover Plantation near Clarksbury Church in 1860. Educated at the Murfreesboro Academy, Randolph-Macon, and the Medical College of Virginia, he opened his first medical practice in the village of Ivor. Dr. Drewry became superintendent of the Petersburg Hospital in 1894 and, in the next twenty-eight years, won national recognition in psychiatric circles. City manager of Petersburg for a period after 1924, he spent the final six years of his life as head of the Bureau of Mental Hygiene in Richmond. He died there in 1934.[21]

Outstandingly the most successful and celebrated Southampton-ian in these years, however, was Colgate W. Darden, Jr. After his marriage to Constance S. Du Pont of the multimillionaire Delaware Du Ponts in 1927, Darden two years later made his initial bid for political office by seeking and gaining a seat in the Virginia House of Delegates as a Democrat. Following his term in that body, he won election to the United States House of Representatives, where he served until unseated in 1936. With the backing of the Byrd machine, Darden returned to Congress in 1939, resigning in 1941 to run for the governorship of Virginia. He was successful by a large majority and took office at Richmond at the beginning of 1942.

Darden's somewhat regressive service in Congress contrasted notably with his more progressive term as governor. In the former role he had been, by his fiscal conservatism and in other ways, a typical representative of the Byrd organization. Darden also sup-ported the infamous Dies Committee, progenitor of the House Committee on Unamerican Activities. His votes helped to foster exports and loans to the European belligerents as early as 1939. He was an opponent of antilynching legislation passed by the House in 1940, though he stoutly supported Virginia's strong legislation aimed at the same crime.

As Virginia's governor, Darden set in motion measures which eliminated the state debt and built up a sizable surplus, most of which was allocated to vocational schools, institutions of higher learning, hospitals, and other public services. More than a million dollars was earmarked at his urging for the expansion of visual-aid programs in the public schools, and steps were taken to complete the electrification of all Virginia's educational institutions.

Addressing the state legislature in 1944, Darden called for steps to improve the living conditions of black citizens. This, he indicated, must include better facilities and support for the all-black staff at the Piedmont Tuberculosis Sanitarium; it would also mean state funds to help educate young blacks wishing to study medicine at Meharry Medical College in Tennessee. The governor called for legislative remedies for the obstacles to service by blacks on juries, and in 1945 he proposed that the states of the South cooperate to provide blacks with greater educational opportunities generally.[22] Darden remained no less a segregationist than any other southern political figure of the time, but his championship of a better life for black people offered a contrast with the heritage of lingering prejudice that still characterized white attitudes throughout the South. It was more remarkable still that the strongest voice in the state for minority interests should be that of a native of the county of Nat Turner and Dred Scott. Only the willfully obtuse could fail to recognize in this that America was nearing an epochal turning point in relations between its major races and that the "strange career of Jim Crow" was finally approaching its close.

Momentum

The Albemarle Steam Navigation Company died its slow death by economic strangulation in the first two decades of the twentieth century, but not without providing Southampton with a few more exciting moments. One of its boats, the *Nanticoke* (formerly the *Chowan* and, before that, the *Ella*),[23] was the object of some sensation-mongering in the big northern dailies in the spring of 1909 when word got abroad that it was to be acquired by Venezuelan filibusters on behalf of former President Castro. The truth appears to have been that the *Nanticoke* was wanted by Venezuela for the Orinoco coffee trade, but the rumors were enough to cause the

United States to send the Coast Guard cutter *Pamlico* up to Franklin in June to make sure no contraband of war was being sent away on the steamboat. Her holds loaded with 125 tons of coal, the *Nanticoke* departed Franklin on June 17, and after an uneventful voyage through the Caribbean, she reached Maracaibo in late August. Youthful Robert M. Fagan of Southampton went along for the trip and kept the *Tidewater News* informed by postcard and cablegram of the boat's progress south.[24] It was a poignant end for the *Nanticoke,* which in her earliest incarnation more than half a century earlier, had been a daring Rebel blockade-runner. It's a fair guess that a filibustering expediton would have suited the old girl better.

In 1911 the ASN acquired from Newport News two new steel screw-steamers, the *Carolina* and *Virginia,* as replacements for its older boats, the *Hertford* and *Keystone.* The *Carolina* went promptly into service on the company's Murfreesboro-Edenton run and her sister ship on the route from Franklin to Tunis and other ports of the upper Chowan. Both of these vessels, however, were purchased by the federal government in November 1917, the *Carolina* being dispatched to Fort Dupont on the Delaware River and the *Virginia* to Fort Slocum, New York.[65] The ASN remained in operation a while longer with the remodeled *Hertford* and a boat with the retrospectively symbolic name of *Appomattox* before a new form of competition, the motortruck, drove the firm into dissolution.[25] But there were pleasures about steamboating which, for the passenger at least, would never be equaled in the steel cocoons of the age of gasoline and wheels.

Little impeded by depression and considerably stimulated by war, the age of the wheel had grown to maturity in Southampton and across the nation, altering the faces of cities, reorganizing lines of transport and communication, touching at last every facet of life. A celebration of the end of innocence for the motorcar in Southampton was the opening of the Franklin-Murfreesboro road in May 1926. The *Tidewater News* took special notice of the last trip of old Smith's Ferry over the Nottoway, its place taken by a new steel bridge, just as the ferries at Monroe and South Quay had also been replaced. Principal speaker for the road opening was Governor Harry F. Byrd, but the North Carolina lieutenant governor was also on hand, along with the State Senator C. C. Vaughan, general chairman of "Virginia-Carolina Day" at Franklin. Thousands gathered for the ribbon cutting at Smith's Ferry Bridge where representatives of the two states met and exchanged greetings. There was a free dinner at Franklin's high school athletic field, and 6,500 people showed up. The day's program concluded with a baseball game between Suffolk and Roanoke Rapids and a street dance at night.[26]

In 1924 the Old Dominion Transit Corporation began a Nor-folk-Richmond bus service daily along the "ridge road," surveyed by Vaughan in 1907 and completed in 1922. This road placed Franklin, Courtland, and other Southampton communities on a major automotive artery and was equivalent in economic impact to the establishment of a major new industry in the county.[27]

Automotive transport brought the mushrooming of gas stations and garages, but it also spelled disaster for blacksmiths, wheel-wrights, and many other artisans, including all those employed by Southampton's prolific but short-lived buggy manufacturers. The bus routes threw the final spades of dirt over the graves of the steam-boat companies, and the fire that destroyed Franklin's municpal stables and mules in 1925 could not be much regretted. Nor was the fact lost on Franklin a few days later when, in response to a fire at the Camp mill, Suffolk's Stutz fire engine was pumping water on the blaze within forty-seven minutes.[28] No town that could afford one dared continue much longer without its own motor fire engine.

The motor car and truck seemed often to bring two or three problems for every one they solved. A new experience in the life of South-ampton was the use of a Dodge touring car on the night of February 10, 1927, by the kidnappers of Al Young, manager of the Franklin Theatre. Young was released unharmed and, to hear him tell it, mystified as to why he had been taken. (The local Ku Klux Klan, active since at least 1924, may have had a hand in it.) The blessings of paved streets also received another look when, at the end of 1934, Franklin's progress-minded city fathers proposed to cut down four-teen High Street elms in order to guarantee a forty-foot right-of-way from curb to curb. But residents in early 1935 voted 110 to 96 to let the trees be cut, the automobile still winning virtually every battle in which it engaged.[29]

Railroads, though losing passenger fares, continued to prosper as bulk carriers. The old Surry, Sussex and Southampton Railway, which for many years had connected Dory with Scotland Wharf on the James River, was remodeled by J. A. Pretlow and others in 1928. The closing of the mill on which the line depended led to the dismantling of the road in 1931, but other lines fared better. The Franklin and Carolina, connecting Franklin and the Atlantic Coast Line in Nansemond, was incorporated in 1944 as a subsidiary of the Camp Manufacturing Company. The Seaboard Air Line (along the tracks of the old P. & R.), the Norfolk and Western (formerly the Petersburg and Norfolk), and the Southern Railroad (once the Atlantic and Danville) continued to serve the county well. The Virginian Railroad, completed in 1906, offered an eastern commercial route to Joyner, Sebrell, Sedley, and Burdette.[30]

It already seemed difficult to believe that the first automobiles had clattered along Franklin's muddy thoroughfares only in 1907, so powerfully had the age of the wheel wrought on the life of Southampton. Still harder to accept was the possibility that the internal combustion engine would in a few more decades begin sipping voraciously at the last drops of the planet's crude oil.

13

A Winter of Discontent

Autumn of Apprehension

When Judge J. Segar Gravatt addressed a mass meeting of whites at Southampton High School on January 3, 1956, he tried to sound the appropriate note of warning to the bureaucrats in Washington. "Any man who knows and understands the temper of the people, in that section . . . between James River and . . . Lynchburg," he declared, "knows that there will be no public schools in this area . . . if compulsory integration is placed upon these communities by the NAACP.[1]" Any federal administrator who doubted whether Gravatt truly represented the constituency for whom he spoke had only to review the events of the preceding three weeks to realize that his remarks were not those of an irresponsible demagogue.

Reacting to demands by the federal government for the racial integration of public schools, the Southampton School Board and the Franklin PTA in early December 1955 had gone on record as being unreservedly opposed to any integration of the schools. Before Christmas, the Southampton Education Association had added its opposition and called for approval of the January 9 referendum on amending the state constitution to facilitate continued segregation.[2] All across the South the lines of resistance were being drawn, and the issue by now seemed clear enough: either the public schools would remain segregated, or there would be no public schools.

There was dramatic affirmation of Judge Gravatt's view on January 9 when, in the largest vote ever cast in Southampton County, the citizens endorsed by 3,325 to 423 a referendum convention to allow state funds to be used for private schools. The Southampton Chapter of Defenders of State Sovereignty and Individual Liberties met in February to hear an attack on federal interposition between local and state authorities,[3] and the marshaling of forces of resistance continued during the following spring and summer. But everything depended on the attitude of the federal government and whether such signs of public opposition might cause it to back away from its goal of total school integration. The early indications seemed encouraging.

Eighteen months of legislative and constitutional sparring on the issue between federal and state authorities brought no integration, but neither did Washington appear to weaken noticeably in its resolve. In October 1957 concerned whites in Southampton began holding meetings to consider ways of blocking the threatened integration of their schools. A house-to-house survey in Franklin was said to have produced almost 90 percent endorsement of its efforts, and in January 1959 the group was chartered as the Southampton Educational Foundation. The objectives of the foundation were spelled out publicly on March 12 by its president, S. W. Rawls, Jr., in an address before the Franklin PTA.

A basic consideration, Rawls explained, was that black children made up 72 percent of the county's school enrollment and that the proportion of blacks to whites was still increasing. Most of the county's black population was "not pressing for integration," and it "would be a tragedy if outside influences" were allowed to bring about the decline of the public schools. But the time was at hand, he added, when people must begin preparing for the worst, and the foundation was using its efforts not merely in behalf of "whites with money" but for "all white families."

In its editorial endorsement of Rawls's remarks a few days later, the *Tidewater News* praised the speaker for having made, not "a race-baiting speech," but only "a calm statement of facts."[5] In Southampton as elsewhere throughout the South, the voices of reason and moderation appeared to be those that foresaw tragedy in the realization of social justice. In such a climate of concern, it seemed unpromising to inquire what the extremists foresaw. If the people in Washington could not be discouraged from imbibing their sociology from the NAACP, the possibility seemed strong for an intersectional crisis in the 1960s that would rival that of the 1860s. The approaching decade looked distinctly ominous even before John Steinbeck launched it with a novel entitled *The Winter of Our Discontent*. Before the decade ended, another novelist was to shock Southampton as no other had done in the two centuries of its existence.

The Happy Warriors

The next generation was to look retrospectively upon World War II as the last of the really fine wars. Adolph Hitler, the distilled and concentrated essence of perfect wickedness, had been villain enough to make the Bolshevik army look like a band of freedom fighters. Southampton boys who went away to fight against Fascism had no qualms about the righteousness of their cause or the absolute neces- sity of crushing the enemy. Never again, perhaps, would a war seem so undeniably just or the difference between right and wrong so certain. In a way, the war had been the closing episode in a long age of innocence when good and bad, and black and white, seemed clearly separable and distinct.

Delaware Thomas Worrell, the county's last Civil War veteran, passed away in April 1941 at the age of 93 in order, perhaps, that different phases of Southampton's history should not overlap un- tidily into one another. On December 16, with the fires of Pearl Harbor still smoldering, county Civil Defense leaders put South- ampton on a war footing with G. Hinson Parker, Jr., appointed chief aircraft warning observer and Frank R. Day in the role of com- munications chief. The Franklin Fire Department organized a res- cue squad and emergency utilities repair unit, while Dr. Morgan B. Raiford headed up the Emergency Medical Division and town employees instituted a Public Works Emergency Division.[6] With the situation stabilized west of Blackwater, the first wartime Christ- mas could be observed in the serenity that is the reward of vigilance and foresight.

Citizens of Southampton rallied to the war effort with becoming energy and patriotism. Before the beginning of the new year over 2,300 people had volunteered their services to Civil Defense Co- ordinator Junius W. Pulley, whose advisory committee included A. B. Doles of Ivor, representing the black community. The Red Cross drive to raise $3,500 in the county was already under way, and Franklin Municipal Airport was in the hands of army engineers who were converting it to military purposes. The 1942 scrap drive brought in more than 370 tons of metal, including such oddities as the Shady Brook highway bridge between Courtland and Frank- lin and the iron fence from around the Confederate Monument on the courthouse green. But Allegheny County took the prize in the state competition with substantially over a thousand tons.[7]

Shortages of many different kinds of goods were borne with patience by Southamptonians, most of whom were still farmers who could rely on their own resources for most commodities. But the theft of ration coupons worth over 30,000 gallons of gasoline from Courtland's War Price and Rationing Board office in September 1942 made for inconvenience that a wheel-happy generation found hard to tolerate. War bond sales and war loan drives usually went well over quotas as the conflict progressed, but shortages of labor sometimes meant problems for the farm community. To help make up the labor deficit, the county's black schools were closed for three weeks in the fall of 1942 and white schools for two weeks, with British sailors from Norfolk available at $2 a day plus room and board. Virtually every community in the county held a celebration on June 6, 1944, at the announcement of the Allied invasion of "Fortress Europe."[8] By now it was certain that the Axis powers were doomed.

As in all the wars since that of secession, Southampton was more helped than hurt by the effort, though some of her young men, beginning with Jack Whitehead of Sebrell, were killed in action and others seriously injured. The Starkes of Capron and the Carters of Newsoms were among those families who sent as many as six sons into service, but many came back from the war with valuable trades and skills and with guarantees of government aid in furthering their educations. With the enlargement of the Franklin Airport (used as a naval auxiliary base)[9] and the added spur given to commerce and industry, Southampton could look back on the war with a good deal of satisfaction. The evil had been arrested, and nearly everybody had profited in the process. If the United States were to be thrust into the role of world's policeman in the postwar epoch, the prospect could not seem altogether burdensome.

Tilling and Milling

Postwar economic gains in Southampton fulfilled the expectations raised by the bustling war years. Besides its continuing importance in peanut, corn, and pork production, the county's herds in 1946 provided almost six million quarts of milk. Southampton was now ranked officially as the twelfth largest peanut-growing county in the nation, and advances in production technology and disease control were to raise production enormously in the years ahead. By 1970 Southampton farmers were growing well over 3,000 pounds of peanuts per acre on over 31,000 acres and generating from this crop more than a third of the county's annual farm income of $30 million. The last mules had almost disappeared from peanut farming, along with walking cultivators and other relics of the past. Huge machines now dried and winnowed the peas in a single operation before depositing them in large drying bins where heated air further reduced moisture content. Boykins's Sunnyside-Up Egg Farm was one of the state's largest chicken farms, and the Virginia Cattle Feeding Corporation's facility at Branchville included the world's largest upright farm silo. Newsoms had won an enviable reputation as "watermelon capital of the South."[10]

A trend toward larger and more complex farming operations steadily drove down the number of farmers in the county, so that there were only 875 by the opening of the 1970s. But increasing numbers of workers were being drawn into the county's developing industries. Camp Manufacturing Company had stretched its far-flung operations into North and South Carolina in the years before the war and in 1936 joined the Chesapeake-Camp Corporation to produce pulp and paper at its Franklin mills. By 1946 the paper plant was turning out 190 tons a day, a capacity which was doubled within another decade. By 1955 the lumber division of the firm was producing 100,000 feet of lumber a day and the plant site occupied an area six times larger than that of the parent Neely mill a century earlier.[11]

The mid-1950s brought a rush of new industry to Southampton, beginning with the St. Regis Paper Company's bag factory at Franklin in 1954 and the Hercules Powder Company's multimillion dollar plant at Delaware on the Nottoway in 1955. In the following year, the Union Bag and Paper Corporation of New York united with Camp to form the Union Bag–Camp Paper Corporation, and in 1961 work was started on the facilities of the Boykins Narrow Fabric Corporation, a weaving concern of advanced design. In 1962 the

Allen & Smith Candy Company switched its operations from Richmond to Boykins to be nearer the raw materials for its peanut brittle and peanut candy bars. White Way Foods at Boykins was another significant business, packaging and selling some 50,000 sandwiches a week by 1963 and distributing them as far away as Washington, D.C.[12] By this time industry had long since overcome the historic lead of agriculture as the chief employer and principal source of income for Southampton. Indeed, agriculture itself, with its expensive and complicated machines for nearly every operation, was increasingly an industrial enterprise and one in which only the well-financed capitalist could hope to succeed.

Dividends

Although literacy had advanced notably in the early decades of the twentieth century, Southampton in the years immediately following the Second World War was not yet a place where literary culture or artistic talent need look for encouragement. Franklin's Community Concert Association, organized in 1946, fanned the faint embers of musical appreciation, but the public, for the time being at least, was more interested in baseball. The Southampton Kildees, organized in 1948 in the Class D Virginia League, won the league pennant in the following year but not a secure niche in the affections of its fans. Poor attendance in the 1951 season forced dissolution of the team.[13]

A sign of broadening popular culture was the interest shown by the postwar generation in books. Franklin's town library, opened in 1926, was able at first to serve its public on a schedule of four hours a week. Three years later the institution could offer a choice among only 770 volumes, but by 1951 the library, now liberated from its cramped quarters in furniture stores and bank buildings, had its own building and a collection of nearly 5,000 volumes. But better opportunities were opened by the offer of Ivor native Walter C. Rawls in 1955 to give Southampton a combination library and museum. Rawls, a St. Louis investment banker, donated an initial $150,000 for the building, which was built at Courtland in 1957. The Rawls Library opened with 30,000 volumes, and Rawls con-

tinued to furnish additions to the endowment and in other ways
until his contributions had passed $500,000.[14] The salary of a full-
time museum curator and funds for the purchase of exhibits were
furnished from the Rawls donation.

Education and culture in Southampton received another important impetus in 1968 with the selection of Franklin as the site for a
state community college. The two-year institution, known as Paul
D. Camp Community College, opened in the fall of 1971 with an
enrollment of not quite four hundred students. Its growth in subsequent years reflected the rising faith of the surrounding community in the benefits of higher education in cultural as well as economic respects. In the meantime, the construction in 1961–62 of the
110-bed Southampton Memorial Hospital promised benefits for the
body comparable to those of the libraries for the mind.[15]

The advance of library and hospital facilities would not have been
possible had it not been for the new income pouring into Southampton from its combined farming and industrial operations. Even the
business slump of the mid-1970s saw the county's economy stable
and prosperous and most of its residents enjoying a standard of
living undreamt of by their parents. In particular, the black community was finally beginning to realize good returns from its
labor and talent, though the gap between median white and median
black earnings remained conspicuous. There were grounds for optimism about the future, and the celebration of the nation's Bicentennial appeared to underscore the faith of both races that the fruits
of progress might not be much longer denied to any who deserved
them.

Southampton in the late 1970s still had its "ghettoes," and economic justice had not followed social and political equality as
rapidly as many had hoped it would in the liberating years of the
1960s. There remained, in fact, visible scars from the ordeal of the
'60s and the tensions associated with the "winter of our discontent."

Backlash

The movement for private all-white schools in Southampton was
delayed throughout the period from 1959 to 1969 pending the out-

Champs. The Southampton County High School football team, 1977 runner-up in Virginia's AA League, is the latest in the school's series of exceptional teams, winners of 72 of 77 games played in the past six years. The school produced state championship teams in 1973 and 1976. (Southampton County High School)

come of legal and judicial maneuvering. As case after case went against the proponents of segregation, Southampton continued to construct and operate racially segregated facilities, begrudgingly admitting token numbers of blacks to formerly all-white schools. In an era of civil rights violence, Southampton was fortunate to avoid bloodshed, though Capron had its civil rights march[16] and Franklin knew a moment of anguish when it seemed that the community might well erupt in racial combat.

The circumstance was the appearance in Franklin on September 30, 1967, of a group of robed Ku Klux Klansmen and a march by them double file down Main Street. The *Tidewater News,* which published an account six days later, on page ten, spoke of a black child having reportedly been "roughed up" by Klansmen at the Open Air Market No. 2 on South Street. The incident drew an assemblage of between 300 and 400 blacks to the vicinity, and a rock-throwing melee occurred in which several people were injured and $1,000 in property damage was caused. Two blacks were arrested and sentenced to a year in jail and $500 each in fines, but the trouble seems to have passed with the departure of the hooded agitators from the scene.[17] The primly discreet coverage of the incident by the newspaper was an index of the alarm generated in a community that had more cause than most to fear the consequence of racial discord.

With the School Board under heavy federal pressure o achieve full desegregation of the system for the coming school year, the Southampton Educational Foundation in January 1969 began work in earnest on its own private, all-white institution. Leaders of the movement announced that they had $16,000 on hand and sought enough to construct, equip, and staff a seven-grade school by the opening of the fall term. Scores of parents promptly enrolled their children so that by the beginning of March, Southampton Academy, though lacking either a building or teachers, had 131 students, enough to fill the first grade to capacity and several other grades nearly so. Construction of the school began in June on an 11½-acre tract near Courtland.[18]

Sensing a serious threat to the public schools from so many withdrawals, a parents' group from Boykins and Newsoms in February petitioned the School Board to redouble its efforts to save and improve the schools. A spokesman for the group complained that the voices of moderation in the county were being drowned out by those seeking full, immediate desegregation, on the one hand, and those still insisting on segregation, on the other.[19] "Freedom of choice" was the rallying cry of tokenism, while moderates acknowledged the necessity for at least a limited assignment of black students to predominately white schools and consequent busing if serious difficulty was to be avoided.

The issue was resolved on June 9 when Judge Walter E. Hoffman of the United States District Court instructed the Southampton School Board to begin pupil assignments for the fall term. The result was a notable upsurge in black enrollment at predominately white schools, though no whites in 1969 were assigned in the other direction. Five years later, enrollment figures showed desegregation to be very near reality with more than 1,000 white children integrated with about 3,000 blacks.[20] The public schools of Southampton had weathered the crisis and racial integration had come to the county of Nat Turner and Dred Scott.

The New Jerusalem

The publication of William Styron's *Confessions of Nat Turner* in 1967 propelled the half-forgotten leader of the 1831 revolt back into the American consciousness at a difficult moment in race relations. It also thrust Southampton County into a limelight which it had not sought and found uncomfortable. But the jarring element in the novel, in the view of many of the county's whites, was its sympathetic portrayal of Nat Turner. In Styron's assessment Nat was almost unrecognizably different from the fanatic described by William S. Drewry in 1900. As the subject of the novel, the rebel leader was neither more nor less than a human being, with perfectly human motives and desires. The book was accorded high critical praise and commercial success, and in the year after its publication, it won the Pulitzer Prize in fiction.

Southampton had little time to adjust to the upsurge of interest in Nat and the locale of his exploits when in September 1969 it became known that a Hollywood studio was planning to film the novel on location in Southampton County. Twentieth-Century Fox representatives were quick to announce that they would not make the film in Southampton if there was significant local opposition, but they added that better than a third of the $4 million budgeted for the film was to be spent in the county. They also indicated a desire to correct certain historical inaccuracies in the story as related by Styron and to build a replica of the antebellum village of Jerusalem that might remain as a tourist attraction when the filming was completed. Black actor James Earl Jones, a fine success in his latest film, *The Great White Hope,* had agreed to play the title role and filming was set to begin on April 1, 1970.[21]

Whatever qualms some may have felt about such a film at such a troubled moment in race relations were swept away as the project won the endorsement of the Boykins Town Council, the County Board of Supervisors, and the Franklin-Southampton Chamber of Commerce. The filmmakers contracted for the use of land near Boykins owned by Mrs. Roy A. Lassiter and the old Johnny Mason place west of Drewryville owned by L. J. Bain and Son.[22] The prospect seemed certain that an audience of many millions would be witnessing hours of Southampton scenery within a matter of months. The tourist benefits of so much exposure and publicity were difficult to assess but could not help but be substantial.

The whole thing exploded with an announcement by Fox in early 1970 that an escalating budget had forced postponement and probable cancellation of the film. The studio was suffering from heavy losses on earlier films and dared not undertake the risk of a project that might, indeed, prove to be an unfortunate gamble. Black activists were by now striking viciously at Styron for what they felt was a distortion of Nat's character in the novel, a debasement of heroic motives into petty personal aims that bore no resemblance to the Nat of either history or mythology.[23] The moment of fame and glory slipped past and Southampton returned to the reality of living one day at a time.

But Styron's novel had served as a catalyst for an interest in Nat Turner that did not depend upon the production of a film. A barrage of books and articles followed in the decade after the appearance of the novel, ranging from scholarly efforts at reconstructing the story more accurately to popular accounts aimed at turning a dollar on a shifting market. For the time being, at least, Nat was accorded the status of a folk hero, a symbol for the aspirations of a generation of blacks who were seeking to complete the process that he had begun. The symbolic Nat became a figure of more important dimensions than the historical Nat, and a literature developed over the proper view that a twentieth-century American was entitled to hold in regard to the deeds of the rebel chieftain.

A spin-off from the interest generated by Styron in the Turner story was that the names of obscure antebellum figures such as Thomas R. Gray and Nathaniel Francis, Margaret Whitehead and Joseph Travis became widely familiar to the reading public. A good deal of ink was expended on such questions as whether Nathaniel Francis was or was not, as Styron alleged, "a mean son of a bitch" to his slaves and just what sort of relationship Nat Turner may have had with Margaret Whitehead.[24] Curious amateurs and professional researchers returned again and again to the courthouse at Courtland or roamed back and forth along Southampton's byways interviewing elderly people who might expose some secret that recorded history had held back for 140 years and more. The family recollections of Percy Claud of Boykins and the political leanings of Boykins' attorney Gilbert Francis became the stuff of scholarly rumina-tions.[25] As the national Bicentennial year ended, there was little indication if any that interest in the Turner story had begun to dissipate. For good or ill, Bill Styron had put the county perma-nently on the literary map of the United States.

Enclave

At the beginning of the twentieth century, Virginia Camp Norfleet tried to tell her grandchildren of the times before the Civil War. She wanted them to know that "children lived in awful terror" that the slaves would " 'rise again,' " and "would tremble with fear at the barking of a dog, or the cracking of a twig."[26] It was fortunate, she felt, that her own had not been required to live in such a situa-tion, and she thought her society well rid of slavery even though there had sometimes been warm and close relations between masters and slaves.

Half a century later, Colgate Darden, who had contributed so much as governor of the state and as president of the University of Virginia, addressed a Ruritan gathering in Southampton. He wanted his audience to be mindful of the danger of the white race being overwhelmed in a world where they represented but a tiny fraction of the population.[27] Southampton whites, sensitive to the local inferiority of their numbers, were perhaps more attuned than most Americans to the dangers he foresaw, having lived for more than a century and a half in the conditions he described.

Again and again the county's history reveals that Southampton whites seem to have lived with a sense of foreboding about the society they were helping to build. The problem, usually unac-knowledged, was national as well as local, but it was magnified in Southampton by the peculiar circumstances of the county's herit-age. History sometimes seemed to be a burdensome weight that was dragged about, inhibiting the realization of some of Southampton's highest hopes.

Like the Spartans of old who lived in terror of the helot masses, Southampton whites seem apprehensive about the keys of the treasury of privilege and power. They were gradually coming to accept their black neighbors as partners but it would be a long time, perhaps, before the partners might see themselves as brothers. For the time being black and white still deal with one another, by mutual consent, largely in formal and exterior modes. There remain stark reminders of the old separation of slave from master, have from have-not.

Local whites who declined to serve as guardians of the shrine of racial and class privilege had ended as expatriates from the county and state. The names of David Barrow, George Henry Thomas, William Mahone—these might have served as models of inspiration and achievement for generations of the county's youth. The attainment by Anthony W. Gardner of the presidency of a foreign country might have been deemed a signal example of merit on the part of a native son. And then there was Nat Turner, greatest of slave rebels, who might have been recognized—ax-murderer though he was—for having resisted an unalloyed evil in the only way open to him. The great novel about Nat Turner's Revolt was from the pen of a Tidewater Virginian, but Styron's name seems anathema among those who might have taken the most pride in the author's success.

On the other hand counterexamples are not hard to find: the young black graduate student who was tracing the genealogy of his Stith ancestors, antebellum Southampton blacks; the appointment of William Engram in 1969 as the first black member of the County School Board;[28] the election in 1967 of S. O. Sykes to the county's Board of Supervisors. There are other promising signs that a new age is dawning when the yoke of race might be lifted from the county's shoulders. There appear to be reservoirs of good will and optimism on both sides, an unspoken consent to the proposition that tomorrow must be as much better than today as today is than yesterday. There remain, however, still two sides.

Appendix
Southampton County Historical Society
Notes
Index

Appendix

Members of the
Southhampton County Historical Society

November 1, 1977

*John D. Abbitt
Mrs. T. T. Andrews, Jr.
*John A. Bailey
*Daniel T. Balfour
Charles S. Barnes
Mrs. Charles S. Barnes
J. Irving Beale III
Mrs. J. Irving Beale III
Charles E. Beaton
Mrs. Charles E. Beaton
F. N. Boney
*Mrs. N. Stephenson Boykin
Mrs. Lemuel A. Branch
Dr. John Mills Britt, Jr.
S. S. Britt, Jr.
Mrs. Curtis T. Brooks, Jr.
*Mrs. M. Kenneth Brown
Mrs. Dorothy B. Bryant
*Mrs. J. Winston Camp
Mrs. S. V. Camp III
Mrs. William M. Camp
*E. Beale Carter
*Mrs. E. Beale Carter
*E. Beale Carter, Jr.
Mrs. E. Beale Carter, Jr.
Julian L. Carter
Mrs. Julian L. Carter
James F. Channing
Miss Robbie Claud
*Herbert G. Cobb, Jr.
Mrs. R. Gordon Cobb

Mrs. E. J. Cogsdale
Thomas N. Cogsdale
*Mrs. Thomas N. Cogsdale
William W. Cole
Mrs. H. G. Coleman
F. D. Cossitt
Mrs. J. Paul Councill
J. Paul Councill, Jr.
Mrs. Janice Crawford
Mrs. David E. Crockett
Mrs. Betty Gray Culverhouse
Ashley P. Cutchin
Mrs. Ashley P. Cutchin
*Frank Story Cutchin
Mrs. Frank Story Cutchin
*Mrs. Clifford A. Cutchins, Jr.
The Hon. Colgate W.
    Darden, Jr.
Mrs. Colgate W. Darden, Jr.
John T. Darden
Mrs. Lloyd A. Darden
Pretlow Darden
*Mrs. Richard N. Darden, Jr.
*Mrs. W. Frank Daughtrey, Jr.
Miss Alma Ruth Davis
Mrs. Beaman Davis
Mrs. George M. Davis, Jr.
Mrs. S. L. Doles
Mrs. L. L. Doughty
Mrs. George Thomas Drake
Mrs. L. F. Draper, Jr.

*Charter Member

Mrs. Joseph S. Drewry
Mrs. Samuel B. Drewry
*Mrs. E. Ennis Eanes
Arthur J. P. Edwards
Bruce M. Edwards
Mrs. Hoen M. Edwards
Hoen M. Edwards, Jr.
Mrs. Roy Edwards
Thomas R. Ellington
Mrs. Thomas R. Ellington
*Miss Winnie Frances Eubank
Mrs. Deaton F. Faucett
Mrs. W. Trent Fox
*Mrs. Elizabeth L. Francis
*Gilbert W. Francis
Mrs. Joseph L. Francis
Mrs. Kermit Francis
Mrs. Phyllis W. Francis
Milton T. Futrell
*Mrs. Milton T. Futrell
*Mrs. Archie R. Gardner
Mrs. Joe Bynum Gay, Jr.
*Miss E. Lucille Gillette
Mrs. Terry P. Gillette
Edward F. Gilliam
W. H. Goodwin
Mrs. W. H. Goodwin
*Mrs. E. E. Goodwin
Henry W. Gould
Mrs. Frank Graves
James A. Grizzard
*Mrs. Lois E. Hann
*Charles Baker Harding
*Mrs. Charles Baker Harding
Mrs. Essie Mae Harrell
Mrs. Julian D. Harrison
J. W. Harville

Mrs. J. W. Harville
Mrs. Mary Boothe Healey
James E. Henry
Mrs. James E. Henry
Mrs. L. Britt Holland
Stanley T. Holland
Mrs. Stanley T. Holland
Emmett W. Holt
Mrs. Emmett W. Holt
Mrs. Maxine R. Howard
Mrs. Romine C. Hundley
Joseph F. Inman
Stuart Jenkins
Mrs. Stuart Jenkins
*Louis P. Jervey
*Miss Elizabeth C. Johnson
*Miss Nelle M. Johnson
Mrs. Owen W. Johnson
W. Delbroe Johnson
Mrs. W. Delbroe Johnson
Mrs. William Tall Jones
Mrs. Betty D. Joyner
Ulysses P. Joyner
Mrs. Ulysses P. Joyner
Mrs. Silas S. Kea
Robert Francis Kello
T. B. Kingsbury III
Mrs. T. B. Kingsbury III
Miss Mabel R. Kitchen
*James T. Knight
Mrs. Roy A. Lassiter
S. Womack Lee
Mrs. S. Womack Lee
Mrs. Ruby J. Leigh
*Mrs. Edward T. Lemmon, Jr.
*Henry W. Lewis
Mrs. Katherine D. Lindsay

*Charter Member

Charles M. McDowell
Mrs. Charles M. McDowell
*Mrs. Lucius M. Manry
*Wilbur J. Manry
*Mrs. Wilbur J. Manry
Mrs. Robert F. Marks
Mrs. Betty McD. Mason
Robert L. Mason
Mrs. Maria Holland Matthews
Mrs. Jacqueline R. Meade
J. Edward Moyler
Mrs. J. Edward Moyler
*Miss Gladys Musgrave
*Thomas P. Musgrave
Dr. Jorge A. Naranjo
Mrs. Jorge A. Naranjo
Mrs. John J. Nunn
Mrs. G. Hinson Parker, Jr.
George H. Parker III
*John C. Parker
Mrs. John C. Parker
Thomas C. Parramore
Daniel K. Peak
G. E. Pillow
V. S. Pittman, Jr.
Mrs. V. S. Pittman, Jr.
E. J. Pope
Mrs. Harvey G. Pope
Sam E. Pope, Jr.
Mrs. Sam E. Pope, Jr.
Ralph L. Porter
Mrs. Ralph L. Porter
Charles Cutchin Powell
The Hon. Lewis F. Powell, Jr.
Mrs. R. H. Powell, Jr.
Mrs. Anne P. Prince
Kyle R. Purvis, Jr.
*Charter Member

Richard E. Railey
Mrs. Richard E. Railey
*Mrs. George W. Reese
William E. Richard, Jr.
Mrs. Churchill G. Ridley
Herschel B. Rochelle
Mrs. Herschel B. Rochelle
Hubert B. Rochelle
Mrs. William S. Rogers
*John W. Rollison, Jr.
*Charles B. Rowe
Mrs. Charles B. Rowe
Miss Virginia Lee Rowe
J. Rucker Ryland
Mrs. J. Rucker Ryland
*Mrs. Homer S. Saunders
Miss Martha L. Savage
*Mrs. B. M. Scott
*Miss Bessie Thomas Shands
*Miss Letitia C. Shands
*Mrs. Reine Musgrave Simmons
Mrs. W. M. Simmons
Bernard W. Smith
Mrs. Charles Lee Smith
Mrs. R. C. Smith, Jr.
W. Eldridge Smith
Mrs. W. Eldridge Smith
*Waring W. Smith, Jr.
Mrs. Willie W. Smith
Fred W. Stanton
Mrs. G. Carl Steinhardt
E. Maupin Stewart
Mrs. E. Maupin Stewart
*Mrs. Beaman Story
*Hatcher P. Story
Miss Louise F. Story
R. B. Story, Jr.

Mrs. R. B. Story, Jr.
Keith A. Strand
Mrs. Keith A. Strand
Mrs. J. R. W. Street
Mrs. J. W. B. Thompson
Miss Evelyn C. Thornton
*Mrs. L. L. Thorpe
Marvin D. Tower
Mrs. Marvin D. Tower
Col. Henry I. Tragle
Edward M. Trice
Mrs. Edward M. Trice
Mrs. James T. Turner, Jr.
*William A. Turner
Mrs. Linda T. Updike
*Mrs. Charles F. Urquhart, Jr.
Charles F. Urquhart III
Mrs. Charles F. Urquhart III
Miss Mildred Varner
*Charter Member

Roland Vaughan
Mrs. Roland Vaughan
Dean Wagenbach
H. Paige Watkinson
Mrs. H. Paige Watkinson
William L. Wellons
Garnett Lee White
Mrs. Charles A. Wieters
Mrs. A. Clifton Williams
*Mrs. A. G. Williams
Ben A. Williams, Jr.
Mrs. Ben A. Williams, Jr.
Miss Dorothy V. Williams
Gary M. Williams
*Mrs. William T. Woodley
Bobby B. Worrell
Mrs. Bobby B. Worrell
*Miss Elizabeth R. Wynns

Notes

Chapter 1: The Passing of the Nottoways

1. Lewis R. Binford, "An Ethnohistory of the Nottoway, Meherrin, and Weanock Indians of Southeastern Virginia," *Ethnohistory* 14 (Summer-Fall 1967): 125-33.
2. Lewis R. Binford, "Archaeological and Ethnohistorical Investigation of Cultural Diversity and Progressive Development among Aboriginal Cultures of Coastal Virginia and North Carolina" (Ph.D. diss., University of Michigan, 1964), pp. 6-66.
3. Binford, "Ethnohistory," p. 160.
4. Ibid., pp. 134-37.
5. Ibid., p. 133.
6. Ibid., pp. 152, 155.
7. Ibid., p. 147.
8. Ibid., pp. 147-48.
9. Ibid., p. 174.
10. Ibid., pp. 157-58.
11. Ibid., pp. 159-61.
12. Ibid., pp. 156-61, 179-81, 192-93. The Meherrins in 1756 numbered only 20 individuals. Their town at that time was located on Potecasi Creek, 15 miles west of their former town at the mouth of Meherrin River (F. Roy Johnson, *The Algonquians*, vol. 2: *History and Traditions* [Murfreesboro, N.C.: Johnson Publishing Co., 1973], p. 220.
13. Binford, "Ethnohistory," pp. 175-78.
14. Ibid., pp. 167-72.
15. Ibid., pp. 171, 178.
16. Ibid., pp. 172-74.
17. William K. Boyd, ed., *William Byrd's Histories of the Dividing Line betwixt Virginia and North Carolina* (Raleigh: North Carolina Historical Commission [State Department of Cultural Resources], 1929), pp. 112-16.
18. "Virginia Council Journals, 1726-1753," *Virginia Magazine of History and Biography* 33 (Jan. 1925): 20.
19. "An Act to enable the Nottoway Indians to sell Certain Lands therein mentioned: and for discharging the Indian Interpreters," William Waller Hening, ed., *The Statutes at Large: Being a Collection of All the Laws of Virginia, from the First Session of the Legislature in the Year 1619* (23 vols., Richmond, etc., 1809-23), 4: 459.
20. Binford, "Ethnohistory," p. 189.
21. Ibid.
22. "Diary of John Blair," *William and Mary Quarterly*, 1st ser., 8 (July 1892): 11.

23. "Proceedings of the Visitors of William and Mary College, 1716," *Virginia Magazine of History and Biography* 4 (Oct. 1895): 167.

24. Binford, "Ethnohistory," p. 190.

25. "Henry Blow, Wm. Blow, Sam'l. Blunt, Trustees N. Indians, to the Governor, Feb. 17, 1809," H. W. Flournoy, ed., *Calendar of Virginia State Papers and Other Manuscripts from January 1, 1808, to December 31, 1835: Preserved in the Capitol, at Richmond* (11 vols., Richmond: James E. Goode, 1875–93), 10: 46–47.

26. Ibid.; "Notes to Council Journals," *Virginia Magazine of History and Biography* 33 (July 1925): 299.

27. *Calendar of Virginia State Papers* 10: 46–47.

28. Petition no. 7228 (Nottoway Indians, Dec. 16, 1818), Legislative Petitions, Archives Division, Virginia State Library, Richmond (hereafter cited as VSL).

29. Petition of Nottoway Indians to Virginia Legislature, Dec. 10, 1821, ibid.

30. Petition no. 8054 (William G. Bozeman, Dec. 13, 1823), ibid.

31. Ibid.

32. *Acts Passed at a General Assembly of the Commonwealth of Virginia, Begun and Held at the Capitol, in the City of Richmond, on Monday, First Day of December, in the Year of Our Lord One Thousand Eight Hundred and Twenty-three, and of the Commonwealth the Forty-eighth* (Richmond: Thomas Ritchie, 1824), pp. 213–14; Petition no. 12075 (Nottoway Indians, Feb. 28, 1838), Legislative Petitions.

33. *Acts of the Commonwealth*, 1856, pp. 274–75.

34. Binford, "Archaeological and Ethnohistorical Investigation," p. 246.

35. "Petition of Henry Lawrence for grant of Patent . . .," *Calendar of Virginia State Papers* 1: 147; "Indians in Southampton County, Virginia," *Virginia Magazine of History and Biography* 36 (April 1928): 197–98.

36. "Indians in Southampton County Virginia," pp. 197–98.

37. Binford, "Archaeological and Ethnohistorical Investigation," p. 247.

38. Ibid., pp. 380, 386–87, 467.

39. Ibid. p. 463.

Chapter 2: The Borderland

1. "Boundary Line Proceedings, 1710," *Virginia Magazine of History and Biography* 5 (July 1897): 5–6.

2. Ibid., pp. 7, 9, 10.

3. Ibid., pp. 7–13.

4. Boyd, *William Byrd's Histories*, p. xxix.

5. William P. Cumming, *The Southeast in Early Maps* (Chapel Hill: University of North Carolina Press, 1962), pl. 32: "Nicholas Comberford. The South Part of Virginia Now the North Part of Carolina," pl. 39: "Joel Gascoyne. A Map of the County of Carolina, 1682," pl. 41: "William Hack. North Carolina. Ca. 1684 MS B," and pl. 47: "Guillaume Delisle. Carte de la Louisiane. 1718."

6. "The Indians of Southern Virginia, 1650–1711," *Virginia Magazine of History and Biography* 7 (July 1899): 347, 351, 8 (July 1900): 2, 3.

7. "Boundary Line Proceedings," pp. 41–42.

8. Cumming, *Southeast in Early Maps,* pp. 131–32.

9. Hugh T. Lefler and William S. Powell, *Colonial North Carolina, A History* (New York: Charles Scribner's Sons, 1973), pp. 25–26. This source mistakenly implies that Ocamahawan may be identified with Ohanoack, a Chowanoke Indian town on Chowan River. Cf. Cumming, pp. 131–32.

10. Lefler and Powell, *Colonial North Carolina,* p. 25; William S. Powell, *Ye Countie of Albemarle in Carolina* (Raleigh: State Department of Archives and History, 1958), p. xv.

11. Lefler and Powell, *Colonial North Carolina,* pp. 26–27.

12. Binford, "Ethnohistory," pp. 126–27. Binford gives the name as "Hocomawananck."

13. William H. Gaines, Jr., "Courthouses of Isle of Wight and Southampton Counties," *Virginia Cavalcade* 20 (Summer 1970): 5–6.

14. Ibid., pp. 6–7; Floyd McKnight, "Warrosquyoake Shire or Isle of Wight County, 1634–1657," in Roger Dey Whichard, *History of Lower Tidewater* (3 vols., New York: Lewis Historical Publishing Co., 1959), 2: 251; George Carrington Mason, "The Colonial Churches of Isle of Wight and Southampton Counties," *William and Mary Quarterly,* 2d ser., 23 (Jan. 1943): 42.

15. "Isle of Wight County Records," *William and Mary Quarterly,* 1st ser., 7 (April 1899): 291.

16. Richard L. Morton, *Colonial Virginia* (2 vols., Chapel Hill: University of North Carolina Press, 1960), p. 318; Floyd J. McKnight, "The County of Southampton, 1749–1957," in Whichard, *History of Lower Tidewater* 2: 286; Binford, "Ethnohistory," p. 168.

17. Binford, "Ethnohistory," p. 168; Morton, *Colonial Virginia,* p. 363.

18. David Leroy Corbitt, *Exploration, Description, and Attempted Settlement of Carolina, 1584–1590* (Raleigh: State Department of Archives and History, 1953), p. 40; John Crump Parker, "Old South Quay in Southampton County," *Virginia Magazine of History and Biography* 83 (April 1975): 161–62.

19. Bruce Cotten, *The Cotten Family of North Carolina* (Tucson, Ariz.: Hauck-Tucson, 1963), p. 9; Parker, "Old South Quay," p. 164; "Boundary Line Proceedings," p. 21; William L. Saunders, ed., *Colonial Records of North Carolina* (10 vols., Raleigh: State of North Carolina, 1886–90), 1: 760, 893. South Quay, originally part of Nansemond County, was in that part of Nansemond taken into Southampton in 1786. A Carolina woman absconding from her husband sought to use the South Quay route in 1697. See Mattie Erma E. Parker, ed., *The Colonial Records of North Carolina,* vol. 3: *North Carolina Higher Court Records, 1697–1701* (Raleigh: State Department of Archives and History, 1971), p. 127.

20. Saunders, *Colonial Records* 2: 22, 25, 26, 79; Cotten, *The Cotten Family,* p. 10.

21. Boyd, *William Byrd's Histories,* p. xxxii.

22. Ibid., p. xxxii.

23. William P. Palmer, ed., *Calendar of Virginia State Papers and Other Manuscripts, 1652–1781, Preserved in the Capitol at Richmond* (10 vols., Richmond: W. H. Wade, 1875–92), 1: 201, 203.

24. Boyd, *William Byrd's Histories,* pp. xxxii, 40–43.

25. Ibid., pp. 106–7. It is presumed that Braswell's, the only Virginia habitation within less than a quarter mile of the line in this region, was the place where Fitz-William and Lovick stopped for the day. See Alexander Irvine, "A Journal or Field Book of the Proceedings of the Surveyors Appointed for Determining the Bounds between the Colonies of Virginia and Carolina," in Saunders, *Colonial Records* 2: 807.

26. Irvine, "Field Book of the Proceedings," p. 807; Boyd, *William Byrd's Histories,* p. 94.

27. Irvine, "Field Book of the Proceedings," pp. 807–8; Boyd, *William Byrd's Histories,* p. 113.

28. Boyd, *William Byrd's Histories,* pp. 113, 123.

29. Mason, "Colonial Churches," pp. 59, 60, 112–13.

30. Undated clipping from *Tidewater News* (Franklin, Va.), in Edgar B. Jackson Papers, Southampton County Historical Society, Boykins, Va. Rose Hill, better known as the Kello Place, is believed to have been built around 1730. Boyd, *William Byrd's Histories,* p. 112.

31. McKnight, "County of Southampton," p. 286; Gaines, "Courthouses," p. 7.

32. Morgan Portiaux Robinson, "Virginia Counties: Those Resulting from Virginia Legislation," *Bulletin of the Virginia State Library,* no. 9 (July 1, 1916), pp. 206–7; McKnight, "Warrasquyoake Shire," p. 256.

33. Lyon Gardiner Tyler, ed., *Encyclopedia of Virginia Biography* (5 vols., New York: Lewis Historical Publishing Co., 1915), 1: 22.

34. Southampton County Order Book No. 1 (1749–1754), Clerk's Office, Courtland, Va.; see also *Tidewater News* (Franklin, Va.), Feb. 6, 1948. The latter source cites a manuscript by Fannie M. Pretlow which indicates that the house inherited from Richard Ricks by his wife Elizabeth Ricks stood between Bloomfield plantation and the present Courtland.

35. Gaines, "Courthouses," p. 8; McKnight, "County of Southampton," p. 287; Order Book No. 1, June 8, 1749.

36. Southampton County Court Minutes, July 13, 1749–Nov. 18, 1759, passim, Clerk's Office, Courtland, Va.

37. Ibid., Aug. 12, Nov. 5, Oct. 16, 1762, July 11, Jan. 13, 1764.

38. "A List of Tithables in the Dominion of Virginia, 1755," Southampton Historical Society, *Bulletin,* no. 3 (Winter 1967), p. 22; "Journal of James Auld, 1765–1770," *Publications of the Southern Historical Association* 8 (1904): 259.

39. Order Book No. 1, July 13, 1749.

40. Ibid. Other officers at this time were Joseph Gray, colonel; Jesse Brown, major; Howell Edmunds, Albridgton Jones, and Timothy Thorpe, captains; and James Jones and John Simmons, lieutenants.

41. Southampton County Judgments, Box B, 1749, Southampton County Court Records on deposit in VSL.

42. Order Book No. 1, July 13, 1749, May 9, 1751; Isle of Wight County Order Book for 1746–1756, entry for March 13, 1746, microfilm copy in VSL.

43. McKnight, "Warrasquyoake Shire," p. 257; Mason, "Colonial Churches," pp. 59–63.

44. Order Book No. 1, Nov. 9, 1749; Joseph Blount Cheshire, *Sketches of Church History in North Carolina* (Wilmington, N.C.: Wm. L. DeRosset, Jr., 1892), p. 37; William Wilson Manross, *The Fulham Palace Papers in the Lambeth Palace Library* (Oxford: Clarendon Press, 1965), pp. 80, 210, 308; Albert Ebenezer Gurley, "Some of the Genealogical Notes Collected by the Late A. E. Gurley," typescript by John Miller Bradley, Birmingham, Ala., 1951, p. 22, in my possession.

45. Cheshire, *Sketches of Church History,* pp. 83–84.

46. Mason, "Colonial Churches," p. 63; Mrs. David C. Anderson and others, eds., *History of Burleigh Church and Mill Swamp Baptist Church* (n. p., 1964), pp. 12–13.

47. *Virginia Gazette* (Purdie and Dixon), Jan. 3, 1771.

Chapter 3: The Tale of the Spanish Cannons

1. William N. Still, Jr., *North Carolina's Revolutionary War Navy* (Raleigh: North Carolina Department of Cultural Resources, 1976), p. 9; G. Melvin Herndon, "A War-Inspired Industry: The Manufacture of Hemp in Virginia during the Revolution," *Virginia Magazine of History and Biography* 74 (July 1966): 307.

2. Still, *Revolutionary War Navy,* p. 9; Walter Clark, ed., *The State Records of North Carolina* (16 vols. and 4-vol. index, Winston, Goldsboro, and Raleigh: State of North Carolina, 1895–1914), 19: 708–11.

3. Still, *Revolutionary War Navy,* p. 10.

4. Ibid., pp. 10, 12.

5. Ibid., pp. 7, 12, 28.

6. Ibid., pp. 7, 12, 21.

7. Ibid., pp. 10–11; Log of the *Conclusion,* English Records, HCA 32/279, item no. 73.2168.1, copy in Division of archives and History, Raleigh. The entry for July 14 says: "A twenty guns ship of [f] the Stocks."

8. Clark, *State Records of North Carolina* 19: 708.

9. "Proceedings of the Committees of Safety of Caroline and Southampton Counties, Virginia, 1774–1776," *Bulletin of the Virginia State Library* 17 (Nov. 1929): 141.

10. Ibid., pp. 142–43; *Virginia Gazette* (Dixon and Hunter), April 1, 1775.

11. "Proceedings of the Committees of Safety," pp. 143, 145.

12. Ibid., pp. 146–47, 149, 151.

13. Ibid., pp. 151–52; Methodist itinerant Francis Asbury, however, passed through Southampton in early November 1775 and was "stopped by one who had an order from the committee to examine strangers" (Elmer T. Clark, ed., *The Journal and Letters of Francis Asbury* [3 vols., Nashville: Abingdon Press, 1958], 1: 168).

14. "Proceedings of the Committees of Safety," p. 155. See, e.g., Revolutionary War Pension File of James Barham, Record Group No. 15A, National Archives, Washington, D.C. Barham, a Southampton native who died in Greene Co., Mo., in 1865, was one of the last surviving veterans of the Revolution.

15. "Proceedings of the Committees of Safety," pp. 153–54.

16. Johann David Schoepf, *Travels in the Confederation* (Philadelphia: William J. Campbell, 1911), p. 113.

17. Parker, "Old South Quay," pp. 165–66; Deposition of Wilson Roscow Bayley, Edenton District Court Records, Box 24, folder no. 1, Division of Archives and History, Raleigh. This deposition, dated April 1770, states that the *Dolphin* was built on the south bank of the Nansemond by Kedah and Webb. It was sold by Tembte and Fisher to Kinchen Taylor.

18. *Virginia Gazette* (Purdie and Dixon), Jan. 26, 1769.

19. Ibid., June 6, Oct. 10, Dec. 19, 1777.

20. *Conclusion* Log, Jan. 31, 1778.

21. Ibid., March 14, 1778.

22. Ibid., May 2, May 14, July 13, July 16, May 20, June 8, June 2, Aug. 1, April 22, May 8, and June 18, 1778.

23. Ibid., Oct. 14, Oct. 16, 1778.

24. Log of the *Esther,* English Records, HCA 32/279, item no. 75. 116.1, copy in Division of Archives and History, Raleigh.

25. "The Old Cannon in Edenton," *North Carolina Historical and Genealogical Register* 1 (1899): 595; Clark, *State Records of North Carolina* 19: 485.

26. "Old Cannon," p. 594; Thomas Newton to the Governor, Norfolk, June 2, 1797, in Palmer, *Calendar of Virginia State Papers* 8: 437; Clark, *State Records of North Carolina* 21: 1036; *The Observer* (Raleigh, N.C.), Oct. 6, 1877.

27. "Old Cannon," p. 595.

28. Col. William Davies to the Governor, War Office, March 29, March 31, 1781 (endorsed by Thomas Jefferson), Nov. 24, 1782, in Palmer, *Calendar of Virginia State Papers* 1: 604, 612, 3: 378.

29. Still, *Revolutionary War Navy,* pp. 17, 18, 11.

30. Ibid., pp. 24, 27, 28.

31. Parker, "Old South Quay," p. 169.

32. Clark, *State Records of North Carolina* 15: 571–72, 561.

33. Alice Barnwell Keith, ed., *The John Gray Blount Papers* (2 vols., Raleigh: Department of Archives and History, 1952), 1: 20.

34. Thomas C. Parramore, "The Saga of 'The Bear' and the 'Evil Genius,' " *Bulletin of the History of Medicine* 42 (July-Aug. 1968): 330; Randolph B. Campbell, "The Case of the *Three Friends:* An Incident in Maritime Regulation during the Revolutionary War," *Virginia Magazine of History and Biography* 74 (April 1966): 200–204.

35. "Nansemond County Legislative Petitions," *Virginia Genealogist* 6 (July-Sept. 1963): 105; Arthur G. Peterson, "Commerce of Virginia, 1789–1791," *William and Mary Quarterly,* 2d ser., 10 (Oct. 1930), 309; Parker, "Old South Quay," pp. 171–72.

36. William Meade, *Old Churches and Families of Virginia* (2 vols., Philadelphia: J. B. Lippincott & Co., 1857), 1: 308; Frederick Lewis Weis, *The Colonial Clergy of Virginia, North Carolina and South Carolina* (Boston: n.p., 1955), p. 8; Cheshire, *Sketches of Church History,* pp. 83–84; *Virginia Gazette* (Purdie and Dixon), Oct. 17, 1771; Manross, *The Fulham Papers,* p. 304; *Virginia Gazette* (Dixon and Hunter), May 15, 1779.

37. Hening, *Statutes at Large* 13: 173–74; Meade, *Old Churches and Families* 1: 308.

38. Hening, *Statutes at Large* 1: 203–4; McKnight, "Warrosquyoake Shire," p. 256; Thomas J. Wertenbaker, *Norfolk: Historic Southern Port* (Durham, N.C.: Duke University Press, 1962), p. 159. A canal company was formed in 1787 to dig a canal from Deep Creek, on the Southern Branch of Elizabeth River, to Pasquotank River. Digging began several years later, but no boats were able to use the canal until 1814.

39. "Petition to Establish a Town at Southampton Courthouse," Southampton County Historical Society, *Bulletin,* no. 2 (Winter 1971), p. 20; Hening, *Statutes at Large* 13: 297.

40. G. MacLaren Brydon, "A List of Clergy of the Protestant Episcopal Church Ordained after the American Revolution, Who Served in Virginia between 1785 and 1814, and a List of Virginia Parishes and Their Rectors for the Same Period," *William and Mary Quarterly,* 3d ser., 19 (Oct. 1939): 405–6. In 1793 Gurley moved to Murfreesboro and was active for several decades thereafter in the North Carolina church.

41. Henry W. Lewis, *Southampton Ridleys and Their Kin* (Chapel Hill, N.C.: privately printed, 1961), p. 25; Anderson, *History of Burleigh Church,* p. 13; "Hebron Baptist Church," p. 1, typescript in Edgar B. Jackson Papers, Southampton County Historical Society, Boykins, Va.

42. Clark, *Journal and Letters of Francis Asbury* 1: 574, 351.

43. John Ferdinand Dalziel Smyth, *A Tour in the United States of America* . . . (2 vols., Dublin: G. Perrin, 1784), 1: 50. Smyth, who traveled from Petersburg to Halifax, N.C., passing through Southampton County about the year 1763, commented that "this part of America is noted for its stock of extraordinary swift horses."

44. Henry W. Lewis, "Nineteenth Century Horses and Horsemen in Southampton County, Virginia," typescript, 1976, p. 2, copy in my possession.

45. Letters and Papers of Elkanah Watson, Journal B, 6: 358–59, New York State Library, Albany. For Watson's tenure in North Carolina, see Thomas C. Parramore, "A Year in Hertford County with Elkanah Watson," *North Carolina Historical Review* 41 (Oct. 1964): 448–63.

46. William Sidney Drewry, *The Southampton Insurrection* (Washington, D.C.: The Neale Co., 1900), p. 108.

Chapter 4: Incident at Black Creek

1. David Barrow, *Circular Letter, Southampton County, Virginia, February 14, 1798* (Norfolk: Willett & O'Connor, 1798), p. 4; Lorenzo Dow, *History of Cosmopolite; or, the Four Volumes of Lorenzo's Journal, Concentrated in One: Containing His Experiences and Travels, from Childhood to Near His Fortieth Year* (Philadelphia: Joseph Rakestraw, 1816), p. 196; Theophilus B. Gates, *The Life and Writings of Theophilus B. Gates* (Philadelphia: David Dickinson, 1818), pp. 133–34.

2. "From the Diary of John Early, Bishop of the Methodist Church, South" *Virginia Magazine of History and Biography,* 88 (July 1930): 251.

3. Drewry, *Southampton Insurrection,* p. 104; Southampton County Minute Book, 1811–1816, p. 142, microfilm copy in VSL; Robert Arnold, *The Dismal Swamp and Lake Drummond* (Norfolk: Evening Telegram, 1888; rept. Murfreesboro, N.C.: Johnson Publishing Co., 1969), p. 52.

4. *The Intelligencer* (Petersburg, Va.), May 11, 1804; *American Beacon* (Norfolk), Oct. 7, 1830; *American Turf Register and Sporting Magazine* 2 (Sept. 1830): 46.

5. Lewis, "Nineteenth Century Horses and Horsemen," pp. 4, 2.

6. *North Carolina Chronicle* (Murfreesboro, N.C.), April 21, 1827. The marriage was performed in Murfreesboro.

7. Barrow, *Circular Letter,* p. 11.

8. Ibid., p. 4.

9. Ibid., pp. 8, 13, 5.

10. *Edenton Gazette* (Edenton, N.C.), Dec. 9, 1830.

11. "Historical Sketch," p. 71, typescript in Edgar A. Jackson Papers, Southampton County Historical Society, Boykins, Va.

12. Petitions no. 6939 (Clements Rochelle, Dec. 3, 1817), no. 7214 (Clements Rochelle and Benjamin W. Johnson, Dec. 14, 1818), Legislative Petitions, VSL.

13. Virginius Cornick Hall, Jr., "Virginia Post Offices, 1798–1859," *Virginia Magazine of History and Biography* 81 (Jan. 1973): 77; Southampton County Minute Book, 1810–1824, deed of Tyler Edwards to John Marchant, p. 513, Southampton County Court Records, Clerk's Office, Courtland, Va.

14. Nelson M. Blake, *William Mahone of Virginia, Soldier and Political Insurgent* (Richmond: Garrett & Massie, 1935), passim; Diary of Dr. Thomas O'Dwyer, Jan. 27, 1825, Southern Historical Collection, Chapel Hill, N.C.

15. "Another Congressman Named Gray," typescript in Edgar B. Jackson Papers, Southampton County Historical Society, Boykins, Va. The account is based on the *Biographical Directory of the American Congress.*

16. See, e.g., Beth G. Crabtree, *North Carolina Governors, 1585–1968* (Raleigh: Department of Archives and History, 1968), pp. 59–60, 66–67, and Samuel A. Ashe and others, eds., *Biographical History of North Carolina* (8 vols., Greensboro, N.C.: Charles L. Van Noppen, 1906), 3: 412–14.

17. Douglas Summers Brown, *Historical and Biographical Sketches of Greensville County, Virginia, 1650–1967* (Richmond: Whittet and Shepperson, 1968), pp. 120–23.

18. Ibid., p. 126.

19. "First School Commissioners, 1818," typescript in Edgar B. Jackson Papers, Southampton Co. Hist. Soc.; "Report of the School Commissioners, 1831," dated Dec. 27, 1831, Judgments, Box 28 (L–W), Southampton County Court Records, VSL. Teachers listed for the year were, besides those mentioned in the text, Josiah Joyner, Nathan Walker, Joseph Pretlow, William Blow, Richard Barrett, William Stephens, Samuel Drake, George G. Gurley, Jere. Stephenson, James Harris, Miles Spivey, Thomas Harris, Samuel H. Holmes, Thomas J. Brister, Eliza Lightfoot, and Lewis W. Cobb.

20. *Tidewater News* (Franklin, Va.), Dec. 30, 1949. Denegre's letter was written from St. Paul, Minn., in 1895.

21. Journal of Elliott L. Story, vol. 1 (1838–1840), in possession of F. Story Cutchin, Franklin, Va.; see summary for year 1832 in opening pages of this volume, John Timothee Trezevant, *The Trezevant Family in the United States* (Columbia, S.C.: State Company, 1914), p. 25.

22. Story Journal, vol. 1, Dec. 14, 1838, vol. 3, Feb. 22, 1842.

23. Ibid., vol. 5, April 9, 1847.

24. Ibid., Vol. 3, March 16, 1843, vol. 5, Jan. 27, 1848.

25. Minutes, Virginia Portsmouth Association, for 1791, 1797, 1801, 1810, 1820, and 1831, Xerox copies in possession of Prof. Donald G. Mathews, University of North Carolina, Chapel Hill; Joshua Leigh, Meherrin Circuit Steward's Book (1839–1881), pp. 110–18, MS in possession of Southampton County Hist. Soc., Courtland, Va.; Durward T. Stokes and William T. Scott, *A History of the Christian Church in the South* (Burlington, N.C.: United Church of Christ, 1975), 51; "Hebron Baptist Church," pp. 5–6; *Tidewater News* (Franklin, Va.), April 29, 1926.

26. "The Church at Black Creek in Southampton County, Minute Book, 1783–1804," typescript in possession of Prof. Donald G. Mathews, University of North Carolina, Chapel Hill; Black Creek Church Minute Book (1818-1882), entry for Sept. 22, 1820, Virginia Baptist Historical Society, Richmond.

27. Black Creek Church Minute Book (1818-1882), entry for fourth Sunday in December, 1825.

28. Ibid., entry for fourth Sunday in December, 1827.

29. David Barrow, *Involuntary, Unmerited, Perpetual, Absolute, Heredity Slavery, Examined; on the Principles of Nature, Reason, Justice, Policy, and Scripture* (Lexington, Ky., 1808), pp. 43–44.

30. Ibid., p. 41.

31. Black Creek Church Minute Book (1818–1882), entry for fourth Sunday in September, 1831.

Chapter 5: Element of Surprise

1. Palmer, *Calendar of Virginia State Papers* 6: 452–53, 488–89, 524, 571–72; *North Carolina Journal* (Halifax, N.C.), Sept. 17, Oct. 30, Dec. 22, 1794.

2. Southampton County Minute Book, 1799–1803, entries for Oct. 25, Nov. 20, 1799, microfilm copy in VSL. Whether the executions actually took place is not certain. Following the convictions, a lengthy jurisdictional issue arose between authorities in Virginia and Maryland. Defendant Sam died in jail during this period. See H. W. Flournoy, ed., *Calendar of Virginia State Papers and Other Manuscripts from January 1, 1799 to December 31, 1807; Preserved in the Capitol at Richmond* (11 vols., Richmond: James E. Goode, 1890), 9: 51, 52.

3. Herbert Aptheker, *American Negro Slave Revolts* (New York: International Publishers, 1943), pp. 219–26.

4. Southampton County Court Judgments, Box A-2, 1797–1830, entry for Oct. 4, 1800, Southampton County Court Records, VSL.

5. *Columbian Centinel* (Boston), Dec. 8, 1801; *Virginia Argus* (Richmond), Jan. 15, 1802; James Monroe to Virginia Assembly, Jan. 16, 1802, Frank Carn to Monroe, Jan. 19, 1802, Thomas M. Bayley to Monroe, Jan. 19, 1802, Executive Papers, VSL; Monroe to John Harris, Jan. 23, 1802, Executive Letter Book, Oct. 5, 1800–Oct. 18, 1803, p. 247, microfilm copy in VSL.

6. James Gee to William Amis, Feb. 1802, William R. Davie to Gov. Benjamin Williams, Feb. 4, 1802, Governor's Letter Book, 14 (1799–1802): 64–68, Division of Archives and History, Raleigh.

7. "J.L." to "the Representative of the lower Company," enclosure in William R. Davie to Gov. Williams, Feb. 4, 1802, ibid.

8. William R. Davie to Gov. Williams, Feb. 1802, ibid.

9. Flournoy, *Calendar of State Papers* 9: 279–80.

10. *Pennsylvania Gazette* (Philadelphia), Feb. 22, 1802.

11. Minute Book, 1799–1803, entries for May 18, July 30, Aug. 10, 1802.

12. Court Orders, Halifax County, April 23, April 26, 1802, microfilm copy in VSL; *Norfolk and Portsmouth Herald* (Norfolk), May 19, 1802; Commonwealth v. Paul Thilman's Glasgow and Tom, May 5, 1802, Thomas Roane to James Monroe, April 12, 1802, John B. Scott to Monroe, April 30, 1802, Executive Papers; *The Intelligencer* (Petersburg, Va.), July 6, 1802.

13. John B. Scott to James Monroe, April 21, 1802, Richard Corbin to Monroe, April 23, 1802, Executive Papers.

14. Commonwealth v. William Farrer's Arthur, May 17, 1802, ibid.; Thomas C. Parramore, "The Great Slave Conspiracy," *The State* 39 (Aug. 15, 1971): 7–10, 19.

15. Those executed in Virginia included two in Nottoway, five in Halifax, two in Brunswick, and one in Norfolk. There were unconfirmed reports of others killed or executed in Orange and elsewhere. The North Carolina executions included eleven in Bertie, one in Hertford, two in Currituck, four in Camden, one in Perquimans, one in Halifax, and two in Martin. There were also reports of executions in Washington, Edgecomb, and elsewhere.

16. Flournoy, *Calendar of Virginia State Papers* 9: 307–8.

17. F. Nash Boney, "The Blue Lizard: Another View of Nat Turner's Country on the Eve of the Rebellion," *Phylon* 31 (Winter 1970): 353–55.

18. *North Carolina Free Press* (Halifax, N.C.), May 7, 1824; *Norfolk and Portsmouth Herald* (Norfolk), June 14, 1824; *The Minerva* (Halifax, N.C.), May 7, 1824.

19. Petition of Anthony (Dec. 20, 1826), Legislative Petitions, VSL.

20. *Eighth Annual Report of the American Society for Colonizing the Free People of Colour of the United States* (1825), p. 32. The chapter was formed in August 1824 by William McKenney.

21. Emigration Register (*Cyrus*, 1824), microfilm copy in Records of the American Colonization Society, ser. VI, vol. 15, Library of Congress, Washington, D.C. See also registers for the *Hunter* (1825) and *Valador* (1830).

22. *Sixty-second Annual Report of the American Colonization Society with the Minutes of the Annual Meeting and of the Board of Directors, January 21 and 22, 1879* (Washington, D.C., 1879), p. 11; *Sixty-ninth Annual Report of the American Colonization Society*, p. 6.

23. Charles Morrow Wilson, *The Dred Scott Decision* (Philadelphia: Auerback Publishers, 1973), pp. 3–4.

24. Peter Blow and wife Elizabeth to Robert Nicholson, Oct. 20, 1818, Southampton County Deed Book, 21: 154, Clerk's Office, Courtland, Va. This 860–acre tract was adjacent the head of Gum Branch and bounded by lands of Thomas Ridley, Mary Jarrell, Samuel Blunt, Edwin Reese, Nathaniel Simmons, and Benjamin Lewis.

25. Wilson, *Dred Scott Decision,* pp. 5–14.

26. Ibid., pp. 18–90; Bruce Catton, "Black Pawn on a Field of Peril," *American Heritage* 15 (Dec. 1963): 90.

27. *The Courier* (Charleston, S.C.), Aug. 16, 1831; Benjamin Hollowell, "The Solar Phenomenon," *Christian Advocate* 9 (Sept. 1831): 489–90.

28. Quoted in *Miners' and Farmers' Journal* (Charlotte, N.C.), Aug. 31, 1831.

29. *The Courier* (Charleston, S.C.), Aug. 16, 1831; quoted in *Miners' and Farmers' Journal* (Charlotte, N.C.), Aug. 31, Aug. 21, 1831.

30. *The Courier* (Charleston, S.C.), Aug. 16, 1831.

31. Quoted in *Scioto Gazette* (Chillicothe, Ohio), Sept. 7, 1831.

32. *Star, and North Carolina Gazette* (Raleigh, N.C.), Aug. 18, 1831.

33. Ibid.; *Scioto Gazette* (Chillicothe, Ohio), Sept. 7, 1831.

34. Thomas R. Gray, "The Confessions of Nat Turner . . .," in Henry Irving Tragle, *The Southampton Slave Revolt* (Amherst: University of Massachusetts Press, 1971), p. 310.

35. Ibid., p. 306; see n. 4 above. Nat refers in his confession to his grandmother and his first owner, Benjamin Turner, as key religious influences in his early life, besides "other religious persons who visited the house, and whom I often saw at prayers."

36. *Richmond Enquirer,* Sept. 30, 1831. According to this source, Nat's baptism had occurred "more than four years ago." Gray, "Confessions of Nat Turner," p. 310.

37. Gray, "Confessions of Nat Turner," p. 310.

38. Drewry, *The Southampton Insurrection,* frontispiece map.

39. Southampton County Marriage Register, 2: 402, Southampton County Court Records, Clerk's Office, Courtland, Va. The marriage bond is dated Oct. 5, 1829. See also F. Roy Johnson, *The Nat Turner Story* (Murfreesboro, N.C.: Johnson Publishing Co., 1970), p. 67.

40. Johnson, *Nat Turner Story,* pp. 67, 54, 45; Southampton County Will Book, 9:254, Southampton County Court Records, Clerk's Office, Courtland, Va.

41. *Religious Herald* (Richmond), Sept. 2, 1831. This is a letter from Jerusalem, dated Aug. 27, 1831. "It is an aggravation of the crime perpetrated," says the writer, "that the owners of slaves in the county are distinguished for lenity and humanity. Cotton and corn are the staples here, and the labor of attending them is trifling compared with what is necessary in other parts of the state."

42. *Constitutional Whig* (Richmond), Sept. 26, 1831; Gray, "Confessions of Nat Turner," p. 308.

43. Samuel Warner, "Authentic and Impartial Narrative of the Tragical Scene . . .," in Tragle, *Southampton Slave Revolt,* p. 296. Warner's authorities included newspaper sources and at least one correspondent from the afflicted area. His source for stating that Nat's wife belonged to "Mr. Reese" is not cited. This woman

has been tentatively identified by F. Roy Johnson, *Nat Turner Story,* p. 54, as Cherry, who belonged first to Samuel Turner's estate and afterward to that of Giles Reese. On this question, see Southampton County Accounts, 1819–1831 (I-O), Box 41, Southampton County Court Records, VSL. A document pertaining to the estate of Thomas Moore cites money owing to the estate for the purchase of slaves Hark, Sam, "girl Charry," and "Mariah and child." The present writer supposes that Mariah and child are as readily identifiable as Nat's wife (and child) as Cherry, and perhaps more so since Cherry was still a girl in 1830. Hark, in this list, is evidently Hark Travis, while Sam may be identical with Sam Francis.

44. Gray, "Confessions of Nat Turner," p. 310; Johnson, *Nat Turner Story,* p. 67.

45. Gray, "Confessions of Nat Turner," p. 310.

46. *American Beacon* (Norfolk), July 19, 1831. A sizable gathering of celebrants congregated at Buckhorn Chapel in Hertford County. They included S. Jordan Wheeler, Solon Borland, and others who would assist in quelling the revolt seven weeks later. Presumably there were similar gatherings throughout the area.

47. Gray, "Confessions of Nat Turner," p. 310.

48. Drewry, *Southampton Insurrection,* p. 75; *The Globe* (Washington, D.C.), Aug. 27, 1831.

49. Johnson, *Nat Turner Story,* p. 85.

50. Gray, "Confessions of Nat Turner," p. 310. It was Nat's habit to hold himself somewhat apart from fellow slaves in order to enhance his impression of a special mission in life.

51. *Richmond Enquirer,* Nov. 8, 1831; "Verbatim Record of the Trials," in Tragle, *Southampton Slave Revolt,* p. 195.

52. Gray, "Confessions of Nat Turner," p. 311; "Record of Trials," pp. 220, 196. Moses Travis testified that Jack came to the Travis house Sunday night complaining of illness, "was in the kitchen when the witness went to sleep—and when the witness awoke a few hours after the prisoner was in the yard sick."

53. Johnson, *Nat Turner Story,* p. 90.

54. *Christian Advocate and Journal and Zion's Herald* (New York), Sept. 9, 1831. Rev. Mr. Powell stated that his own "niece and nephew" were the first two families attacked. He evidently was referring to Mrs. Joseph Travis and her brother, Salathiel Francis. Drewry, *Southampton Insurrection,* pp. 42–43.

55. David Walker, *Walker's Appeal, in Four Articles; . . . Written in Boston, State of Massachusetts, Sept. 28, 1829* (Boston, 1830).

56. *The Liberator* (Boston), Jan. 15, 1831.

Chapter 6: The Southampton Rebellion

1. Gray, "Confessions of Nat Turner," p. 311.

2. Ibid. See also *Constitutional Whig* (Richmond), Sept. 26, 1831, which says that "one blow seems to have sufficed for the two little boys, who were sleeping so close, one blow nearly severed each neck."

3. Gray, "Confessions of Nat Turner," p. 311. Nat told Gray that they found four guns that would shoot, besides "several old muskets, with a pound or two of powder."

4. "Record of Trials," p. 220. Moses testified that he was "compelled to go with the insurgents." A further military gesture was the apparent designation of titles of rank for leaders of the company. Nat is said to have used the names "Gen. Jackson" (*Raleigh Register and North-Carolina Gazette*, Sept. 18, 1831) or "Gen. Cargill" (*Richmond Compiler*, Sept. 3, 1831). Hark Travis became "Capt. Moore," adopting the surname of his former master (*Richmond Enquirer*, Aug. 30, 1831), while Henry Porter (the "paymaster" of the rebels) and Nelson Edwards became, respectively, "Gen. Porter" and "Gen. Nelson" (*American Beacon* [Norfolk], Aug. 29, 1831). Evidence showed that Davy Waller was known to fellow rebels as "brother Clements" ("Record of Trials," p. 194). "Their banner was a red-cross in a white field," wrote one source. "Some of the wretches wore red caps, and others had their hats ornamented with red bands of various materials" (*Constitutional Whig* [Richmond], Sept. 8, 1831).

5. Gray, "Confessions of Nat Turner," p. 311. Francis is cited as brother-in-law of Mrs. Travis by Drewry, *Southampton Insurrection*, p. 38.

6. Gray, "Confessions of Nat Turner," p. 311. Drewry, *Southampton Insurrection*, p. 38, alleges that the letter was supposed to be from Nathaniel Francis.

7. Federal Census, 1830, Southampton County, p. 260, microfilm copy at Division of Archives and History, Raleigh. Postmaster Theodore Trezevant reported on Sept. 5 that the rebels "recruited their force at Francis's" (letter in *Raleigh Register*, Sept. 4, 1831).

8. Petition no. 9915–D (Piety Reese, Dec. 29, 1831), Legislative Petitions, VSL.

9. Court Notes in trial of Moses Barrow, Southampton County Judgments, Box 28, 1820–1841, Southampton County Court Records, VSL (hereafter cited as Court Notes). These rough notes represent the summaries of statements made to officers of the court by both witnesses and participants in the rebellion. Some were entered verbatim into the court minute book, some in slightly altered form, and some were not entered. In this instance the statement asserts that "Mrs. Newsome . . . was sister of [Hark's] master." See also Southampton County Minute Book, 1830–1835, p. 121, Clerk's Office, Courtland, Va., for reference to Mrs. Newsome (or Newsom) as widow of James B. Newsom(e).

10. Gray, "Confessions of Nat Turner," p. 311.

11. "Record of Trials," p. 185. Moses Travis testified that Davy was at Mrs. Turner's when the rebels arrived there and that Davy was told "that if he did not join them he would die there." See Court Notes for allegation against Jack and Shadrack, slaves of Elizabeth Turner, that on Aug. 30 they gave aid to Sam Turner and received from him a gold watch and "a large sum of money" which he had "received by robbery during the insurrection" and tried to use to insure his "own escape and safety." See Petition no. 9915–E (distributees of Elizabeth Turner, Dec. 29, 1831), Legislative Petitions, for reference to Jordan Turner having "united himself with the Insurgents."

12. Gray, "Confessions of Nat Turner," p. 312; *Richmond Enquirer,* Aug. 30, 1831; *Norfolk and Portsmouth Herald* (Norfolk), Aug. 26, 1831. For identification of Bryant's wife's name as Sally, see Minute Book, 1830–1835, p. 113.

13. "Record of Trials," p. 207. Nat was initially listed as a slave of Edwin Turner's estate, but the entry was corrected in Minute Book, 1830–1835, p. 153.

14. *Norfolk and Portsmouth Herald* (Norfolk), Aug. 26, 1831. For identification of Mrs. Williams's name as Louisa, see Minute Book, 1830–1835, p. 104.

15. Drewry, *Southampton Insurrection,* p. 45. Drewry's account, though based on oral tradition, would explain Francis's absence from home.

16. "Record of Trials," pp. 196–97. Jack was at first identified as belonging to William Reese, but the error was corrected to read Joseph William Reese in Minute Book, 1830–1835, p. 127.

17. Court Notes, concerning trials of Jack and Andrew Whitehead. This document summarizes Tom Whitehead's account of his own flight from and return to the farm.

18. Ibid., concerning trial of Thomas Haithcock. A white witness mentioned visiting Haithcock's house on Aug. 26 and finding two blankets which were identified by Mrs. Haithcock as having been left there by Andrew and Jack, who "rode on them the Monday morning after the insurrection." See also "Record of Trials," p. 182.

19. "Record of Trials," pp. 180, 181, 277.

20. Gray, "Confessions of Nat turner," p. 313. Decapitations and other forms of brutality were widely reported from the scenes of slaughter. In addition, O. M. Smith, writing from Sussex County, a few miles from the scene of disturbance, to the *New Hampshire Post* (Haverhill), Sept. 14, 1831, reported that "in the course of the murders, one negro singled out a father, & requested of the others the privilege of killing him in his own way. He took him and then threw him down, put his knee upon his breast, and stuck him like a pig. The negro after being taken was stuck in the same way."

21. Gray, "Confessions of Nat Turner," p. 312; "Record of Trials," p. 207. Doyel's name is often rendered Doyle, but see his signature in Petition no. 8402, Legislative Petitions.

22. Petition no. 9803 (Richard Porter, Dec. 12, 1831), Legislative Petitions. Porter states that Jacob was aged 22 and Moses 19. See also "Record of Trials," pp. 177–79, for trial of Daniel.

23. Southampton County Minute Book, 1824–1830 (Sept. 21, 1829), Clerk's Office, Courtland, Va., contains a record of Nathaniel Francis's appointment as guardian to Samuel and John L. Brown. See also Drewry, *Southampton Insurrection,* p. 47, for the purported ages of the boys. They were orphans of Thomas D. Brown.

24. Drewry, *Southampton Insurrection,* p. 47. Contemporary lists of victims agree in including Francis's overseer, but I know none that gives the man's name.

25. Gray, "Confessions of Nat Turner," p. 318; "Record of Trials," pp. 200–201. The three were said to be "not more than 15" years old.

26. "Record of Trials," pp. 198–99.

27. Gray, "Confessions of Nat Turner," pp. 312–13; Petition no. 9804-A (Peter Edwards, Dec. 12, 1831), Legislative Petitions. Edwards gives Austin's age as 19, Jim's as 22. For the role of Sam Edwards, see "Record of Trials," pp. 217–19.

28. *Carolina Observer* (Fayetteville, N.C.), Sept. 17, 1831.

29. Samuel Warner, "An Authentic and Impartial Narrative of the Tragical Scene . . .," in Tragle, *Southampton Slave Revolt,* pp. 283–84. This account was published in New York in 1831.

30. "Record of Trials," p. 208; *Constitutional Whig* (Richmond), Sept. 26, 1831.

31. *Constitutional Whig* (Richmond), Aug. 29, 1831; Drewry, *Southampton Insurrection,* pp. 51–52.

32. Gray, "Confessions of Nat Turner," p. 313.

33. Ibid.

34. "Record of Trials," p. 221. Waller testified that it was "between 9 and 10 o'clock" when he "heard that the negroes had risen."

35. Court Notes, statement by Levi Waller.

36. Ibid., in case of Daniel Porter. Waller's testimony was that Daniel "came out of the house with the Scissors of his wife."

37. "Record of Trials," pp. 194, 232; Waller, witness in Davy's trial, asserted that Davy was called "brother Clements" by the other rebels. Petition no. 9804-A (Peter Edwards, Dec. 12, 1831), Legislative Petitions; see Waller's affirmation accompanying this petition; *New Hampshire Post* (Haverhill), Sept. 14, 1831.

38. "Record of Trials," p. 178. In Daniel Porter's trial, Waller testified that he returned to the house and "found his wife and the small girl murdered as well as many other members of his family and an infant child mortally wounded who died Wednesday evening following." The *Constitutional Whig* (Richmond), on Aug. 29, reported that a child at Waller's had been "cruelly wounded and left for dead, and probably will not survive." It does not appear that Waller sought aid for the child.

39. *Constitutional Whig* (Richmond), Aug. 26, 1831; John Hill Wheeler, *Historical Sketches of North Carolina, from 1584 to 1851* (Philadelphia: Lippincott, Granbo and Co., 1851), p. 210. Wheeler, a Murfreesboro attorney in 1831, stated: "Well does the writer recollect Levi Waller running into town, and describing with painful effort that his wife and ten children (one at the breast) were murdered."

40. Gray, "Confessions of Nat Turner," p. 313; Drewry, *Southampton Insurrection,* p. 59.

41. "Record of Trials," pp. 193–94.

42. Ibid., p. 194. Nelson Williams, executed for his role in the revolt, has been incorrectly identified by historians with Nelson Edwards, one of Nat's original conspirators. An examination of the trial record of Nelson Williams indicates the strong likelihood that he had nothing to do with the rebellion before the rebels reached his master's farm. See also Petition no. 9804-A (Peter Edwards, Dec. 12, 1831), Legislative Petitions, where Nelson Edwards is described in terms more nearly compatible with the original conspirator.

43. *The Liberator* (Boston), Sept. 17, 1831; *Constitutional Whig* (Richmond), Sept. 3, Aug. 29, 1831. Miss Vaughan may have been the "young lady of 17 years of age, who . . . was to have been the day following united in marriage to a young gentle-

man of North Carolina, and who left home on the fatal night preceding with the pleasing expectation of conveying there the succeeding day," mentioned by Warner, "Authentic Narrative," p. 287.

44. *The Liberator* (Boston), Sept. 17, 1831; *Constitutional Whig* (Richmond), Sept. 3, 1831; "Record of Trials," p. 183.

45. *National Gazette* (Philadelphia), Aug. 29, 1831; Drewry, *Southampton Insurrection*, p. 65; *Richmond Compiler*, Sept. 3, 1831.

46. Drewry, *Southampton Insurrection*, p. 65.

47. *The Observer* (Raleigh, N.C.), Nov. 3, 1877. This account was related by one "N." of Sanford, N.C., who said that he had it many years before from "Dr. C." The writer thought that he recalled French as a law student at Fayetteville, N.C., in 1830. "Dr. C." is identified as "probably . . . Dr. William C. Caruthers, 1802–1846," in the *Tidewater News* (Franklin, Va.), "Golden Anniversary Historical Edition," 1955.

48. *North Carolina Free Press* (Tarboro), Sept. 13, 1831. Pope was initially reported to have been killed. The *Richmond Compiler*, Sept. 3, 1831, states that one of the patrol at Parker's field was "knocked from his horse" and "about to be dispatched by the banditti" when the second party of whites rode up to prevent it.

49. Gray, "Confessions of Nat Turner," p. 314.

50. Ibid., p. 315.

51. Ibid., pp. 314–15. Nat mentions visiting Thomas's and Spencer's after the Parker's field fight. Jacob Williams, testifying against his slave Nelson, noted that the rebels also came to his farm a second time, on Monday evening ("Record of Trials," p. 193).

52. "Record of Trials," pp. 186–88. Curtis and Stephen were apprehended by John C. Turner between 8 and 9 A.M. on Tuesday and handed over to authorities at Cross Keys.

53. Gray, "Confessions of Nat Turner," p. 315.

54. "Record of Trials," p. 182; *Connstitutional Whig* (Richmond), Sept. 3, 1831. The rebels at this time were said to number "from 15 to 20." See also Petition no. 9915-F (legatees of Thos. Fitzhugh, Dec. 29, 1831), Legislative Petitions, for the role of Fitzhugh's Negroes at Blunt's.

55. "Record of Trials," pp. 182–83; *Constitutional Whig* (Richmond), Sept. 3, 1831.

56. Gray, "Confessions of Nat Turner," p. 315.

57. Register of Free Negroes, entry no. 1589 (Aug. 26, 1826), Southampton County Court Records, VSL. Artis is described as aged 29, "rather light complexion, 6 feet 1 Inch High," and with various scars. He was freeborn.

58. "Record of Trials," pp. 203–4, 227.

59. Petition no. 9915-F (legatees of Thos. Fitzhugh), Dec. 29, 1831, Legislative Petitions.

60. Ibid.

61. The time of the arrival of the first alarm in Murfreesboro is uncertain. A report from there states that it "was late in the day" before news could be transmitted from there to those white men of the community who had left that morning

for court at Winton, 12 miles south (*Norfolk and Portsmouth Herald* [Norfolk], Aug. 29, 1831).

62. *Roanoke Advocate* (Halifax, N.C.), Sept. 8, 1831; *Richmond Compiler,* Aug. 24, 1831.

63. Dr. Thomas Borland to Gov. Montford Stokes, Murfreesboro, Sept. 18, 1831, Governor's Letter Book, 30 (June 1–Oct. 1, 1831), Division of Archives and History, Raleigh.

64. *Richmond Enquirer,* Aug. 30, 1831. A thousand women were reported to have found refuge at Halifax and as many more at Murfreesboro (Robert S. Parker to Mrs. Rebecca Maney, Enfield, N.C., Aug. 29, 1831, John Kimberly Papers, Southern Historical Collection, Chapel Hill, N.C.).

65. *Norfolk and Portsmouth Herald* (Norfolk), Sept. 3, 1831; Borland to Gov. Stokes, Sept. 18, 1831, Governor's Letter Book, 30 (June 1–Oct. 1, 1831); Wheeler, *Historical Sketches,* p. 210.

66. "Carlton" [Col. D. H. Hardee], in *Patron and Gleaner* (Lasker, N.C.), Aug. 29, 1895. The identification of "Carlton" as Hardee is based on Drewry, *Southampton Insurrection,* p. 80, who quotes from the same letter.

67. *Roanoke Advocate* (Halifax, N.C.), Sept. 1, 1831; *Petersburg Intelligencer,* Aug. 26, 1831; *Richmond Compiler,* Aug. 24, 1831; "Governor Floyd's Diary and Correspondence," in Tragle, *Southampton Slave Revolt,* p. 252.

68. Tragle, *Southampton Slave Revolt,* pp. 16–21; Herbert Aptheker, *Nat Turner's Slave Rebellion* (New York: Grove Press, 1966), p. 50; *Roanoke Advocate* (Halifax, N.C.), Sept. 8, 1831.

69. Petition no. 10110-A (Richard Darden, Dec. 10, 1831), Legislative Petitions.

70. *New Hampshire Post* (Haverhill), Sept. 14, 1831.

71. *The Globe* (Washington, D.C.), Sept. 9, 1831; *Roanoke Advocate* (Halifax, N.C.), Sept. 9, 1831.

72. Thomas J. Harper, Littlebury Mason, and [G. D. Cummings?] to Gov. Montford Stokes, Cross Keys, Va., Aug. 25, 1831, Governor's Letter Book, 30 (June 1–Oct. 1, 1831).

73. Petition no. 9803 (Richard Porter, Dec. 1, 1831), Legislative Petitions; *North Carolina Free Press* (Tarboro), Sept. 6, 1831.

74. *Roanoke Advocate* (Halifax, N.C.), Oct. 13, 1831; *Niles' Weekly Register* (Baltimore), Sept. 3, 1831; *New Hampshire Post* (Haverhill), Sept. 14, 1831.

75. *Roanoke Advocate* (Halifax, N.C.), Oct. 13, 1831; "Petition of Levi Waller for Reimbursement for Loss of a Negro," in Tragle, *Southampton Slave Revolt,* pp. 462–64. Drewry, *Southampton Insurrection,* p. 64, credits the act of hamstringing to Samson C. Reese: *New Hampshire Post* (Haverhill), Sept. 14, 1831.

76. *North Carolina Free Press* (Tarboro), Sept. 8, 1831; Petition no. 9804-A (Peter Edwards, Dec. 8, 1831), Legislative Petitions; *American Beacon* (Norfolk), Aug. 29, 1831.

77. Petition no. 7804-A (Peter Edwards, Dec. 8, 1831), Legislative Petitions.

78. "Record of Trials," pp. 218, 194; *Constitutional Whig* (Richmond), Sept. 3, 1831; *Richmond Compiler,* Sept. 3, 1831; *American Beacon* (Norfolk), Sept. 9, 1831.

79. *Constitutional Whig* (Richmond), Aug. 29, 1831.

80. *Petersburg Intelligencer,* Aug. 26, 1831; Harper, Mason, and [Cummings?] to Gov. Stokes, Aug. 29, 1831, Governor's Letter Book, 30 (June 1–Oct. 31, 1831).

81. *Richmond Compiler,* Aug. 27, 1831; *American Beacon* (Norfolk), Aug. 29, 1831; *Lynchburg Virginian,* Sept. 8, 1831; *Raleigh Register,* Sept. 5, 1831; *Constitutional Whig* (Richmond), Sept. 3, 1831.

82. *Christian Advocate and Zion's Herald* (New York.), Sept. 9, 1831; R. S. Parker to Mrs. Maney, Aug. 29, 1831, John Kimberly Papers, Southern Hist. Collection; *The Globe* (Washington, D.C.), Sept. 9, 1831; *North Carolina Free Press* (Tarboro), Aug. 30, 1831.

83. Borland to Gov. Stokes, Sept. 18, 1831, Governor's Letter Book, 30 (1830–31); R. S. Parker to Mrs. Maney, Aug. 29, 1831, John Kimberly Papers, Southern Hist. Collection.

84. *American Slavery As It Is: Testimony of a Thousand Witnesses* (New York: American Anti-slavery Society, 1839), p. 91.

85. *Constitutional Whig* (Richmond), Aug. 29, 1831.

86. See n. 38 above.

87. Gray, "Confessions of Nat Turner," p. 318; Drewry, *Southampton Insurrection,* pp. 43–44.

88. The only source to mention any other casualty at Piety Reese's besides herself and son William is the *Religious Herald* (Richmond), Sept. 2, 1831, which lists the name "Barham" there. Drewry, *Southampton Insurrection,* p. 40, tells of one James Barmer (or Balmer?), overseer for Mrs. Reese, who was attacked and left for dead by the rebels, but later recovered. Barham and Barmer may be the same.

89. *American Beacon* (Norfolk), Aug. 30, 1831. The list of victims here includes the Felts girls, who may have been among the pupils killed at Levi Waller's. This list in the *Religious Herald* (Richmond), Sept. 2, 1831, includes Mrs. Doyel and Jacob Williams.

90. *Norfolk and Portsmouth Herald* (Norfolk), Aug. 31, 1831.

91. See n. 43, chap. 5, above.

92. *Constitutional Whig* (Richmond), Sept. 26, 1831; *Richmond Enquirer,* Sept. 2, 1831.

93. *New Hampshire Post* (Haverhill), Sept. 14, 1831.

Chapter 7: Requiem for a God-fearing Man

1. Will of Thomas Gray, Sept. 6, 1831 (probated Sept. 18, 1831), Southampton County Will Book, 10: 343, Clerk's Office, Courtland, Va. The estate was left in equal shares to Gray's son Edwin, daughter Ann, and granddaughter Ellen Douglas Gray, daughter of Thomas Ruffin Gray. The testator willed that if any of these three should die intestate and without issue, the "Survivors of these three shall inherit the rights and emoluments of the other." In regard to slaves left to Thomas Gray's children, by Joseph Ruffin, should any claim be made on their account, "or on any account of any nature or kind whatsoever, . . . in that case I give and bequeath to such one Either or All to each the sum of one dollar, as . . . his, her or their full portion." With reference to a joint security with Thomas R. Gray

to Louis W. Kaifer of Portsmouth, the testator relinquished claim against his son and made the estate liable for full payment of the debt.

2. See Southampton County Minute Book, 1824–1830, microfilm copy in VSL. Gray is here allowed $10 each for defending Davy Turner, Sam Francis, and Jack Reese. No reference is made to payment for other cases, but it may be supposed that he also received similar compensation for defending Moses Travis and for assisting in the defense of Nathan, Tom, and Davy Francis, who were tried together.

3. Stephen B. Oates, *The Fires of Jubilee: Nat Turner's Fierce Rebellion* (New York: Harper & Row, 1975), p. 124.

4. "Record of Trials," pp. 177–97.

5. Ibid., pp. 197–221. Of the Negroes on trial, evidence indicates that the following joined in the rebellion as members of Nat's raiding party: Hark Travis, Sam Francis, Jack Reese, Moses Moore, Davy Turner, Joe Turner, Daniel Porter, Moses Barrow, Nathan Blunt, Davy Waller, Nelson Williams, James and Elizabeth Turner's Nat, Dred Francis, and Sam Edwards. Other evidence adduced in chap. 6 above indicates the participation in the same party of Henry Porter; Nelson Edwards; Will Francis; Austin Travis; Jordan Turner; Jacob, Moses, and Aaron Porter; Nathan, Tom, and Davy Francis; Austin and Jim Edwards; Alfred Waller; one of the Whitehead slaves; and slaves named Tom and Marmaduke. In addition, Stephen and Curtis Ridley went on a recruiting mission for Nat, and Lucy Barrow tried to give assistance to the rebels. Finally, William Artis, Ben Blunt, Cherry Artis, and Tom Haithcock were accused of forming a separate rebel party. These names appear to leave some 20 rebels unidentified. For identification of Moses as a slave of Putnam Moore rather than Joseph Travis, see Southampton County Minute Book, 1830–1835, p. 142, Clerk's Office, Courtland, Va.

6. The fate of Thomas R. Gray's wife is speculative, based on absence of reference to her in Thomas Gray's will and on the guardianship appointed for Ellen Douglas Gray in 1832 (see n. 61 below). I have found no reference to Gray's wife in records so far consulted. As the child was an infant in 1832, her mother must have died not long previous to that time.

7. Southampton County Land Tax, 1829, 1830–31, 1832, and Southampton County Personal Property Tax, 1829, 1827–31, and 1832, VSL.

8. Minute Book, 1824–30, entry for Oct. 18, 1830, certification that Gray "wishes to obtain a license to practice as an Attorney in the courts of the Commonwealth." See also entry for Dec. 20, 1830: "Thomas R. Gray qualified atto: at Law in this court."

9. *Norfolk and Portsmouth Herald* (Norfolk), Nov. 4, 1831; *The Liberator* (Boston), Nov. 19, 1831; Henry Irving Tragle, "Styron and His Sources," *Massachusetts Review* 11 (Winter 1970): 143.

10. *Virginia Herald* (Fredericksburg), Sept. 7, 1831; *Norfolk and Portsmouth Herald* (Norfolk), Sept. 28, 1831; Gray, "Confessions of Nat Turner," p. 315.

11. Gray, "Confessions of Nat Turner," p. 315. This hiding place was said to be on the Travis farm (*National Intelligencer* [Washington, D.C.], Nov. 2, 1831).

12. Gray, "Confessions of Nat Turner," pp. 315–16.

13. *Constitutional Whig* (Richmond), Nov. 7, 1831.

14. *The Liberator* (Boston), Nov. 5, 1831. This source carries a letter dated from Petersburg, Va., on Oct. 31 and stating that a slave named Nelson brought to Jerusalem on Oct. 15 information that he had seen Nat "in the woods" that day, was hailed by Nat, but, noting that the fugitive was armed, ran away. The stick with forty-one notches was reported in the *Constitutional Whig* (Richmond), Nov. 7, 1831. If the assumption is correct that this was Nat's mode of keeping track of time spent in this hideout, he must have been there from Sept. 5 to Oct. 15 and some other place between Aug. 25 and Sept. 5.

15. *Constitutional Whig* (Richmond), Nov. 7, 1831; *Richmond Enquirer,* Nov. 15, 1831. The site is identified as being on the Francis farm by the *National Intelligencer* (Washington, D.C.), Nov. 9, 1831.

16. *Star, and North Carolina Gazette* (Raleigh), Nov. 10, 1831.

17. *Norfolk and Portsmouth Herald* (Norfolk), Nov. 4, 1831; *Constitutional Whig* (Richmond), Nov. 7, Nov. 11, 1831.

18. *Norfolk and Portsmouth Herald* (Norfolk), Nov. 4, 1831; *Petersburg Intelligencer,* Nov. 4, 1831; *American Beacon* (Norfolk), Nov. 2, 1831; *Star, and North Carolina Gazette* (Raleigh), Nov. 10, 1831.

19. "Report about the Jail 1831 June," Southampton County Judgments, Box 28 (I-M), Southampton County Court Records, VSL; *Constitutional Whig* (Richmond), Aug. 29, 1831. General Eppes is quoted as stating that there were 48 prisoners on Aug. 28.

20. "Record of Trials," pp. 182–228.

21. *Richmond Enquirer,* Nov. 8, 1831.

22. *Norfolk and Portsmouth Herald* (Norfolk), Nov. 4, 1831.

23. *Constitutional Whig* (Richmond), Nov. 7, 1831; *Norfolk and Portsmouth Herald* (Norfolk), Nov. 4, 1831.

24. *Richmond Enquirer,* Nov. 8, 1831.

25. *Constitutional Whig* (Richmond), Nov. 7, 1831.

26. Gray, "Confessions of Nat Turner," p. 307.

27. Ibid., p. 310.

28. *American Beacon* (Norfolk), Nov. 14, 1831; Tragle, "Styron and His Sources," p. 141.

29. *The Globe* (Washington, D.C.), Nov. 22, 1831 (see ad of Coale & Co.); *American Beacon* (Norfolk), Nov. 24, 1831; *Norfolk and Portsmouth Herald* (Norfolk), Nov. 14, 1831.

30. Gray, "Confessions of Nat Turner," pp. 304–5, 316–17.

31. Ibid., p. 317.

32. *The Liberator* (Boston), Dec. 17, 1831.

33. Robin W. Winks and others, *Four Fugitive Slave Narratives* (Redding, Mass.: Addison-Wesley Publishing Co., 1968), p. 232.

34. Caleb White to R. R. Gurley, Sept. 7, 1831, John C. Ehringhaus to Gurley, Sept. 27, 1831, John W. McPhail to Gurley, Sept. 23, 1831, Incoming Letters, Domestic, ser. I-A, Records of the American Colonization Society, Library of Congress.

35. *Tidewater News* (Franklin, Va.), Aug. 20, 1909; Henry Lenow to R. R. Gurley,

Sept. 9, 1831, Incoming Letters, Domestic, ser. I-A, Records of the American Colonization Society.

36. John W. McPhail to R. R. Gurley, Sept. 22, 1831, Oct. 30, 1831, Incoming Letters, Domestic, ser. I-A, Records of the American Colonization Society.

37. *American Beacon* (Norfolk), Dec. 6, 1831.

38. John W. McPhail to R. R. Gurley, Nov. 27, 1831, Incoming Letters, Domestic, ser. I-A, Records of the American Colonization Society.

39. Emigration Register, *James Perkins,* ser. VI, vol. 15, ibid.

40. John W. McPhail to R. R. Gurley, Nov. 10, 1831, Incoming Letters, Domestic, ser. I-A, ibid.

41. Emigration Register, *James Perkins,* ser. VI, vol. 15, ibid. For James Cotton and Hamilton Tann as Southampton landowners, see "List of Free Negroes and Mulattoes with the District of Benj. Griffin . . ." (1826), Judgments, Box 27, Polls.

42. Seth Crowell to R. R. Gurley, March 25, 1832, John W. McPhail to Gurley, Nov. 27, 1831, Incoming Letters, Domestic, ser. I-A, Records of the American Colonization Society.

43. Emigration Register, *Jupiter* and *Roanoke,* ser. VI, vol. 15, ibid.

44. "Record of Trials," p. 227; Johnson, *Nat Turner Story,* p. 176.

45. Registry of Free Negroes, no. 2002 (June 13, 1832), Southampton County Court Records, VSL. Haithcock is here described as 5 ft. 6¼ in. tall, with scars near the corner of his left eye and left side of his forehead. His good fortune in escaping conviction probably may be accounted for, in part, by Virginia legislation making the testimony of a slave or free Negro insufficient for conviction unless "pregnant circumstances" supported the testimony. See *Richmond Enquirer,* Sept. 30, 1831.

46. Court Notes, statement by Burwell Vick, slave of William Vick. Burwell Vick stated that he was ordered by Bolling S. B. Barrett on Tuesday, Aug. 23, to go to the houses of Lemuel and James Story and William Vick and get them to come to Mrs. Gurley's with their families. He was delivering the message to Lemuel Story when Artis came up and interrupted him. Later, as Burwell was arriving at Mrs. Gurley's, Artis appeared with a pistol, making "considerable noise." Artis was told that if he kept this up the whites would come and shoot him, whereupon he was said to have replied to the effect cited in the text. Burwell's statement was corroborated by Ben, another of William Vick's slaves.

47. Ibid., statement by Henry. This witness testified that on Monday morning, Aug. 22, he found Newsom at his master's new ground and asked if he had seen his master. Newsom replied that "yes he had seen the D——rascal & would have him before night." On Wednesday, Henry heard Newsom say "that if Capt Nat came on he would join him."

48. Some newspaper reports mention two or three others hanged on the same day as Nat Turner, but court records contain no reference to them. See, e.g., *Norfolk and Portsmouth Herald* (Norfolk), Nov. 9, 1831.

49. *Constitutional Whig* (Richmond), Sept. 3, 1831.

50. *Niles' Register* (Baltimore), Sept. 10, 1831.

51. Harriet Whitehead "to the Honorable Judge of the Circuit Superior

Court . . . of Southampton County . . ." (Nov. 1848), John R. Kilby Papers, Manuscripts Division, Duke University, Durham, N.C.

52. Ibid.

53. Ibid.; Meherrin Circuit Steward's Book, Southampton County Historical Society, Courtland, Va. The latter source gives a list of members of Clarksbury Church (formerly Turner's Meeting House) in 1839, showing Nathaniel Francis as "class leader" and Harriet Whitehead as a member, as well as Lavinia Francis.

54. Whitehead, "to the Superior Court," copy of Superior Court decree, Nov. 1848, and copy of Harriet Whitehead's will, dated June 1, 1842, probated May 5, 1852, John R. Kilby Papers, Manuscripts Division, Duke University; F. Nash Boney, "Nathaniel Francis, Representative Antebellum Southerner," *Proceedings of the American Philosophical Society* 118 (Oct. 1974): 456.

55. *New Hampshire Post* (Haverhill), Sept. 14, 1831.

56. Petition no. 10110-A (Richmond Darden, Dec. 10, 1832), Legislative Petitions, VSL. The petition of Henry B. Vaughan for over $800 was not found among these papers and was presumably withdrawn before action could be taken on it.

57. *Religious Herald* (Richmond), Sept. 16, Sept. 23, 1831.

58. *The Globe* (Washington, D.C.), Aug. 27, 1831; Drewry, *Southampton Insurrection,* p. 75.

59. *Richmond Enquirer,* Sept. 12, 1831; Thomas H. S. Hamersly, *Complete Army and Navy Register of the United States of America, from 1776 to 1887* (New York: T. H. S. Hamersly, 1888), p. 79. Blunt was appointed midshipman in June 1838, lieutenant in July 1842, and died in service on April 27, 1854.

60. Tragle, *Southampton Slave Revolt,* p. 402. This printing was published in Richmond.

61. Southampton County Personal Property Tax, 1832–1836; Judgments, Box A-2.

62. Minute Book, 1824–1830, entry for Dec. 20, 1830; Judgments, Box A-2 and Box 43 (Dec. 21, 1829).

63. Norfolk County Court Minute Book 26, entry for Nov. 18, 1839, VSL. Gray on this date qualified as attorney in the Norfolk County court. See also Southampton County Judgments, Box A-2, for several letters from Gray at Portsmouth to the Southampton clerk of court.

64. *Norfolk and Portsmouth Herald* (Norfolk), Aug. 27, 1845.

65. Ibid., Nov. 14, 1831; *Constitutional Whig* (Richmond), Nov. 11, 1831.

66. *Norfolk and Portsmouth Herald* (Norfolk), Aug. 27, 1831.

Chapter 8: Trojan Horsepower

1. *Norfolk and Portsmouth Herald* (Norfolk), July 29, 1835.

2. Richard E. Prince, *Seaboard Air Line Railway: Steamboats, Locomotives, and History* (Green River, Wyo.: R. E. Prince, 1969), p. 6.

3. *Norfolk and Portsmouth Herald* (Norfolk), July 29, 1835.

4. Ibid.

5. Ibid.

6. *American Beacon* (Norfolk), Aug. 9, June 22, Aug. 11, 1834.

7. *Knickerbocker, or New York Monthly Magazine,* 8 (July 1836): 45.

8. *American Beacon* (Norfolk), March 17, 1836; *The Corporate History of the Sea-board Air Line Railway Company Compiled by the Valuation Department, Seaboard Air Line Railway Company, Norfolk, Va.* (Norfolk; Burke & Gregory, 1922), p. 7.

9. Joseph Martin, *A New and Comprehensive Gazetteer of Virginia and the District of Columbia* (Charlottesville, Va.: Moseley and Tompkins, 1836), p. 279.

10. Journal of Elliott L. Story, vol. 1, in possession of F. Story Cutchin, Franklin, Va. The opening pages of the volume synopsize the year of 1837.

11. *Norfolk and Portsmouth Herald* (Norfolk), Nov. 4, 1835.

12. Story Journal, vol. 8, Sept. 28, 1858; R. Crawford Barrett, "Franklin, Va.," p. 2, copy of typescript, dated Aug. 12, 1922, in my possession.

13. *Norfolk and Portsmouth Herald* (Norfolk), Dec. 13, 1837; *American Beacon* (Norfolk), Dec. 13, 1837.

14. *American Beacon* (Norfolk), Oct. 3, 1840.

15. Ibid., Sept. 1, 1836, Oct. 3, Sept. 29, 1840.

16. Prince, *Seaboard Air Line,* pp. 7, 8.

17. E. M. Babb, *History of Ivor and Its Environs* (n.p., 1965), p. 8.

18. *Albemarle Enquirer* (Edenton, N.C.), Aug. 5, 1886.

19. *American Beacon* (Norfolk), Nov. 8, 1850. The *Fox* was built in New York in 1834 of live oak and cedar and was 103 ft. long, with 13½ ft. across the beam and 5 ft. 8 in. depth in the hold. She was copper fastened and drew 3 ft. of water.

20. Ibid., Jan. 28, 1851.

21. Story Journal, vol. 1, Nov. 10, 1838.

22. Barrett, "Franklin, Va.," pp. 1, 2.

23. Ibid., pp. 3, 9.

24. *Raleigh Register,* Aug. 27, 1851.

25. Diary of William D. Valentine, Aug. 23, 1851, Southern Historical Collection, Chapel Hill, N.C. The diarist was a resident of Hertford County, N.C.

26. *Patron and Gleaner* (Rich Square, N.C.), March 18, 1897. This article was written by Pulaski Cowper, a native of Hertford County.

27. Hugh T. Lefler and Albert Ray Newsome, *North Carolina: The History of a Southern State* (Chapel Hill, N.C.: University of North Carolina, 1954), p. 362.

28. *Daily Express* (Petersburg, Va.), Nov. 3, 1857.

29. Lefler and Newsome, *North Carolina,* p. 562; James G. Scott and Edward A. Wyatt, *Petersburg Story* (Petersburg, Va.: Titmus Optical Co., 1960), p. 104.

30. *Daily Express* (Petersburg, Va.), Jan. 15, 1859.

31. Ibid.

32. *American Banner* (Edenton, N.C.), Aug. 7, 1856.

33. Thomas C. Parramore, "The Ironic Fate of the 'Southern Star,'" *North Carolina Historical Review* 13 (July 1965): 336–40. The builder of the vessel, Jesse A. Jackson, was a resident of Franklin for some years after the Civil War.

34. See, e.g., advertisement by Riddick and Burbage in *The Citizen* (Murfreesboro, N.C.), Nov 23, 1859.

35. Ibid., Oct. 17, 1860.

36. *Semi-Centennial Memoir of the Harlan & Hollingsworth Company, Wilmington, Delaware, U.S.A.* (n.p., 1886), p. 380. The *Virginia Dare* was built for the Albemarle Steam Packet Co. in 1861. She was a 400-ton ship, 155 ft. long, 27 ft. in the beam, 8 ft. 3 in. deep, and was "afterward called Delaware & sold to U.S. Govt.," according to this source.

37. Stephen Barton, Jr., to Samuel R. Barton, Bartonsville, July 13, 1859, Xerox copy in my possession.

38. See p. 103 below.

39. "Porte Crayon" [D. H. Strother], "North Carolina Illustrated," *Harper's New Monthly Magazine* 14 (April 1857): 435–36.

40. *Daily Express* (Petersburg, Va.), July 14, 1857.

41. Cecil D. Eby, Jr., *"Porte Crayon": The Life of David Hunter Strother* (Chapel Hill: University of North Carolina Press, 1960), p. 121.

42. William M. Lytle, comp., and Forrest R. Holdcamper, ed., *Merchant Steam Vessels of the United States, 1807–1868: "The Lytle List"* (Mystic, Connecticut: The Steamship Historical Society of America, 1952).

Chapter 9: The Restless Calm

1. James Atkins Shackford, *David Crockett, the Man and the Legend* (Chapel Hill: University of North Carolina Press, 1956), pp. 254–65.

2. *The Observer* (Raleigh, N.C.), Nov. 3, 1877.

3. Shackford, *David Crockett*, p. 262.

4. James S. French, *Elkswatawa; or The Prophet of the West: A Tale of the Frontier* (2 vols., New York: Harper and Brothers, 1836). Shackford, *David Crockett*, p. 258, calls attention to the derivation of "Earthquake" from Crockett.

5. French, *Elkswatawa* 1: 210, 95, 109, 210.

6. According to Bassett French, "French, James Strange," microfilm copy in S. Bassett French Biographies, VSL, James S. French was born at Petersburg in 1807, reared in Norfolk, graduated from William and Mary in 1826, was a student of law at the University of Virginia in 1826, settled at Alexandria, and practiced his profession there.

7. French, *Elkswatawa* 1: 40, 42.

8. Ibid., 1: 45–52.

9. Curtis Carroll Davis, "A Digest of 'Elkswatawa,'" typescript summary of both volumes, contained in vol. 2 of the book in VSL.

10. George H. Thomas to John W. Thomas, May 10, 1838, in possession of Misses Bessie and Letitia Shands, Courtland, Va., relatives of the Thomas brothers, hereafter cited as Shands Papers.

11. Southampton County Marriage Register, 2: 485, VSL.

12. French, "French, James Strange."

13. George H. Thomas to John W. Thomas, Oct. 19, 1840, Shands Papers.

14. *Christian Sun* (Suffolk, Va.), June 8, 1860.

15. Ibid.
16. *Religious Herald* (Richmond), Aug. 30, 1833.
17. Story Journal, vol. 3, March 16, 1843.
18. Henry W. Lewis, *Southampton Ridleys and Their Kin* (Chapel Hill, N.C.: privately published, 1961), p. 56.
19. *Daily Express* (Petersburg, Va.), Jan. 8, 1859; Story Journal, vol. 8, Nov. 14, 1858.
20. Story Journal, vol. 5, Dec. 25, 1848, May 13, 1847.
21. Ibid., vol. 3, June 1, 1843, vol. 1, Sept. 5, 1839.
22. Ibid., vol. 3, Dec. 22, 1842.
23. Ibid., vol. 5, March 6, 1847, March 18, 1848.
24. Ibid., vol. 4, Aug. 13, 1846.
25. Ibid., vol. 1, March 6, 1840.
26. Ibid., vol. 8, Jan. 1, 1858.
27. Ibid., vol. 5, Jan. 8, 1848.
28. Ibid., May 3, 1848.
29. Ibid., vol. 4, Jan. 29, 1846.
30. Ibid., vol. 5, June 6, 1848, Nov. 4, 1847.
31. Ibid., Feb. 9, 1848.
32. Ibid., vol. 8, April 29, 1858, vol. 1, June 24, 1839, vol. 8, Dec. 29, 1857.
33. Ibid., vol. 5, May 3, 1848.
34. Ibid., Sept. 9, 1847.
35. Luther Porter Jackson, *Free Negro Labor and Property Holding in Virgina, 1830–1860* (New York: D. Appleton-Century Co., 1942), p. 108.
36. *Register of Officers of the Confederate States Navy, 1861–1865* (Washington, D.C.: U.S. Government Printing Office, 1931), p. 167; William Couper, ed., *Register of Former Cadets, Centennial Edition: Virginia Military Institute, Lexington, Va.* (Roanoke, Va.: Roanoke Printing Co., 1939), p. 11, 15, 18, 30.
37. Couper, *Register of Former Cadets*, p. 18.
38. Wilbur Thomas, *General George H. Thomas, the Indomitable Warrior: A Biography* (New York: Exposition Press, 1964), p. 52.
39. George H. Thomas to John W. Thomas, Oct. 19, 1840, Shands Papers; Thomas, *General George H. Thomas*, p. 60.
40. George H. Thomas to John W. Thomas, July 25, 1841, Shands Papers; Thomas, *General George H. Thomas*, p. 72.
41. Thomas, *General George H. Thomas*, pp. 97–98.
42. George H. Thomas to John W. Thomas, Oct. 25, 1848, Shands Papers.
43. George H. Thomas to John W. Thomas, April 28, 1850, Feb. 28, 1857, ibid.
44. Story Journal, vol. 8, Oct. 13, 1858.
45. *Daily Express* (Petersburg, Va.), Sept. 20, Sept. 24, 1859.
46. Ibid., Dec. 14, 1859.
47. *The Press* (Petersburg, Va.), Dec. 1, 1859.
48. *Daily Express* (Petersburg, Va.), Dec. 14, 1859; *The Citizen* (Murfreesboro, N.C.), Aug. 30, 1860; Story Journal, vol. 8, Aug. 2, 1860.
49. Story Journal, vol. 8, Aug. 30, Nov. 3, Oct. 27, Oct. 12, 1860.

50. Ibid., Nov. 9, 1860, May 11, 1861.

51. Ibid., May 11, 1861.

52. George H. Thomas to John W. Thomas, March 23, 1857, Shands Papers.

Chapter 10: The Civil War

1. *Daily Express* (Petersburg, Va.), June 26, 1861.

2. Edgar B. Jackson, ed., *Three Rebels Write Home* (Franklin, Va.: News Publishing Co., 1955), p. 40.

3. *Daily Express* (Petersburg, Va.), June 26, 1861.

4. Jackson, *Three Rebels Write Home,* p. 40.

5. Ibid., p. 41.

6. R. N. Scott and others, eds., *The War of the Rebellion: A Compilation of the Official Records of the Union and Confederate Armies* (Washington, D.C.: U.S. Government Printing Office, 1880–1901), ser. I, 9: 110, 196.

7. Ibid., ser. I, 9: 438; 305.

8. Jackson, *Three Rebels Write Home,* pp. 58, 77.

9. Richmond Rush and others, eds., *Official Records of the Union and Confederate Navies in the War of the Rebellion* (Washington, D.C.: U.S. Government Printing Office, 1894–1914), ser. I, 7: 440. The Nottoway railroad bridge, reported in May 1862 to have been burned, was evidently rebuilt not long afterward.

10. See n. 36, chap. 8, above; *Official Records,* ser. I, 9: 196.

11. J. Marsden Smith, Norfolk, to W. N. H. Smith, March 21, 1862, Kader Biggs to W. N. H. Smith, March 22, 1862, Edward C. Smith Papers, Manuscripts Division, Duke University Library, Durham, N.C.

12. *Official Naval Records,* ser. I, 7: 440.

13. Ibid.

14. Ibid., 7: 632–33; *Official Records,* ser. I, 18: 16.

15. *Official Naval Records,* ser. I, 8: 108.

16. George H. Allen, *Forty-Six Months with the Fourth Rhode Island Volunteers, in the War of 1861–1865, Comprising a History of Its Marches and Battles and Camp Life* (Providence, R.I.: J. A. and R. A. Reid, 1887), p. 59.

17. R. J. Roske and Charles Van Doren, *Lincoln's Commando: The Biography of Commander W. B. Cushing, U.S.N.* (New York: Harper and Brothers, 1957).

18. Ibid., p. 128.

19. Ibid., p. 129.

20. *Official Naval Records,* ser. I, 7: 113.

21. *Official Records,* ser. I, 18: 40. Pryor took command of the Blackwater line in early December.

22. *Tidewater News* (Franklin, Va.), Jan. 15, 1962.

23. *Official Records,* ser. I, 18: 38; John G. Barrett, *The Civil War in North Carolina* (Chapel Hill: University of North Carolina Press, 1963), p. 139.

24. *Official Records,* ser. I, 18: 42–44.

25. Undated newspaper clipping from *Tidewater News* (Franklin, Va.) in Edgar B. Jackson Papers, Southampton County Historical Society, Boykins, Va. The

article includes excerpts from Captain Webb's diary. These entries are dated Nov. 20, Nov. 21, and Dec. 7, 1862.

26. Ibid., Dec. 12, 1862.

27. *Official Records,* ser. I, 18: 549–52.

28. Ibid., ser. I, 18: 958.

29. *Tidewater News* (Franklin, Va.), Jan 15, 1962.

30. Ibid., July 30, 1953.

31. Barrett, "Franklin, Va." p. 2.

32. *Tidewater News* (Franklin, Va.), March 25, 1932.

33. Virginia Camp Norfleet, "To My Grandchildren," typescript in possession of Southampton County Historical Society, Courtland, Va. This document was evidently composed about 1910.

34. *The Freedman's Journal* (Boston), Jan. 1865. This letter from Sarah E. Foster was dated Norfolk, Nov. 1864.

35. *Tidewater News* (Franklin, Va.), "Golden Anniversary Historical Edition," 1955; Southampton County Order Book, 1875–1881 (Dec. 21, 1875), p. 16, Clerk's Office, Courtland, Va.

36. Jackson, *Three Rebels Write Home,* p. 64.

37. Blake, *William Mahone,* p. 10.

38. William Henry Tappey Squires, *The Days of Yester-Year in Colony and Commonwealth: A Sketchbook of Virginia* (Portsmouth, Va.: Printcraft Press, 1928), p. 189.

39. Blake, *William Mahone,* p. 10; Squires, *Days of Yester-Year,* p. 185.

40. Bruce Catton, *This Hallowed Ground: The Story of the Union Side of the Civil War* (New York: Pocket Books, 1976), p. 111.

41. Ibid., p. 347.

42. Ibid., p. 454.

43. Blake, *William Mahone,* p. 40; Catton, *This Hallowed Ground,* pp. 411–14.

44. Ibid.

45. James Norcom, "The Eastern Shore of North Carolina, 1861 and 1862," *Historical Magazine* 18 (Nov. 1870): 302–3.

46. *Official Records,* ser. I, 42: 958–59.

47. *North Carolina Times* (New Bern), Aug. 2, 1864.

48. *Official Naval Records,* ser. I, 2: 423.

49. Capt. Baldy A. Capehart to Mrs. Capehart, Jan. 5, 1865, Meeta A. Capehart Papers, Southern Historical Collection, Chapel Hill, N.C. Captain Capehart was with the 15th Cavalry Battalion, North Carolina Troops.

50. *Official Naval Records,* ser. I, 2: 424, 10: 163.

51. George H. Gordon, *A War Diary of Events in the War of the Great Rebellion, 1863–1865* (Boston: James R. Osgood & Co., 1882), pp. 388, 381–82.

52. Norfleet, "To My Grandchildren."

Chapter 11: The Convalescence

1. Norfleet, "To My Grandchildren," p. 14.

2. Barrett, "Franklin, Va.," pp. 5–6; *Semi-Centennial Memoir of the Harlan and Hollingsworth Company, Wilmington, Delaware, U.S.A.* (n.p., 1886), p. 384.

3. *Norfolk Virginian,* Aug. 19, 1874.

4. *Tidewater News* (Franklin, Va.), June 1, 1926; Fanny Webb, *Recollections of Franklin and Historical Sketches of Southampton County* (Raleigh: Edwards and Broughton, 1863), p. 59; Barrett, "Franklin, Va.," p. 7.

5. Barrett, "Franklin, Va.," p. 6.

6. *Murfreesboro Enquirer* (Murfreesboro, N.C.), Jan. 1, 1877. This source cites publication of the *Tribune* at Franklin. The same paper for Oct. 4, 1877, cites the *Monitor.* See also Lester J. Cappon, *Virginia Newspapers, 1821–1935: A Bibliography with Historical Introduction and Notes* (New York: D. Appleton-Century Co., 1936).

7. *Norfolk Virginian,* Dec. 16, 1870.

8. Webb, *Recollections of Franklin,* pp. 3, 28.

9. Southampton County Deed Book, 23: 363, Clerk's Office, Courtland, Va. This indenture, dated April 1, 1878, leases a wharf and warehouse at Franklin, formerly used by the Clyde Line, to the Farmers and Merchants Steam Transportation Company.

10. *Rural Messenger* (Petersburg, Va.), May 17, 1879.

11. Typescript copy of Franklin Council Minutes, entries for March 28, 1876, Jan. 5, 1880, March 13, 1877, Edgar B. Jackson Papers, Southampton County Historical Society, Boykins, Va.

12. Barrett, "Franklin, Va.," p. 6.

13. Ibid.

14. *Tidewater News* (Franklin, Va.), March 11, 1938.

15. Southampton County Deed Book, 31: 476, Clerk's Office, Courtland, Va.

16. "Camp Manufacturing Company," *Tidewater News* (Franklin, Va.), "Golden Anniversary Historical Edition," 1955; Southampton County Deed Book, 31: 413, Clerk's Office, Courtland, Va.

17. "Camp Manufacturing Company," *Tidewater News* (Franklin, Va.), "Golden Anniversary Historical Edition," 1955.

18. F. Roy Johnson, *The Peanut Story* (Murfreesboro, N.C.: Johnson Publishing Co., 1964), pp. 37–38.

19. Ibid., p. 78.

20. *Rural Messenger* (Petersburg, Va.), June 1, 1872.

21. F. Roy Johnson, " 'Chic' Tall among the Inventors," MS copy of article in Edgar B. Jackson Papers, Southampton County Hist. Soc., Boykins, Va.

22. Johnson, *Peanut Story,* pp. 118–19.

23. Edward F. Gilliam, "County's Early Peanut Industry Developed by Pretlow Family," *Tidewater News* (Franklin, Va.), "Golden Anniversary Edition," 1955.

24. Southampton County Record of Postmasters: Names, Post Offices, and Dates, photostatic copy in records of Southampton County Historical Society, Courtland, Va.

25. *Tidewater News* (Franklin, Va.), Sept. 21, 1906.

26. Record of Postmasters.

27. *Rural Messenger* (Petersburg, Va.), Nov. 2, 1878.

28. "The Tourney," MS copy of description in Edgar B. Jackson Papers, Southampton County Historical Society, Boykins, Va. The tourney was held on Dec. 9, 1869.

29. *Norfolk Journal,* May 24, May 25, May 21, 1872.

30. Ibid., May 24, May 21, 1872.

31. Norman S. Beaton, *History of Boykins Depot and Boykins, Virginia, 1835-1955* (Franklin, Va.: The Tidewater News, n.d.), p. 2.

32. Prince, *Seaboard Air Line,* p. 24.

33. *Rural Messenger* (Petersburg, Va.), May 24, 1879.

34. Babb, *History of Ivor,* p. 50.

35. *Norfolk Virginian,* July 27, 1868.

36. Wertenbaker, *Norfolk,* p. 246.

37. *Norfolk Virginian,* June 24, June 25, 1869.

38. Ibid., July 27, 1868, May 31, 1870, Dec. 7, 1875.

39. "Southampton County's Representatives to the General Assembly," typescript copy in Edgar B. Jackson Papers, Southampton County Hist. Soc., Boykins, Va.

40. *Norfolk Virginian,* Sept. 27, 1872; "Representatives in the General Assembly"; "Franklin Doctor Organizes County School System," *Tidewater News* (Franklin, Va.), "Golden Anniversary Historical Edition," 1955.

41. Drewry, *Southampton Insurrection,* pp. vi-vii, 181, 186, 193; see also Aptheker, *Nat Turner's Slave Rebellion,* p. 109.

42. Blake, *William Mahone,* p. 269.

43. Ibid., pp. 144-45, 254, 234.

44. *Norfolk Virginian,* Dec. 18, 1879.

45. Squires, *Days of Yester-Year,* pp. 194, 188.

46. MS copy of obituary, dated Courtland, Va., April 3, 1889, in Edgar B. Jackson Papers, Southampton County Hist. Soc., Boykins, Va.

47. Data on Rochelle's early cruises are found in marginal notes made by his mother, Martha F. B. Rochelle, in her Book of Common Prayer, pp. 276, 285, 290, 295, 308, 326, 345, 346, 374, 375, in possession of Misses Bessie and Letitia Shands, Courtland, Va.; Parramore, "The Ironic Fate of the 'Southern Star,'" p. 341.

48. James H. Rochelle, *Life of Rear Admiral John Randolph Tucker* (Washington, D.C.: Neale Publishing Co., 1903), p. 89.

49. *Norfolk Virginian,* Nov. 10, 1884.

50. "Vaughan & Company, Bankers, Southampton's Oldest, Biggest Banking Institution, Has Played Leading Role in Tidewater Area's Business and Commercial Development," "Original Killdees Represented Franklin 60 Years Ago," and "Franklin's Features Have Changed Greatly in Past 70 Years," *Tidewater News* (Franklin, Va.), "Golden Anniversary Historical Edition," 1955.

51. *Norfolk Journal,* Dec. 5, 1872; "Franklin's Features Have Changed Greatly in Past 70 Years," *Tidewater News* (Franklin, Va.), "Golden Anniversary Historical Edition," 1955.

52. "Royal Welcome Given Franklin's Company I on Returning Home from

War with Spain," *Tidewater News* (Franklin, Va.), "Golden Anniversary Historical Edition," 1955.

Chapter 12: The Age of Wheels

1. "Line Squall Sinks 'Olive' in Lower Chowan, with Terrible Loss of Life," *Tidewater News* (Franklin, Va.), "Golden Anniversary Historical Edition," 1955.
2. Ibid., Jan. 10, 1908, Oct. 7, 1910, May 11, 1906, March 17, 1911, Dec. 13, 1912.
3. Ibid., June 19, 1908, Nov. 9, 1909, April 22, April 29, July 29, 1910.
4. Minutes of Franklin Town Council, June 10, 1901, Dec. 10, 1906, June 13, 1910, June 29, 1914, typescript copy in Edgar B. Jackson Papers, Southampton County Hist. Soc., Boykins, Va.
5. Ibid., 1876–1911; *Tidewater News* (Franklin, Va.), Oct. 1, 1909, April 19, 1912, Jan. 3, 1913.
6. *Tidewater News* (Franklin, Va.), April 9, 1909, May 14, 1926, Jan. 31, Feb. 21, 1913, April 3, 1914.
7. Ibid., Sept. 10, 1937.
8. Ibid., April 6, 1917, and "Golden Anniversary Historical Edition," 1955.
9. Ibid., April 13, April 27, 1917, Jan. 1, 1918, June 9, April 20, Sept. 7, 1917.
10. Ibid., June 28, July 5, 1918.
11. Ibid., April 19, July 21, 1918.
12. Ibid., June 27, July 25, 1919.
13. "History of Public Education in Southampton County," typescript in Edgar B. Jackson Papers, Southampton County Hist. Soc., Boykins.
14. *Tidewater News* (Franklin, Va.), Dec. 12, 1924.
15. Ibid., March 13, 1931, Sept. 25, 1914.
16. Cappon, *Virginia Newspapers,* pp. 73, 89–90.
17. *Tidewater News* (Franklin, Va.), Jan. 21, 1916.
18. Ibid., Feb. 15, 1924.
19. Ibid., Oct. 2, 1931, May 26, July 21, Dec. 1, 1933, March 30, July 27, 1934, Dec. 18, 1936.
20. Ibid., Nov. 12, 1926, Oct. 29, 1937.
21. Ibid., Oct. 26, 1934.
22. "Colgate Whitehead Darden, Jr.," *Current Biography* 9 (Sept. 1948): 132–34.
23. See n. 2, chap. 11, above; see also newspaper clipping based on interview with Capt. Jasper Wiggins, Edenton, N.C., Aug. 10, 1964, in Edgar B. Jackson Papers, Southampton County Hist. Soc., Boykins.
24. *Tidewater News* (Franklin, Va.), April 9, June 18, Sept. 2, Sept. 10, 1909.
25. Ibid., June 16, 1911, Nov. 23, 1917, 1918–23 passim.
26. Ibid., May 14, 1926.
27. Ibid., Nov. 17, 1922.
28. Ibid., Sept. 6, Sept. 11, 1925.
29. Ibid., Feb. 11, 1927, Aug. 8, 1924, Jan. 1, 1935.
30. Ibid., Aug. 31, 1928; H. Temple Crittenden, "Lost: Two Towns," *Virginia*

Cavalcade 10 (Winter 1960–61): 32; "Franklin & Carolina R. R.," MS note in Edgar B. Jackson Papers, Southampton County Hist. Soc., Boykins; Florence Pierce Jackson, *Southampton County Geography Supplement* (Charlottesville: University of Virginia Press, 1930), pp. 16–17.

Chapter 13: A Winter of Discontent

1. *Tidewater News* (Franklin, Va.), Jan. 5, 1956.
2. Ibid., Dec. 15, Dec. 29, 1955.
3. Ibid., Jan. 12, Feb. 23, 1956.
4. Ibid., March 12, 1959.
5. Ibid.
6. Ibid., April 11, Dec. 19, 1941.
7. Ibid., Jan. 3, Jan. 9, Oct. 30, 1942.
8. Oct. 2, Sept. 17, June 9, 1942.
9. Ibid., Nov. 12, 1942, July 7, July 28, 1944, Feb. 26, 1943.
10. Ibid., Oct. 11, 1946, May 30, 1947, Oct. 8, 1970, Oct. 21, 1974, Dec. 9, 1963, Sept. 7, 1964, Aug. 1, 1960.
11. Ibid., April 19, 1976, and "Golden Anniversary Historical Edition," 1955.
12. Ibid., Jan. 6, 1955, May 31, 1956, March 20, 1961, May 14, Sept. 10, 1962.
13. Ibid., May 31, 1946, Jan. 9, 1948, Jan. 25, 1952.
14. Ibid., May 2, 1952, Feb. 3, 1955, Jan. 18, 1962.
15. Ibid., July 7, 1968, Oct. 4, 1971, May 18, 1963.
16. Ibid., Feb. 13, 1969.
17. Ibid., Oct. 5, 1967.
18. Ibid., Jan. 16, June 26, 1969.
19. Ibid., Feb. 13, 1969.
20. Ibid., Aug. 14, 1969, Sept. 23, 1974.
21. Ibid., Sept. 25, 1969.
22. Ibid., Sept. 25, 1969, Jan. 26, 1970.
23. Ibid., Jan. 26, 1970; John Henrik Clarke, ed., *William Styron's Nat Turner: Ten Black Writers Respond* (Boston: Beacon Press, 1968).
24. Clarke, *William Styron's Nat Turner*, pp. 6, 20–21.
25. Stephen B. Oates, *The Fires of Jubilee* (New York: Harper and Row, 1975), pp. 148–54.
26. Norfleet, "To My Grandchildren," p. 3.
27. *Tidewater News* (Franklin, Va.), Aug. 5, 1954.
28. Ibid., June 5, 1975, June 3, 1969. The student was Wendell Franklin, of Washington, D.C.

Index

A. R. *Schultz* (steamboat), 129, 130, 138
Abbitt, John D., 201
Accomack County, Va., 66
Adam's Grove, Va., 186
Agar, Rev. William, 32
Agnew, Rev. John, 38
Agriculture, *see* Farming
Ahoskie, N.C., 103
Airfield, Va., 185
Albemarle (ironclad), 163
Albemarle Sound, 47, 124, 134, 160
Albemarle Steam Navigation Co., 135, 160, 181; chartered as Albemarle Steam Packet Co., 134, reestablished in 1866, 178; partially controlled by Pretlow family, 184; fatal accident of, 199; decline of, 210–11
Albemarle Steam Packet Co., *see* Albemarle Steam Navigation Co.
Alexandria, London and Hampshire Railroad, 143
Allegheny County, Va., 217
Allen, Widow, 27
Allen and Smith Candy Co., 219
Amelia County, Va., 67
American (ship), 115
American Colonization Society, 71, 72, 114
Amis, William, 51
Angelico Creek, 28
Anglican church, *see* Church of England
Appomattox (steamboat), 211
Appomattox Courthouse, Va., 176
Argall, Capt. Samuel, 21
Ariel, H.M.S., 43

Armory Hall (Franklin), 196, 202
Arrow (steamboat), 175
Artis, Cherry, 95
Artis, Exum, 116
Artis, George, 115
Artis, Orville, 189
Artis, William, 95, 100, 102
Artis family (Negro), 116
Asbury, Bishop Francis, 47, 48
Assamoosick Swamp, 4, 6, 10, 183
Atkins, Elisha, 87
Atlantic, Mississippi and Ohio Railroad, *see* Norfolk and Western Railroad
Atlantic and Danville Railroad, 213
Augusta County, Va., 66
Auld, James, 30, 31

Balmer (Barham), Mr., 103
Baptists, 47, 52, 53; first church at Mill Swamp, 32; David Barrow's Black Creek congregation, 32, 33; Tucker Swamp Church established, 61; Black Creek ousts Rev. Langston, 62, 63; church at Franklin built, 178
Barham, Mr., *see* Balmer, Mr.
Barham, John, 132
Barham, Dr. W. B., 15, 16, 168
Barnes, Jordan, 85
Barnes, Nathan, 37
Barnes's chapel, 61, 79, 80
Barrett, Mrs., 178
Barrett, Rev. Burwell, 62
Barrett, Fannie, 186
Barrett, John, 27
Barrett, Richard, 129

Bolton's Ferry, 27
Boon's Bridge, N.C., 97
Booth, George, 51
Boritz, Capt. William, 36, 41, 42
Boush, Goodrich, 43
Bowers, Dr. Carr, 58, 114
Bowlin, Henry, 115
Boykin, Rev., 147
Boykin, Elizabeth, 147
Boykin, Francis, 46
Boykin, William, 65
Boykins, Va., 6, 27, 200, 206, 219, 221–24; growth aided by railroad, 125; KGC organized, 155; called "half-horse town," 187; buggy factory, 199; Civic Symphony Orchestra, 207; large egg farm, 218; plan to make film near, 223
Boykins' Camp Meeting, N.C., 50
Boykins Narrow Fabric Corp., 218
Boykins Town Council, 223
Bozeman, William G., 13–16
Brady, Elias, 27
Bragg, Gen. Braxton, 172
Branchville, Va., 27, 125, 188, 190, 218
Brandy, use and production of, 48, 50, 51
Brantley, Etheldred T., 76
Braswell, Richard, 19
Braswell, Valentine, 26, 27
Breckinridge, John C., 155
Briggs, Henry, 20
Britt, Benjamin W., 103
Broadwater, Va., 32, 47, 65
Broughton, Thomas G., 123
Brown, Dr. Jesse, 27
Brown, John, 154
Brown, John L., 87
Brown, Samuel, 87
Brown, Willy, 115
Brown family (Negro), 72, 115
Browne, Thomas, 46
Brown's Ferry, 54
Brunswick County, Va., 29, 37, 52, 66, 154

Bryant, Henry, 83
Bryant, Capt. James, 92
Bryant, Capt. James D., 132
Bryant, James Fenton; soldier in Civil War, 157–59; Conservative politician, 190; county's first school superintendent, 205
Bryant, Mollie, 159
Bryant, Mrs. Sally, 83
Buckhorn plantation (of Thomas Ridley), 94
Buckhorn Swamp (Nottoway Indian reservation), 6
Burbage, Capt. Thomas I., 134
Burdette, Va., 213
Bureau of Mental Hygiene (Richmond), 209
Burges, Rev. Henry John, 32, 46, 47
Burges, Dr. Richard U., 189
Burges, Rev. Thomas, 32, 46
Burgess, Stephen, 19
Burke, Gov. Thomas (N.C.), 45
Burnside expedition, 159
Butler, Gen. Benjamin F., 175
Butler family (Negro), 115
Butte, Joshua, 65
Byrd, Gov. Harry F., 211
Byrd, Col. William: visits Meherrin Indians, 6; describes Nottoway Indians, 8–10; boundary line surveyor, 26–28

Cabin Pond, 78, 79
Cairo, Va., *see* Capron, Va.
Calvert, Christopher, 34
Camp, Pvt., 177
Camp, George, 168, 177
Camp, James L., 182
Camp, John S., 182
Camp, Paul D., 182, 203
Camp, William, 182
Campbell County, Va., 68
Camp Hugo (Va.), 68
Camp Manufacturing Co., 182, 183, 213, 218